D1552862

"*Globalbeliever.com* captures Christ's heart and hope for world harvest. It has impacted me not only for missions, but for evangelism. The message of this book is a no-nonsense, balanced theology of world harvest. I recommend it. I applaud it. The church needs it!"

Raymond F. Culpepper, Senior Pastor
Metropolitan Church of God
Birmingham, Alabama

"Grant McClung's warm, engaging style makes this book a pleasure to read. His superb grasp of mission facts and trends, as well as the Biblical basis of missions, stimulates thoughtful interaction. The church's missionary vision will be greatly sharpened by Grant's analysis and prescription for the future."

Jim Reapsome
Editor at large
Evangelical Missions Quarterly

"*Globalbeliever.com* is a trendsetting book for this new decade and century. As one of the foremost missiologists of our time, Dr. Grant McClung blends the insights of a careful academician with the warmth of a Great Commission enthusiast. His forecasts for this decade are exciting and on target. Here is *a timely book* for this *kairos* season of unique opportunity for the church, *a practical book* for "logging on" and connecting to God's purposes, and *an encouraging book* that will refresh your heart with hope for the harvest."

David Shibley, President
Global Advance

"As its name implies, Grant McClung's *Globalbeliever.com* is as much on the cutting edge as the 21st century and the Internet itself. It contains a futuristic view of world missions that will challenge everyone, especially the Pentecostals and Charismatics. I recommend it for every Great Commission Christian."

Vinson Synan
Dean of The School of Divinity
Regent University

"In today's world of rapidly expanding technology, the communications revolution is shrinking our world, providing greater opportunities than ever before for involvement in global ministry. This book shows believers how to present the eternal message of Christ to the new millennium's "dot-com" culture. It is a must for enlarging the circle of ministry outreach in the 21st century."

Paul L. Walker
Church of God
Cleveland, Tennessee

"The beginning of the third millennium offers exciting new opportunities in mission that Christians living a century ago could not have imagined. *Globalbeliever.com* is written for those who want to be actively involved in fulfilling the Great Commission. One of the foremost missiologists of the Pentecostal Movement, Dr. Grant McClung shares his burden for transforming local congregations into communities of "Globalbelievers." In an easy-to-read fashion, he weaves solid Bible teaching, church history, mission theory, and practical instruction into a blueprint for evangelizing unbelievers. Pentecostals, Charismatics, and evangelicals alike will be challenged by this guide to presenting the good news of Jesus Christ in the power of the Holy Spirit."

Gary B. McGee
Professor of Church History & Pentecostal Studies
Assemblies of God Theological Seminary
Springfield, Missouri

"*Globalbeliever.com* comes on the scene at a crucial time for Pentecostal mission efforts. It provides an entry into negotiating complex changes in missionary strategy for the missions-minded church leader. The object of our missionary efforts during the 20th century has now become our partner in the completion of the missionary task. The "dot-com world" is not a new fad or trend—it is a fundamentally different world. If the power of Pentecost is to have its fullest expression worldwide, the realities described in *Globalbeliever.com* must be heeded. For local church leader and missionary alike, Dr. McClung has offered a negotiable pathway to effective Pentecostal missionary effort in the 21st century."

Byron D. Klaus, President
Assemblies of God Theological Seminary

"Written primarily as a mission primer for Pentecostal and Charismatic pastors and church members, Grant McClung has created a resource for Great Commission Christians. Thoughtful discussion questions and thorough documentation make this book practical. Non-Pentecostals will find that Grant's broad knowledge of both Pentecostal and standard Evangelical mission history and practice make his analysis of current trends particularly valuable."

Gary Corwin, Editor
Evangelical Missions Quarterly

Grant McClung functions as a service provider in this book, connecting pastors and members with God's mission for a "dot-com" world. His insights and suggestions will help many to understand and be more effective in what God is calling them to do in His mission."

Gerald H. Anderson, Director
Overseas Ministries Study Center

"In a world made smaller every day through the reach of electronic technology, the need for world evangelization becomes even more critical. Through his unique approach in *Globalbeliever.com,* Dr. Grant McClung makes the daunting task of fulfilling the Great Commission a practical, positive process in which every "plugged in" believer can participate."

Robert E. Fisher, Director
Center for Spiritual Renewal

"Dr. Grant McClung reminds us in *Globalbeliever.com* that from the very first verse and chapter in Genesis to the last chapter and verse in Revelation, world evangelization is at the heart of God's revelation of Himself and His Son. I urge believers to read this book. It will broaden their vision and increase their burden for the lost of this world, particularly those in the 10/40 Window who have not yet heard the good news that Jesus is both Savior and Lord."

Lovell R. Cary
Church of God World Missions

"Whether the reader is a new Christian just learning about the cause of missions, a pastor seeking material for missionary sermons or a veteran missionary following God's calling and purpose, this book in invaluable."

Roland E. Vaughan
Church of God World Missions

"This book by Grant McClung draws from the Scriptures, missiology and history to give us many relevant lessons for this electronic age. Though broad in scope, his treatment of the various disciplines is deep enough to serve as a great resource for pastors who want their preaching to reflect the heart of God. Pentecost is placed in the context of history and missionary outreach to assist Charismatic leaders in integrating their tradition with the Redeemer's constant movement toward all peoples and nations."

Paul McKaughan, President
EFMA, ACMC

Grant McClung's book, *Globalbeliever.com—Connecting to God's Work in Your World*, leads you into what God's Word says about the world. The reflections at the end of each chapter ask you to take action—to initiate through practical living that which God has revealed to your hearts. Grant's experience as a missiologist, his simple but profound writing gifts and his heart for the lost make this book a treasured textbook for all who seek to touch the world with the gospel.

Ron Williams
Communications Office
International Church of the Foursquare Gospel

Globalbeliever.com

Connecting to God's Work in Your World

Globalbeliever.com

Connecting to God's Work in Your World

Grant McClung

Book Editor: Wanda Griffith
Editorial Assistant: Tammy Hatfield
Copy Editors: Esther Metaxas
Cresta Shawver
Oreeda Burnette
Inside Layout: Mark Shuler

Library of Congress Catalog Card Number: 00-101812
ISBN:0-87148-373-4
Copyright © 2000 by Pathway Press
Cleveland, Tennessee 37311
All Rights Reserved
Printed in the United States of America

Gratefully dedicated to my
missions mentor:

David S. Bishop

Thank you for pointing me and my
generation to God's global cause.

TABLE OF CONTENTS

Foreword

*G*lobalization is a word that means everything and nothing, depending on how it is used. It is a word that has not yet secured a firm place in the dictionary. Mentioning the word summons different emotions ranging from exuberance to fear. Globalization is viewed as either the rose of a new future or the spreading of a terrible virus, depending on your understanding of the word.

Globalization has become the catchword for all sorts of causes. To some, it is no more than shrinking space and disappearing national borders that open the door to a new flow of money and commodities. It signals the growing interdependence of the world's people through the availability of communal resources.

To others, the very thought of moving toward a global community is frightening, perhaps even threatening. It announces the arrival of a new model and order of life. It declares the need for understanding the complexities, contradictions and conflicts associated with living in a global society. The very thought of that kind of radical change has sent people scampering to find an enclave around which the cloak of provincialism may be draped.

God has always had a global view—and so must His church. With today's technology, that reality is within our reach more than ever before. But the choice is ours. We can either anxiously hide behind the shawl of localism or we can "plug in" to what God is doing around the world.

We must develop a global mind-set and become involved in a world that is in rapid transition. It is time for us to recognize the bigger, broader picture of what it means to be a global Christian. We must be open to rethinking boundaries and finding new meaning in being a part of the worldwide family of God. It is essential for us to adopt a global vision and become, not just inspired, but also equipped to fulfill our Lord's Great Commission.

In the end, we must all accept the fact that reaching this world for Jesus Christ is not based on whether or not we have adequate resources—it is based on our commitment and limited only by our vision.

Grant McClung's superb *Globalbeliever.com* could not have arrived at a better time. The church that ministers to this age must have a clear understanding of, and a commitment to, a global future. Dr. McClung, one of the foremost missiologists of our time, answers some important questions. He guarantees us that no behavior in the 21st-century church can ever become routine again. The changing world in which we live screams out for constant examination of new threats and possibilities. Perhaps above all, *Globalbeliever.com* reminds us that our Lord's command to "go into all the world" is not only possible today . . . it is urgent!

Globalbeliever.com gives us a new paradigm for ministry. Any Christian leader interested in formulating a global plan for ministry will find this book inspiring and enlivening.

R. Lamar Vest
Executive Committee
Church of God
Cleveland, Tennessee

ACKNOWLEDGMENTS

By His marvelous grace God placed me in a ministry-sensitive family. My parents, Lloyd McClung (now deceased) and Pauline (McClung) Bird, were hardworking local church members who modeled for me and supervised me in ministry to all races, cultures and socioeconomic classes. Through their careful tutelage and example I accepted Jesus Christ as my Lord and Savior as a child. Through their sacrifice and encouragement I was able to attend high school and college at West Coast Bible College in Fresno, California.

The last 30 years of my life and ministry have been associated with a growing "Great Commission" community of students, local church pastors and laity, missionaries, and international church leaders. Much of the contents of this book is a reflection of this community in the classroom, in special leadership conferences, or traveling with colleagues in various parts of the world. I am grateful to that community, whether it be at West Coast Bible College, the European Bible Seminary (where my family and I served as missionaries), Fuller Theological Seminary School of World Missions, the Church of God Theological Seminary, and numerous seminary and Bible college venues in every region of the globe.

Thanks to Bill George, editor in chief, and his team at Pathway Press, for bringing this manuscript to life in the publishing process. Bill is a veteran "Globalbeliever" who has served as a missionary, missions administrator, and missions professor. Thanks also to my colleagues in Church of God World Missions who have encouraged and promoted this new publication.

Scott and Carol Rains, missionaries to Portugal, assisted me in the technical formatting of the manuscript and diagrams. Teaching Assistant Angeline Hernandez transcribed classroom lectures into a written format and the Spring 1999 class of Introduction to the World Missions of the Church (at the Church of God Theological Seminary) took this book as their special prayer project.

Since the day we met in 1965, Janice Leach McClung has been my closest friend and encourager. On numerous publishing projects (articles, chapters, books) she has provided the word processing and final editing. On this project she exercised her primary spiritual gifts of encouragement and intercession. What I said to her in my dedication of *Azusa Street and Beyond: Pentecostal Missions and Church Growth in the Twentieth Century* (Bridge Publishing, 1986) bears repeating: "To Janice—professional secretary, anointed musician, committed wife and mother—for her partnership in matrimony and ministry."

PREFACE

At the entry of a new decade, a new century, and a new millennium we serve a "global/universal God" in a "dot.com world." Wherever we turn, through virtually any and every medium of communication—billboards, bumper stickers, on the side of a bus or subway car, on gum wrappers, fast-food containers, through TV, radio, and now the World Wide Web—we are invited to log on to "dot.com" information/advertising/conversation sites. We are living in a technological revolution.

There are many "new revolutions" (many of them puzzling and frightening) taking place in our fast-changing world at the outset of this new millennium. Our eternal God (ever existing before the creation of the universe, solar system, and earth) is proactive, dynamic, moving by His Holy Spirit in unprecedented ways. In the exciting mix of theology and technology, followers of Christ are challenged to keep the first-century reality connected to the 21st century context.

Don't be left behind in this final global "spiritual revolution." Bring every energy and focus to "click on" to be online with what the God of history/God of the nations is doing in your world. In connecting to God's work in your world, you—and those you bring with you—will be on your way toward becoming a "Globalbeliever.com" with world Christian values and ministries.

At the end of each chapter you will find a section called "Reflections," which will help you and other "global believers/world Christians" think about, discuss, and pray about the information in that chapter. I suggest that you do this in a Sunday school class, home Bible study, a missions prayer group, and so forth. There will also be a section called "Projections/Actions," which will allow you individually and/or in a group to state some personal ministry goals and list some concrete action steps you will be taking in response to what God is saying to you. At the end of each main section you will find "Resource Connections" to other world Christian resources.

Come on, "global believer," let's make His mission our motivation in this new millennium!

Grant McClung
Cleveland, Tennessee

PART ONE

GETTING ONLINE WITH THE GLOBAL/ UNIVERSAL GOD

Preview

Part I gives a general overview of God's mission in the world through the eyes of the Old Testament. Highlights are given from the four major sections of the Old Testament: Law, History, Poetry and Prophets. It will also survey the New Testament mission of God's people, highlighting the Great Commission passages and some of the parables of Jesus. Finally, Part I will trace the international growth of the gospel through church history to recent times, paying tribute to the missions leadership of students, laity and women.

Globalbeliever.Commandment—"The Great Commandment"

"Love the Lord your God with all your heart and with all your soul and with all your mind. . . . And the second is like it: Love your neighbor as yourself" (Matthew 22:37-39).

Globalbeliever.Commission—"The Great Commission"

"Therefore go and make disciples of all nations, baptizing them in the name of the Father and of the Son and of the Holy Spirit, and teaching them to obey everything I have commanded you" (Matthew 28:19, 20).

In some "Wild West Lore" (with some imagination thrown in), a Native American was sending smoke-signals to his friend across the canyon. "Dear Tonto," he began by lifting his thick Indian blanket gently off the campfire. He continued with various sizes of smoke puffs to emphasize his points. What he didn't know was that many miles away, across the desert, the Atomic Energy Commission had just triggered a nuclear test explosion. A massive mushroom cloud filled the horizon and rose into the sky. Feeling overwhelmed, he quickly sent a highly punctuated smoke-cloud message to his friend on the opposite bluff, "Man, I wish I had said THAT!" When I read the following quote from Pastor John Piper, I had to say, "Man, I wish I had said THAT!"

> Missions is not the ultimate goal of the church. Worship is. Missions exists because worship doesn't. . . . When this age is over, and the countless millions of the redeemed fall on their faces before the throne of God, missions will be no more. It is a temporary necessity. But worship abides forever. Worship, therefore, is the fuel and goal in missions. . . . The goal of missions is the gladness of the peoples in the greatness of God.[1]

So we begin where the Bible begins—with God. The truth declaration, "In the beginning God . . ." (Genesis 1:1) tells us that this missions (global-believer) approach did not begin with today's missionary movement, with the church, with Israel, with Abraham, with Adam and Eve, or with any human institution. It is not even defined by concepts so narrow as "global" and "universal."

> Oh, the depth of the riches of the wisdom and knowledge of God! How unsearchable his judgments, and his paths beyond tracing out! Who has known the mind of the Lord? Or who has been his counselor? Who has ever given to God, that God should repay him? For from him and through him and to him are all things. To him be the glory forever! Amen (Romans 11:33-36).

CHAPTER ONE

GOD'S GLOBAL VIEW

WE NEED TO BECOME GLOBAL CHRISTIANS WITH
A GLOBAL VISION BECAUSE WE HAVE A GLOBAL
GOD. THE LIVING GOD IS A MISSIONARY GOD.
—JOHN R.W. STOTT
RECTOR EMERITUS OF ALL SOULS CHURCH,
LONDON, ENGLAND

It may seem strange that we begin in the Old Testament because many think that world missions is only a concern of the New Testament and the New Testament church. "After all," common reasoning would say, "the Great Commission doesn't actually come until the Gospels (Matthew, Mark, Luke and John) and the Book of Acts."

This Biblical overview is intended to reverse the misconception that the first mention of the universal concerns of God for the whole world, and His heart for all mankind, is only found in the Gospels and the books of the New Testament. It is my purpose to trace the Old Testament foundations for world evangelization.

Categories of Review

There are at least four ways to look at the Old Testament.

1. *Events*. If we did a search under the category "great events," we would see the following: the Creation, the Flood, Abraham's call, Joseph's move to Egypt, the Exodus (deliverance through the Red Sea), the building and dedication of the Temple, the Exile, and so forth.

2. *Biographical*. We could view the Old Testament through the lives and stories of people—a biographical approach. If we looked at the Old Testament this way, we would highlight Abraham, Moses, Deborah, Esther, David, Daniel and others.

3. *Chronological.* Some have traced God's heart for the nations in the Old Testament by producing chronological Bibles that begin with a point in time, trying to show that one book is older than the other. J. Herbert Kane argues that in three time spans—before, during and after the Babylonian Captivity—there is clear evidence of a missions obligation to the Gentiles.[2]

This argument is very important. There would be some who would say that you could look at some postexilic prophets (Ezra, Zechariah and others), and they would say: "Sure, there are all kinds of statements in those Prophets about reaching out to the nations, and being a light to the nations, and reaching out to surrounding people because by this time the people of God had already spent 70 years in Babylonian captivity. And, after all, if you were scattered out among the nations you definitely would have an international/intercultural perspective, wouldn't you?"

While working in broadcast journalism in Los Angeles a number of years ago, I attended a press conference at the Beverly Hilton Hotel where FBI Director Clarence Kelly was explaining the whereabouts of heiress Patty Hearst, who was kidnapped by an American underground movement known as the Symbionese Liberation Army. One thing that was interesting to track was a psychological study of Patty Hearst's statements to the press after she was kidnapped. This is noticeable when people are kidnapped and held, and later make statements to the press. One day she was a regular rich kid, the daughter of publishing billionaire Randolph Hearst. After being captured, her statements to the press sounded very much like she was a radical underground revolutionary. The argument, of course, is that under captivity victims begin to speak their captors' language and say things they really do not mean because of fear, stress and psychological manipulation.

This might be the argument some would take with Israel. They would say that before going into Babylonian captivity, Israel was a pure race—inward, nationalistic, self-oriented. Then, the messages coming out of Israel after the Babylonian

Captivity had an international/intercultural world outlook. There is evidence, however, to suggest that from the opening pages of Scripture, long before the Babylonian Captivity, there is a strong focus on the entire world of nations.

4. *International/Intercultural.* Another possibility is an international/intercultural view of the Old Testament through the eyes of missiology. I am not suggesting that you will find a fully developed "Great Commission" in the Old Testament like the one Jesus preached on the Mount of Olives. What you will find, however, is a well-stated purpose from the heart of God that He wants His people to be a light to the nations.

In the Old Testament we do not necessarily see people forming missionary bands and going out to make disciples of all the nations. What we will see, however, is a definite posture of invitation, inclusion, pluralism and international integration by the people of God throughout the Old Testament.

Four Traditional Divisions

The four traditional divisions of the Old Testament—Law, History, Poetic and Wisdom Books, and the Prophets—will be reviewed from an international and intercultural perspective.

The Bible that Jesus knew was divided somewhat differently. In His postresurrection reflection on the Old Testament foundations for His life and mission, Jesus referred to three main divisions of Scripture: "This is what I told you while I was still with you: Everything must be fulfilled that is written about me in the Law of Moses, the Prophets and the Psalms" (Luke 24:44). This is the so-called TaNaKh: the Torah, the Nebhiim and the Kethubim—the three divisions or sections of the Old Testament as the Jewish scholars divided the Scriptures then.

From the wellsprings of the Old Testament, Jesus demonstrated the prior forecasting of all the events of His life, death and resurrection. What about His mission to establish the church for which

He died? Is that mission not also a part of everything that "must be fulfilled that is written about me in the Law of Moses, the Prophets and the Psalms"? He moves quite naturally, then, from Luke 24:44 to His commission:

> Then he opened their minds so they could understand the Scriptures. He told them, 'This is what is written: The Christ will suffer and rise from the dead on the third day, and repentance and forgiveness of sins will be preached in his name to all nations, beginning at Jerusalem. You are witnesses of these things. I am going to send you what my Father has promised; but stay in the city until you have been clothed with power from on high' (vv. 45-49).

Jesus included the preaching of repentance and forgiveness of sin in His name to all nations, and the necessary enduement of power for that task, to be a part of the context of "all things" that must be fulfilled from the Law, the Prophets and the Psalms (v. 44). He was saying that there is equal evidence in the Old Testament for the preaching of salvation to the nations as there is for the purchase of that salvation in the Cross-Resurrection event.

We use Luke 24:44-49 to demonstrate the fulfillment of the messianic prophecies—the 30 pieces of silver, His ride into Jerusalem on a donkey, His betrayal by a friend, the place where He was born—all the intricacies of His life and ministry, death and resurrection. What about His mission for all of the nations? That is also in the Old Testament (v. 47). From the standpoint of a Pentecostal missiology, the prophecy of the enduement of power for that task is in the Old Testament as well.

Our purpose is to survey the main sections of Old Testament Scripture to draw insights for world evangelization from selected passages . . .

1. In the Law, Genesis 12 (the call of Abraham) and Exodus 19 (the call to Israel)

2. In the Historical Books, 1 Kings 8 (the dedicatory prayer over Solomon's temple)

3. In the Poetic and Wisdom Books, Psalm 67

4. In the Prophets, the "Servant Songs" of Isaiah and the books of Jonah, Daniel and others.

The Law

As we work our way back through the Law (Genesis, Exodus, Leviticus, Numbers and Deuteronomy), where would be the logical point to discuss Old Testament foundations for world evangelization? Perhaps it might be to work in reverse, starting in Deuteronomy on the plains of Moab at the end of the 40-year wanderings when Moses reminded Israel: "[God] defends the cause of the fatherless and the widow, and loves the alien, giving him food and clothing. And you are to love those who are aliens, for you yourselves were aliens in Egypt" (Deuteronomy 10:18, 19).

Numbers 14:12, 15-21. If we take a 40-year step backward from Deuteronomy to Kadesh Barnea in the wilderness of Paran, we find the rebellion of Israel (Numbers 14). Twelve spies were sent into Canaan, but only two believed Israel could take the land. Someone has said that the 12 came back speaking two different languages: 10 were speaking the language of unbelief; two were speaking the language of belief. God was ready to destroy them, but Moses interceded ("God, remember the nations") and God declared that despite the unbelief in Israel, all the earth would be filled with the glory of the Lord (vv.15-21).

Leviticus 16:29; 17:8; 19:33, 34. By working our way back through the Book of Leviticus, we see that the nations are among Israel and included as a part of the community of the King. Consider redefining your definition of Israel in the Old Testament from a purely ethnic, racial understanding to an ecclesiastical Israel that included all the people of God who submitted to and followed Him. Aliens participated in the Day of

Atonement (Leviticus 16:29), and foreigners could become a part of the nation of Israel and offer sacrifices with the people of God (17:8). A separate Bible study emerges out of an Old Testament concordance search under the words *alien, foreigner, sojourner, stranger, nations, Gentiles.*

It is clear in the Book of Leviticus, which was given prior to the wilderness wanderings and before they ever got to Canaan, that the worshiping community involved a variety of peoples. Leviticus 19:33, 34 stresses the proper treatment of Gentiles among the Jews: "When an alien lives with you in your land, do not mistreat him. The alien living with you must be treated as one of your native-born. Love him as yourself, for you were aliens in Egypt. I am the Lord your God." This is an important scripture in light of the tragedies we see in our world today: in South Africa; in former Yugoslavia; in the streets of America; in the "ethnic cleansing" that takes place in different parts of the world; in racial hatred.

In contemporary terms, no bumper stickers would have been allowed that read: "Israel: Love it or leave it!" or "Welcome to the Promised Land; now go home!" The alien could wear a cap or T-shirt that read: "Alien by birth; Israelite by the grace of God."

"You were aliens in Egypt," God reminded Israel. To us, *Egypt* may only be a five-letter word in Biblical history and contemporary Middle East affairs, but to Israel the word *Egypt* had a psychological impact. It was where they spent 400 years as hostage slaves under totalitarianism.

But it was in Egypt, in the midst of the nations, where God displayed His glory—the glory that He later said in Numbers 14:21 would fill the whole earth. God intended for His glory to be shown to the entire earth. This story unfolds in the next book, Exodus.

Exodus 9:13-16; 12:38, 48; 19:4-6 (see also Romans 12:1; 1 Peter 2:9-11; Revelation 1:6; 5:10). To the unbelieving nation of Egypt and to the hardened heart of its Pharaoh, God speaks in Exodus 9:13-16:

"This is what the Lord, the God of the Hebrews, says: Let my people go, so that they may worship me, or this time I will send the full force of my plagues against you and against your officials and your people, so you may know that there is no one like me in all the earth. For by now I could have stretched out my hand and struck you and your people with a plague that would have wiped you off the earth. But I have raised you up for this very purpose, that I might show you my power and that my name might be proclaimed in all the earth."

In the powerful *acts* of God on behalf of His people, there is an ultimate message intended for *all* the peoples of the earth. His primary audience, however, was the most powerful nation on earth at that time. God was extending grace and compassion to Pharaoh and to his entire nation: "I could have wiped you out, but I've let you live this long."

There was also a message of openness and pluralism in the newly formed redeemed community that was saved through the Red Sea in the Book of Exodus. Notice a very interesting word in Exodus 12. Among those that went out there was a "mixed multitude" which joined Israel in the Red Sea deliverance. They were just as surely a part of that redemption and covering as a native-born child of Abraham, Isaac and Jacob. This is a missiological inclusion of all peoples of the earth. A mixed multitude went out of Egypt with Israel, and aliens were allowed to celebrate the Jewish Passover meal (12:38, 48)!

Not only was there a message *for* the nations but a mission *to* the nations was placed upon Israel in Exodus 19:4-6. On the three-month anniversary of their deliverance from Egypt, God covenanted with them at Mount Sinai:

"You yourselves have seen what I did to Egypt, and how I carried you on eagles' wings and brought you to myself. Now if you obey me fully and keep my covenant, then out of all nations you will be my treasured possession. Although the whole earth is mine, you will be for me a kingdom of priests and a holy nation."

The King James rendering of verse 5 begins with "Now therefore," which indicates the context of grace and redemption as well as covenanting. As the listing of the Ten Commandments begins in the next chapter (20:1), God reminds His people that He has brought them out of bondage and therefore expects holy living in the covenant community. This passage also expresses that they should show their gratitude by glorifying God for being carried out on "eagles' wings."

We could almost close our eyes at Sinai and replace the text of Exodus 19:4-6 with Romans 12:1, where, in view of God's mercy, the New Testament Gentile believers are instructed to therefore offer their bodies as living sacrifices in reasonable service to God. Peter draws from the Exodus 19 commissioning of Israel to speak to the *new* Israel—the church: "But you are a chosen people, a royal priesthood, a holy nation, a people belonging to God, that you may declare the praises of him who called you out of darkness into his wonderful light" (1 Peter 2:9). The reason we are saved, set apart and sent as a "peculiar people" (KJV) is to proclaim our redemption and deliverance.

I believe God was saying to them in Exodus 19, "Look what I've done for you. I've called you out of Egypt. I've delivered you. I've set you on eagles' wings, and now I am going to make you a kingdom of priests to be an interceding, proclaiming community for the surrounding peoples of this earth so that you can be salt and light and bring redemption to the surrounding world."

For Old Testament Israel, this was surely their commissioning. It was no less a calling than that which is given to the New Testament church in 1 Peter 2:9-11. The *entire* nation, not just a select group of Levitical priests, was to function in a priestly/prophetic role on behalf of the *surrounding* nations. They were to be mediators with a mission—to witness to the reality of the one true God in the presence of the peoples of the earth. One might say that they were called *out of* the nations to live *among* the nations in order to be a witness *to* the nations. This setting forth of a national priesthood (typifying the New Testament priesthood of all believers in 1 Peter 2:9 and Revelation 1:6; 5:10) comes in Exodus 19, *preceding* the establishment of the Levitical priesthood in Exodus 28. The Levitical priesthood was ordained by God, but it came *after* the ordination of the entire nation as a nation of priests to serve the other nations.

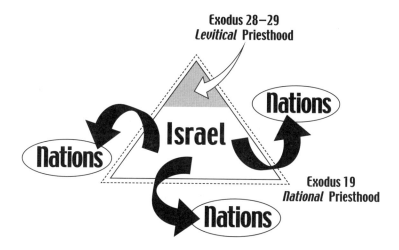

If, then, the special priests in Israel represented the 12 tribes and their families, to serve as healing agents *within* the community of Israel, then the *entire* nation was being commissioned in Exodus 19 to be a mediator for *all* the families of nations! The issue was not only *accessibility* to God for their own salvation, but *accountability* to God for the salvation of the Gentiles.

Reflections

1. What are three new ideas you have learned from God's global view in the Old Testament?

2. The Old Testament law (for example, in Exodus and Leviticus) speaks of loving and accepting the "alien," "foreigner," "sojourner," "stranger," "nations" and "Gentiles." What is God saying to you about foreigners and international immigrants coming to your city and country?

Pause now for personal or group prayer before moving to Projections/Actions.

Projections:

Today's date_____

By this time next year, next month, next week, I believe God for the following ministry goals to connect to God's work in my world (enter calendar dates for accountability):

1. Next year (date_____)

2. Next month (date_____)

3. Next week (date_____)

Actions:

By this time tomorrow—in the next 24 hours—I will . . .

1.

2.

A Telescope and a Microscope

IF YOU LIVE WITHOUT A VISION OF THE GLORY
OF GOD FILLING THE WHOLE EARTH, YOU ARE
IN DANGER OF SERVING YOUR OWN DREAMS
OF GREATNESS.
—FLOYD McCLUNG, JR.
MISSIONS VISIONARY/PASTOR

David Howard depicts the Genesis view of things as God allowing us to look through both a telescope and a microscope. In Genesis 1—11 we see the telescopic picture of the universe—the Creation, the Flood, the foundation of nations and cities, the entrance of universal sin into all of mankind, and so forth. In chapters 12—50, however, it is as if God is laying aside the telescope and picking up the microscope and is saying, "This is where I begin to work My plan through the individual, personal lives of four people." We call them the patriarchs: Abraham, Isaac, Jacob and Joseph.

A Telescope: The Nations (Genesis 1-11)

Genesis 1:1—Creation. Genesis 1:1 begins with the phrase "In the beginning God . . ." Although it may be our tendency to have it otherwise, the first verse of the Bible begins with God. The Bible does not begin with a missions department, a local church, a missions strategist, conference or class. The Bible does not begin with Israel or even the Church of God— the Bible begins with God, the God of the church. Biblically, theologically and missiologically, this is crucial to our understanding of missions. This is why we go to the foundational text of the Word of God, in Genesis 1:1.

In this regard we speak of the *missio Dei*, "the mission of God," as opposed to the *missio ecclesia*, "the mission of the church." In his book *The Bible Basics of Missions,* Robert Hall Glover says this about this mission:

> The missionary enterprise is no human conception or under-taking, no modern scheme or invention, no mere philan-thropy even of the finest kind. It did not originate in the brain or heart of any man, not even of William Carey, or the apostle Paul. Its source was in the heart of God himself. And Jesus Christ, God's great Missionary to a lost world, was the supreme revelation of His heart and expression of His love.[1]

This is expressed in another way by J. Herbert Kane:

> From first to last the Christian mission is God's mission, not man's. It originated in the *heart* of God. It is based on the love of God. It is determined by the *will* of God. Its mandate was enunciated by the *Son* of God. Its rationale is explained in the *Word* of God. For its ultimate success it is dependent upon the *power* of God.[2]

Genesis 1:1 reveals the sovereignty of God as the originator of His mission. There is no participation in God without participation in His mission. When we enter into a relationship with God and follow after Him, we automatically become a part of His mission. This is integral to basic Christian discipleship. This verse continues by saying, "In the beginning God created the heavens and the earth," indicating that from the outset the heavens and the earth were the focus of God. He is not to be limited to a province or people or place, but, "The earth is the Lord's, and everything in it, the world, and all who live in it" (Psalm 24:1).

Genesis 1:28—Command. The universal scope and concern in the opening lines of Scripture is continued in Genesis 1:28—the commission of God to Adam and Eve: "God blessed them and said to them, 'Be fruitful and increase in number; fill the earth and subdue it.'"

From an ecological standpoint of what is called the "cultural mandate," many Christians do not feel any responsibility to care for earth's resources because of their expectations of the return of the Lord. They live a life of wasteful consumerism with no regard for air pollution, the environment or the whole world of God's creation.

Our cultural mandate is to care for the world of resources, the created world and the orderly society of human beings in which we live. The "evangelistic mandate" is to make disciples of all nations, and that takes priority. To deprive people of the opportunity to hear the name of Jesus and be His followers is the greatest social injustice. Winning drug dealers, for example, and getting them off the streets not only brings followers to Christ, it contributes to the social betterment and security of communities. Therefore, making disciples is social action.

Genesis 3:15—Conquest/Comfort. This is the God who, already in the third chapter of Genesis, is sending a Savior as a response to man's sinful disobedience. Genesis 3:15 speaks of the universal Savior for all mankind who will destroy the adversary.

Genesis 9:1—Commission. This is the sending God who repeats His initial commissioning of Adam and Eve to Noah as he and his family emerge from the ark. Genesis 1:28 and 9:1 are identical. God wanted Noah to have the same message that Adam and Eve had, "Be fruitful, multiply, fill the earth."

Genesis 11:1-9—Confusion. It is this sending God whom we see in Genesis 11 whose purposes will not be frustrated by the designs and schemes of evil men at the Tower of Babel. Notice the "ethnocentrism" present in their inwardness and refusal to obey the sending God. This is portrayed in their use of "we" and "us": "Come, let us build ourselves a city, with a tower that reaches to the heavens, so that we may make a name for ourselves and not be scattered over the face of the whole earth" (v. 4).

They were saying "Come" when God was saying "Go, be fruitful, multiply, scatter across the earth." Their ethnocentrism at a national level is the same self-seeking spirit to be found in egocentrism at a personal level and ecclesiocentrism in general and local church life. Just as Babel was doomed to fail, the local church will fail when the "spirit of Babel" enters. Christians are meant to be salt and light, scattered, spread around, doing good.

"Christians are like fertilizer," said one farmer. "When scattered over the field they do a lot of good. But when piled up in one place, all they do is make a big stink!" Babel warns us against the stink and sin of selfishness. "The church," one person said, "is the only institution on earth that exists primarily for the benefit of its *nonmembers*."

Genesis 11 (Babel) and Acts 2 (Pentecost). God did three things at Babel. He came down, He confused their language, and He scattered them abroad. In a parallel blessing in Acts 2, God came down, He gave them a new language as the Spirit gave them the utterance, and God scattered them across the Mediterranean world.

"THE BABEL BLESSING" (GENESIS 11:1–9)

God did three things:	An interesting parallel (Acts 2–Pentecost):
1. He came down.	1. God came down (Holy Spirit).
2. He confused the language.	2. He gave a new tongue(s).
3. He scattered them abroad.	3. He scattered them abroad.

A Microscope: Abraham, Isaac, Jacob and Joseph (Genesis 12–50)

At this point the telescope is laid aside and the microscope focuses on the personal workings of God in the life of one man and his family. From this point on, Israel will be reminded that God is the God of Abraham, Isaac and Jacob—a very personal God.

God chose Abraham in order to build a missionary nation. Through this new people He would raise up from Abraham, He would witness of Himself from a nation to the nations. This is how it reads in Genesis 12:1-3:

> The Lord had said to Abram, "Leave your country, your peo-ple and your father's household and go to the land I will show you. I will make you into a great nation and I will bless you; I will make your name great, and you will be a blessing. I will bless those who bless you, and whoever curses you I will curse; and all peoples on earth will be blessed through you."

According to Walter Kaiser, the key word in this passage is *bless* or *blessing*. Notice how often the word *bless* is used. This word also characterizes the first 11 chapters of the book. Note, for example, Genesis 1:28 (God blessed Adam and Eve) and Genesis 9:1 (God blessed Noah).

After the blessing of God in 12:2, Kaiser points out that there is in the Hebrew language a purpose clause: "so that." In other words, it can read, "You will be blessed *so that* you may be a blessing." Is there any need, then, to search further in the Bible for the evidence of God's richest blessings on a denomination, a local church, a fam-ily, or an individual who will obey God's commission?

Abraham's Call: 12:1–3

There are three dimensions in God's call to Abraham. Abraham's call was first of all a nongeographical call. Second, it had the characteristic of being a call to mobility. Finally, it was a call to universality.

Nongeographical. Abraham's ultimate calling was to a land. His primary calling, however, was not only to a land, but it was also to a lifetime of leading. His calling was not just to property, but to a Person. This is a fundamental realization that takes us beyond a certain syndrome we get into in the ministry. We get hung up about God's will for places. This issue was not a place— it was the lordship of Jehovah God in his life.

According to Hebrews 11:8, Abraham did not know where he was going when he started. He was being called to a life of fol- lowership and discipleship. The land came as he began moving out in faith. As an illustration, it is very difficult to steer a parked automobile. You have to start the automobile moving before you can start steering it in the right direction.

Mobility. There are a number of myths and misconceptions about missions. One of them comes from the statement "*Some* can go; *most* can give; *all* can pray." Notice the progression: some . . . most . . . all. That is a pietistic-sounding slogan heard in churches or missions conferences. The subtle hierarchy limit- ing "some" at the top of the pyramid implies that only special, superspiritual saints can go.

The above statement needs to be rephrased: "*All* can go; *all* can give; *all* can pray." It's a matter of asking how far do we go or what is the nature of our going. To walk across the street and witness to a neighbor is "going." The cultural and geographical distance is left up to God. But all *can* go, and all *must* go.

Universality. The third aspect of Abraham's call was to uni- versality. God promised Abraham that through his seed He would touch all the nations of the earth. This is also possible today. Because of our obedience, life-changing experiences can take place in other parts of the world. In Acts 8, Philip obeys the Lord, leaves Samaria, goes down and speaks to a man on his way home to Ethiopia. This is thought to be the beginning of spread- ing the gospel in northeast Africa, and what is later known as the Coptic church in Egypt and Ethiopia. These movements could trace their roots to one person, a layman, who willingly obeyed the call of God. This set off universal implications.

In the early 1900s two Pentecostal laymen in Chicago obeyed the call to Brazil. As a result, by 2000 there were more than 25 million Pentecostals in that South American country. This was a call with universal implications.

The Building of a Missionary Nation: Israel

God begins to build a missionary nation through Abraham. Here, we have a "come and see" structure. The Old Testament is not as strong on the "going/proclaiming," as it is on the "come in and see" what God is doing. There was the scattering, sending and going out, but it was not as evident as it was in the New Testament.

Two Missionary Structures:

Old Testament   **New Testament**

"Come and See"   **"Go and Tell"**
(centripetal)   **(centrifugal)**

Ralph Winter has suggested that there are "go mechanisms" and "come mechanisms" throughout Scripture. Some are voluntary while others are involuntary. For example, a voluntary "go mechanism" is when Abraham obeyed God's call and went to

Canaan. An involuntary "go mechanism" is when people are reluctant and go against their will (i.e., Joseph being sold into Egypt; Naomi and Ruth; Jonah, the story of the reluctant missionary; etc.). The involuntary dispersion of God's people later turned out to be a blessing not only for them, but also for the surrounding people where they were taken.

The "voluntary coming" is seen in Naaman the Syrian coming to Elisha, the Queen of Sheba coming to Solomon's court, and so forth. The "involuntary coming" can be seen in people being drawn against their will, although it turns to be a matter of God's blessing. We can see this also in the demographical stirring in our world today. Winter believes this has serious missiological implications.

GO **Mechanism** **Voluntary**	Abraham to Canaan Minor Prophets preach to other nations near Israel Pharisees sent out "over land and see"	Jesus in Samaria Peter to Cornelius Paul and Barnabus on their missionary journeys Witness of other Christians in Babylon, Rome, Cyprus, Alexandria, etc.	Patrick to Ireland Celtic peregrini to England and Europe Friars to China, India, Japan, America Moravians to America	William Carey and other missionaries of 1st Era Hudson Taylor and the 2nd Era Missionaries Third Era Missionaries
Involuntary	Joseph sold into Egypt witnesses to Pharaoh Naomi witnesses to Ruth because of famine Jonah—the reluctant missionary Hebrew girl is taken off to Namaan's home Captive Hebrews in Babylon witness to captors	Persecution of Christians forces them out of Holy Land all over Roman empire and beyond	Ulfilas sold as slave to the Goths Exiled Asian bishops go to Gothic areas Christians captured by the Vikings win them Christian soldiers sent by Rome to England, Spain, etc. Pilgrims and Puritans forced to the Americas and to discover their mission to the Indians	WWII Christian soldiers sent around the globe return to start 150 new mission agencies Ugandan Christians flee to other parts of Africa Korean Christians flee to less-Christian South, later sent to Saudi Arabia and Iran, etc. to work
COME **Mechanism** **Voluntary**	Naaman the Syrian came to Elisha Queen of Sheba came to Solomon's court Ruth chose to go to Judah from Moab	Greeks who sought out Jesus Cornelius sends for Peter Man of Macedonia calls to Paul	Goths invade Christian Rome, learn more of the Christian faith Vikings invade Christian Europe, are won to the faith eventually through that contact	The Influx of International visitors, students, and businessmen into the Christian West
Involuntary	Gentiles settled in Israel by Cyrus the Great (II Kings 17).	Roman military occupation and infiltration of "Galilee of the Gentiles"	Slaves brought from Africa to America	Refugees from Communism Boat people, Cubans forced out, etc.

History

Presence/Proclamation: 1 Kings 10:6; 2 Kings 5. God's mission is revealed in the biographies and events of the Historical

Books from Joshua to Esther. Israel is beginning to possess the land and establish the nation in Canaan, in the midst of the nations. Here we see the Old Testament foundation for the missiological concept of "presence," that is, being a specific kind of people living in the presence of other people. Unfortunately, many theologians and missiologists have stopped at this point and have seen presence as the only suitable form of witness to the nations.

For example, Ferdinand Hahn believes that the Old Testament bears a "completely passive character."[3] In other words, the Old Testament people of God are passive participants who have no call to the other nations.

This, however, was not the nature of the intended witnessing community when God commissioned Israel in Genesis 12 and Exodus 19. Surely, there is more than presence. There is also *proclamation* and *persuasion*. We see this in the Historical Books. Throughout the Old Testament, as Gentiles became proselytes and God-fearers, it was because they had *heard* about God and God's mighty deeds. Israel's mission was both in word and deed.

This was the case of the Queen of Sheba, who *heard* and came (1 Kings 10:6), and of Naaman the Syrian, who was healed through the *testimony* of a captive Jewish maiden (2 Kings 5). It includes the story of Rahab, who lived on the wall of Jericho and *heard* what was going on in Israel, and the story of Ruth from Moab, who was brought to faith in God through the *witness* of God's scattered people.

Another example is the story of Esther, whose book closes the historical section of the Old Testament. Esther lived out her testimony in Persia in the presence of the king and non-Jewish people. Mordecai stated that she had come to the kingdom "for such a time as this." Esther's cross-cultural witness bore witness to monotheism, the only true God, and brought blessings and salvation to her people.

Temple Dedication: 1 Kings 8:41-43. This is what we see again in 1 Kings 8. The fact that Israel was to be a proclaiming community, not just a community of presence, is highlighted in Solomon's prayer at the dedication of the Temple.

> As for the foreigner who does not belong to your people Israel but has come from a distant land because of your name—for men will hear of your great name and your mighty hand and your outstretched arm—when he comes and prays toward this temple, then hear from heaven, your dwelling place, and do whatever the foreigner asks of you, so that all the peoples of the earth may know your name and fear you, as do your own people Israel, and may know that this house I have built bears your Name (vv. 41-43).

Second Chronicles 2:17 reveals that while Solomon was praying this prayer, there were already 153,600 aliens living in Jerusalem. Many of these were foremen and builders who had constructed the Temple. The Temple for all the people of God and all nations of the earth was built by representatives from the nations!

Poetic and Wisdom Books

Through the songs, stories and worship of the missionizing community of Israel, we hear the heartbeat of international theology, particularly in the Psalms. In *A Biblical Theology of Missions*, George Peters claims, "The Psalter is one of the greatest missionary books in the world. There are more than 175 references with a universal theme relating to the nations of the world."[4]

Rich applications to the Old Testament foundations of world evangelization are found in Psalms 2, 22, 33, 47, 50, 66, 67, 72, 96, 98, 117 and 145.

In looking at Psalm 67, we see an international consciousness:

> May God be gracious to us and bless us and make his face shine upon us, Selah. That your ways may be known on earth, and your salvation among all nations. May the peoples praise you, O God; may all the peoples praise you. May the

nations be glad and sing for joy, for you rule the peoples just-
ly and guide the nations of the earth. Selah. May the peoples
praise you, O God; may all the peoples praise you. Then the
land will yield its harvest, and God, our God, will bless us.
God will bless us, and all the ends of the earth will fear him.

In comparing Psalm 67 with Genesis 11, notice the different
uses of "us" and "we." Both references have these uses, but
Genesis 11 reveals selfishness, whereas Psalm 67 reveals *selfless-
ness*. Genesis 11 reveals an attitude of self-glorification, whereas
Psalm 67 reveals an attitude of *self-humiliation*. In Genesis 11
there is a concern for security, while in Psalm 67 there is a concern
for *service*. Psalm 67 becomes a prayer toward proclamation.

Walter Kaiser notes that Psalm 67 is derived from the Aaronic
benediction found in Numbers 6:24-26, where Moses says: "The
Lord bless you and keep you; the Lord make his face shine upon
you and be gracious to you; the Lord turn his face toward you
and give you peace." But the psalmist has revised the blessing
somewhat. Rather than using the *Yahweh* of Numbers 6 (meaning "Lord," Israel's covenantal and personal name for God), he
substitutes *Elohim* (meaning "God," the name used when God's
relationship to *all* people and nations is needed). The psalmist is
recognizing that the purpose of the blessing of God is found
when the covenant blessing is shared with all nations.

This agrees with the sense and purpose of God's commission
to Abraham in Genesis 12:2, 3. According to Kaiser, "Three times
this psalm refers to the blessing from God: verses 1, 6 and 7. The
structure is almost an exact replica of Genesis 12:2, 3. Bless us,
bless us, bless us . . . so that all the nations might know the Lord."[5]

A further observation from this missionary psalm will be of
special interest to "globalbelievers." Old Testament researchers
think that Psalm 67 was probably sung at the Feast of Pentecost.
Pentecost took place 50 days after the offering of the firstfruits,
coming at the beginning of the summer harvest season. The
psalmist specifically refers to the ingathering of the harvest (v. 6)

and sees this as symbolic of the ingathering of the spiritual harvest from the ends of the earth.

It was both a present desire for the psalmist and a prophetic word toward the Day of Pentecost in the New Testament. One can almost visualize that day in Acts 2 when representatives from all nations were gathered in Jerusalem for the Feast of Pentecost. When they sang this hymn (Psalm 67) with its international imagery, its message "actualized" by the presence and power of the Holy Spirit.

Let us, then, in the spirit of Psalm 67 and Acts 2, pray that God's Holy Spirit anointing will be "gracious to us and make his face shine upon us" *so that* we may witness in the power of the Holy Spirit and take His message to all nations. When we hoard the blessing of the baptism of the Holy Spirit and misinterpret its meaning, we miss the mission of the God of the Old Testament and we fail the purpose of the Lord Jesus Christ, the Baptizer in the Holy Spirit revealed in the New Testament (Matthew 3:11; Mark 1:8; Luke 3:16; John 1:33).

The Prophets

George Peters, in *A Biblical Theology of Missions,* articulates three truths surrounding Israel's missionary mission. These are clearly stated throughout the writings of the prophets, especially Isaiah.

Israel's mission is a God-appointed mission. God is the source and the originator of His mission. He created Jacob. He formed Israel. He redeemed His people. He is the Creator and Redeemer, the King and Holy One of Israel. These phrases and designations are repeated throughout Scripture. Israel is not a self-made people, nor a nation of a self-appointed destiny; Israel, God said, is "the people I formed for myself that they may proclaim my praise" (Isaiah 43:21). This was not a development, or a humanitarian feeling coming from Israel to help the other nations. Israel is peculiarly God's people for a uniquely divine mission and purpose.

Israel's mission is a God-centered mission. As God is the originator of the mission of Israel, so He is also its center and content. Israel existed principally in Old Testament times for the purpose of upholding ethical monotheism (one true, holy God) in
the midst of a surrounding sea of paganism and false gods. In the
midst of competing worldviews, systems, and allegiances that
were in the nations surrounding Israel, the center of Israel's mission was God: "This is what the Lord says—Israel's King and
Redeemer, the Lord Almighty: I am the first and I am the last;
apart from me there is no God" (Isaiah 44:6).

Israel's mission is a mission to the nations. The mission was
not just in, of, and for Israel. It is for the surrounding nations.
Robert Hall Glover states, "The finest missionary teachings of
the Old Testament are to be found in the Prophets where a worldwide outlook is always clearly recognizable even when the central message is relating to Israel itself."[6] The Book of Isaiah is
particularly clear on this mission to the nations (45:21; 49:6;
52:10; 56:7).

J. Herbert Kane (*Christian Missions in Biblical Perspective*)
notes three developments *before* the Captivity:

- Strangers were permitted to enter the congregation of Israel.

- Entire nations were to be attracted to the God of Israel.

- All the nations were to know and worship the Lord.[7]

During the Exile, Israel's missionary role began to shift from
that of an attracting force to an outward-going force. Instead of
the nations of the world flocking to Jerusalem to learn the Law
of the Lord, the Law was taken by the Jews of Diaspora to the
ends of the earth. For the first time in her history, Israel became
actively involved in winning converts outside of Israel in the
Diaspora. One of the chief characteristics of the Diaspora was
proselyting. Jesus refers to this in Matthew 23:15:

> "Woe to you, teachers of the law and Pharisees, you hyp-
> ocrites! You travel over land and sea to win a single convert,

and when he becomes one, you make him twice as much a
son of hell as you are."

There was aggressive missionary activity occurring more
than 100 years before Christ. From the beginning, the Jews in
Rome exhibited such an aggressive spirit of proselytism that
they were charged with infecting the Romans with their cult,
and the government expelled the chief Jewish propagandist
from the city in 139 B.C.

Six characteristics of religious life among the Jews during this
time identified this outgoing movement:

- The institution of the synagogue: It is difficult to overesti-
  mate the importance of the synagogue in the religious life
  of the Jews in the Diaspora. The synagogue became the
  chief means of making converts. It became the place where
  proselytes and God-fearers could come and learn about the
  one true God.

- The observance of the Sabbath

- The translation of the Scriptures into Greek (the
  Septuagint)

- The teaching of monotheism (one true God)

- The practice of morality: Immorality ranked with idolatry
  as one of the two great sins of the pagan world.

- The prophetic promise of a coming Savior[8]

These contributions of the Jews in the Diaspora helped pave
the way for the "fullness of the time" (Galatians 4:4, *NKJV*).

Reflections

1. In the story of Genesis how does God help us look through a telescope and a microscope?

2. Take a look again at special passages like Genesis 12, 1 Kings 8 and Psalm 67. What is God saying to you through these passages about His work in the world?

*Pause now for personal or group prayer before moving to Projections/Actions.

Projections:

Today's date_____

By this time next year, next month, next week, I believe God for the following ministry goals to connect to God's work in my world (enter calendar dates for accountability):

1. Next year (date_____)
2. Next month (date_____)
3. Next week (date_____)

Actions:

By this time tomorrow—in the next 24 hours—I will . . .
1.

2.

CHAPTER THREE

A *KAIROS* THING

WHEN GOD'S FINGER POINTS, GOD'S
HAND WILL OPEN THE DOOR.
—CLARENCE W. JONES
MISSIONARY TO ECUADOR

E J. and Violet Reynolds were frantic with despair. They had not heard from their daughter, Ronda, in weeks. Thanksgiving, Christmas, and New Year's Day had come and gone—but not a word from Ronda. She had been on an extended vacation trip to Europe with friends and had started her trip keeping her parents posted by mail. They knew that she had been to London, Paris, Brussels, Rome, Madrid, and other cities but eventually had lost touch. They were sick with worry and disappointment. E.J. recalls:

> I did all I could to comfort and reassure my wife, then spent that night and most of the early morning in earnest prayer and thought. I needed help from God. . . . As I was praying, I felt impressed to make a transatlantic call to Barcelona, to see if there was some kind of American restaurant in that area. There was, the operator said, a place called Kentucky Grill in a suburb. I placed a person-to-person call. It was about 9:30 a.m. in the U.S., mid-afternoon in Spain.[1]

"Mid-afternoon in Spain" turned out to be God's *kairos* moment for E.J., Violet and Ronda. Thankfully the owner of the restaurant could speak English. Pastor Reynolds identified himself, explained the situation and asked if there would be anyone in the restaurant named Ronda. At that very moment the man saw three girls passing his doorway on the street.

Recognizing them as Americans he stepped to the door and asked if one of them was named Ronda Reynolds. To his amazement one of the three was in fact Ronda. She came to the phone for a wonderful reunion with her parents!

God had heard and answered prayer and carefully orchestrated His precision *kairos* moment. *Kairos* is a New Testament Greek word meaning a specific, strategic, opportune moment in time (as opposed to *chronos*, from which we get our modern word *chronology*, meaning the passage of time from minute to hour to days to weeks, etc.).

It was a *kairos* thing when Jesus Christ came to this world and began His story in history. This is what Paul meant when he testified, "But when the time [*kairos*] had fully come, God sent his Son . . ." (Galatians 4:4). The *kairos* was ready: There was the "Pax Romana" ("peace of Rome"), a stable world government controlled by Rome, ensuring international commerce and travel. Roman roads across the empire and international shipping lanes made travel accessible on land and sea. There was a universal language—the "koine" Greek which was commonly understood and used in multinational business. The Old Testament Scriptures had been translated into this global medium. Knowledge of the one true Jehovah God had spread throughout the Jewish Diaspora in synagogues and Jewish communities across the Greek-Roman world.

This was God's globalization moment. It was *kairos* in time and space. God was driving the world market toward a new "e-commerce" moment—the convergence and connection of His own "evangelism-commerce," His New Testament people (the early church), the agents of change.

Ekklesia, Koinonia, Diaspora: "A Gathered Fellowship That Is Scattered"

How can a church be gathered and scattered simultaneously? Although it seems it should be one way or the other, Scripture indicates otherwise. James 1:1 gives us some insight on this matter:

"James, a servant of God and of the Lord Jesus Christ, to the twelve tribes scattered among the nations: Greetings."

James uses the word *scattered*, which in the Greek is *diaspora* (dispersion). In dissecting the word we see that it is a combination of the Greek preposition *dia* ("through") and the word *spora* (which is the root word for "seeds"). This word paints the picture of seeds that blow in the wind, take root, and produce plants. James refers to believers who are scattered because of persecution. Like seeds blown in the wind, these believers take root wherever they are and produce churches.

I have a childhood memory from a watermelon feed in my backyard one hot summer night. About 100 people from my church attended. As everyone sat around eating watermelon, they spat the seeds out on the grass. Within days, watermelon plants were everywhere. The combination of the hot, dry central California afternoon climate, and the early morning dew produced these sprouts.

This is the picture of the New Testament diaspora—what the New Testament church is supposed to be. The church is not meant to be a monolithic, centralized conglomerate gathered in one place (one big plant) like the people aspired to be at Babel in Genesis 11. It is meant to be scattered across communities and nations, with new plants sprouting everywhere. Tertullian, an early-church father, described it like this: "We have infiltrated the marketplace, the centers of power, the seats of learning, your senates and your schools, and your exchanges. We have left nothing for you but the temples of your gods." That is the idea of the dispersion and the integration, and the salt and light of the people of God who are meant to infiltrate, to integrate and to participate in every dimension of society.

The Totality of Christ's Command

Everything we need to complete Christ's command is provided in the Great Commission (Matthew 28:9-20). I like to call it the

"Totality of Christ's Command" because of the frequent use of the word *all*. This all-inclusive word appears five times in the original text.

"All hail"—28:9: the Summons of our mission. "And as they went to tell his disciples, behold, Jesus met them saying, All hail. And they came and held him by the feet, and worshiped him" (KJV).

Jesus greeted them with His joyous "All hail," and the women responded in worship. This was more than just a casual, everyday greeting. It was a victorious salutation of the One who had conquered death forever. This was an eternal "Good morning" greeting! Out of this context of worship came the Great Commission, an outflow of the "Great Celebration" because of Christ's resurrection. His joyous eternal life is our summons to mission. He lives—we preach His good news of eternal life!

"All power"—28:18: the Source of our mission. "And Jesus came and spake unto them, saying, All power is given unto me in heaven and in earth" (KJV).

The source of our mission cannot be found in our humanitarian benevolence or in our natural inclination to help hurting, grieving people. We should also not go just because people are dying and going to hell. We should go because of the ultimate glory of God and because Jesus Christ, who is Lord over all nations, commands us to go. This is the source of our mission.

"All nations" (panta ta ethne)—*28:19: the Scope of our mission.* "Therefore go and make disciples of all nations, baptizing them in the name of the Father and of the Son and of the Holy Spirit."

The Greek word that is used for "nations" is *ethne*. The linguistic meaning of this word does not mean "nation" in the modern sense of the word—it means "a cultural, linguistic, ethnic, racial grouping of people, even living within a nation." This meaning also takes the word beyond a mere racial designation. In one way or another, we all have an *ethne*, a people group into which we were born. Jesus tells us that He wants us to make disciples of every one of the *ethne*. Donald McGavran, founder of the Church Growth Movement, called these the "segments of society." All the *ethne* are the scope of our mission.

"All things"—28:20a: the Subject of our mission. "Teaching them to observe all things whatsoever I have commanded you" (KJV).

It is particularly important to understand that the mission of the church involves the fullness of the kingdom of God, in all its miraculous demonstrations, not just the announcement of the message of salvation. It is both a verbal announcement and a demonstration of signs and wonders, healing, and engaging evil powers. This is inclusive in what Jesus is saying.

"All the days"—28:20b: The Strength of our mission. "And, lo, I am with you alway [literally, "all the days"], even unto the end of the world" (KJV).

This is our strength, our encouragement, our fortitude. In doing what we feel God would have us to do, we know He is with us. Two variations on the definition of the "end of the world" include both a geographical and eschatological view. He is with us geographically—to the most distant and remote parts of the earth. He is with us eschatologically—to the very end of time, to the "end of the age."

Other Great Commission Scriptures

Mark 16:15: "And he said unto them, Go ye into all the world, and preach the gospel to every creature" (KJV).

In this passage we see another example of David Howard's "Telescope and Microscope" perspective. We see all the nations and the individual, personal God. In this commission there is the combination of the general ("all") and the individual ("every"). God wants us to win the entire world, but we accomplish this by working with individual people. Jesus had four or five major addresses to large groups of people, but we find 28 occasions in the New Testament where Jesus spoke to individuals. That 1:7 ratio favors individual encounters.

Luke 24:46-49: He told them, "This is what is written: The Christ will suffer and rise from the dead on the third day, and repentance and forgiveness of sins will be preached in his name to all nations, beginning at Jerusalem. You are witnesses of these things. I am going to send you what my Father has promised; but stay in the city until you have been clothed with power from on high."

This commission comes out of the context of worship and includes the command to wait upon the indispensable enduement of power for mission, the baptism in the Holy Spirit.

John 20:20, 21: "After he said this, he showed them his hands and his side. The disciples were overjoyed when they saw the Lord. Again Jesus said, 'Peace be with you! As the Father has sent me, I am sending you.'"

David Howard notes the two different uses of the word *send* in verse 21. The first one is in the aorist (past) tense, meaning, "I have been sent once and for all." This action has been taken once and is not repeated. Jesus has come once and for all. The second sending is in the present active indicative, meaning a continued action—"I am sending you, and I will keep on sending you until the work is completed."

He continues to send today. The sending responsibility of the church is not optional or expendable. It is to continue until Christ comes. Acts 1:8 says, "But you will receive power when the Holy Spirit comes on you; and you will be my witnesses in Jerusalem, and in all Judea and Samaria, and to the ends of the earth."

Mission Central to the New Testament

- Every book in the New Testament was written by a foreign missionary.

- Every letter in the New Testament that was written to an individual was written to a convert of a foreign missionary.

- Every epistle in the New Testament that was written to a church was written to a foreign missionary church.

- The one book of prophecy in the New Testament (Revelation) was written to seven foreign missionary churches of Asia.

- The only authoritative history of the early Christian church is a foreign missionary journal (Acts).

- The disciples were called Christians first in a foreign missionary community (Antioch).

- The map of the early Christian world is the tracing of the journeys of the first missionaries.

- Of the 12 apostles chosen by Jesus, every apostle, except one, became a missionary. The other became a traitor.

- The problems which arose in the early church were largely questions of missionary procedure.

from *The Way*, William Adam Brown

ECCLESIOLOGY AND ESCHATOLOGY

Ecclesiology

Christ's lordship over the church is illustrated in *Seven New Testament Pictures*:

- Humanity, race, nations—Christ is viewed as the "last Adam" over the new creation (1 Corinthians 15:45-47; Romans 5:12-21; Ephesians 2:14-18, 4:13).

- Physical life, body—Jesus is seen as head over the body (1 Corinthians 12:12-27; Colossians 1:18, 24).

- Occupation, work—Jesus is seen as the Great Shepherd over the sheep (John 10; 1 Peter 5:4).

- Food, nutrition, agriculture—Jesus is seen as the Vine over the branches (John 15; Ezekiel 15:2-5).

- Home, shelter, construction—Jesus is seen as the Chief Cornerstone over His "living stones" (Ephesians 2:19-22; 1 Peter 2:4-6).

- Religion—Jesus is seen as the High Priest over His royal priesthood (Hebrews 5:4-10; 1 Peter 2:5-9).

- Marriage, family—Jesus is seen as the Bridegroom over His bride (Ephesians 5:25; Revelation 19:6-8).

Eschatology

The Forgotten Sign of the Times. "And this gospel of the kingdom will be preached in the whole world as a testimony to all nations, and then the end will come" (Matthew 24:14).

Growing up in a Pentecostal church, I have had quite an education in premillennial prophecy. I have heard anything and everything Biblical, sub-Biblical and extra-Biblical preached as a "sign of the times." Added to the lists of things discussed in Scripture—wars, rumors of wars, famines, earthquakes, persecution, false prophets, wickedness—are other events and processes declared signs of the end times.

Various "signs" have included the European Common Market (with its "Beast" computer), the threat of the former Soviet Union, the emergence of new technology, the growth of scientific knowledge, and the increase in air traffic. The list changes annually (as do the candidates for the Antichrist)!

In all of the prognostications, however, I do not recall one incident from the pulpit or in a Sunday school class declaring the *obvious* sign of the end. In fact, after most of the signs proclaimed by Jesus in Matthew 24 are set in order, He said, "The end is not yet" (v. 6). All these things are not the end, but the beginning, He declared (v. 8). The final sign of the end is the worldwide proclamation of the gospel in all the world to every nation. After this, Jesus said, "then the end will come" (v. 14).

The purpose of this overview, therefore, is to demonstrate that the message of missions is an eschatological message and to examine the symbiotic relationship between world evangelization and the end times. This relationship can be examined under four words: *escapism, evangelization, event* and *enduement.*

1. *Escapism.* Each generation faces the imminent return of Christ. "Eternity," said Thomas F. Zimmerman, "is always crowding time." In terms of world evangelization, this either helps or hinders us in accomplishing our task. The facts of the coming of Christ and the impending judgment upon the world have propelled Pentecostal witnesses around the world in order to bring the good news of salvation. On the other hand, some have preferred an escape mentality, getting few into the ark before the rains come.

The church cannot allow a "get your gun and jump in the truck" mentality to form its view of world evangelization. We are commanded to make disciples of all nations, and we are to do this *until* all have heard or *until* Jesus Christ returns and says the task is over. We must occupy *until* He comes!

In addition, we cannot use Matthew 24:14 to justify witnessing to a few people in every nation of the world in order to condemn them because their nation has "heard" the gospel. "Unfortunately it seems to be employed by some," said William Owen Carver, "as if the function of the gospel were to witness to a few of each nation that God might save them under certain conditions, but in the case of the majority to prepare for using this message as a basis of condemning them"[2]

This "gathering a few, condemning the rest" view of world evangelization is inconsistent with the nature of God, "who wants all men to be saved and to come to a knowledge of the truth" (1 Timothy 2:4). God does not want "*anyone* to perish, but *everyone* to come to repentance" (2 Peter 3:9). Escapism is unfaithfulness to the Lord of the harvest. While keeping our eyes on the sky, we must keep our hands on the plow!

2. *Evangelization.* World evangelization is the natural response to the reality of final and universal judgment. People must be told! Following his statement of truth regarding the heart of God for the lost (2 Peter 3:9), Peter goes on to exclaim, "But the day of the Lord will come" (v. 10). "Knowing therefore the terror of the Lord," Paul warned, "we persuade men" (2 Corinthians 5:11, KJV).

In these verses, the relationship between world evangelization and the end times is made evident. Because of the urgency of coming judgment, we must work before the night comes when no man can work (John 9:4). If we believe in the premillennial second coming of Jesus Christ, then our premillennialism must be a reason to *proclaim*, not to *predict*. Our eschatology and evangelization work together. We preach because the end is coming; the end is coming because we preach.

We must be careful, however, to allow our premillennialism to work *for* us and not *against* us in our task of making disciples of *all* nations (Matthew 28:18-20). Jesus spoke of the gospel of the Kingdom being preached in *all* the world to *every* nation (every tribe, linguistic, culture group, even "nations within a nation"). We cannot allow any construction of prophetic interpretation (even pre-millennialism or dispensationalism)—regardless of how carefully systematized or articulated—to hinder the *prior* commission to reach all cultures and nations everywhere with the gospel!

Let me illustrate. Based upon a misunderstanding of Acts 15:14-18, some have declared our current times to be solely the age of Gentile evangelization and that there will come a future time for all of Israel to be saved. This then rules out any possibility of taking seriously the evangelistic mandate of Jesus to make disciples of all people—including the Jews—in *this* generation. If the truth were known, most of our obstacles in reaching Jewish people have been cultural, not theological. Jews do not want to become Gentiles in order to become disciples. Many Jews are finding their Messiah today because cross-cultural witnesses are demonstrating that the gospel can be communicated in Jewish symbols and cultural forms.

Let us take this a step further. If as Christians we pray for the peace of Jerusalem and are considerate of Israel in light of God's present and future dealings with them, we do right. But if, in the name of some eschatological scheme we have inherited from church history, we condone the militaristic adventures of the secular state of Israel, we may have gone beyond the limits of Scripture. When some citizens of Israel themselves are crying out against aggression and the abuse of power in civil strife, how is it that some American Evangelicals blindly agree to everything that is done by the Israeli government without calling for reconciliation and justice in the name of the Prince of Peace?

What about the hopes and aspirations of the Arab peoples of the Middle East? In the name of a particular system of prophetic interpretation, do we forget that the blood of our Lord was also shed for more than 1 billion Muslims in our world today? Will our eschatology cause us to relegate them to outer darkness, or will it commission us to reach them with the light of the gospel?

When we stand before the judgment seat of Christ, our judgment will not be based upon how correct we were in our interpretation of Bible prophecy but rather upon how obedient we were to Jesus' clear-cut instructions to make disciples of *all* nations before the end came. Our eschatology must always motivate us toward evangelization.

3. *Event.* As we participate in world evangelization, we become a part of a prophetic event. In all of the cataclysmic signs in Scripture—such as famines, earthquakes and wars—Christians are often involved as victims. But in the process of world evangelization, we are active participants in the prophetic process! We are actually involved in the coming of the Kingdom.

We must caution, however, against world evangelization being an absolute precondition or prerequisite for the coming of the end. We cannot "use" eschatology to support world missions in the sense that the quicker we get souls saved, the sooner we will see our Lord's return or "bring back the King." Our increased fervor in world evangelization will not accelerate the predetermined times and dates set by the Father's own authority (Acts 1:7). Our task is to be obedient to the command of Christ, knowing that our worldwide preaching is in itself a part of the final sign of His return (Matthew 24:14). The event is God's event; we are only emissaries.

4. *Enduement.* Rather than adopting an escapist approach to eschatology, we must instead accept our responsibility to evangelize and become a part of God's final eschatological event. To do this, we must seek the enduement of power. The outpouring of the Holy Spirit is clearly a fulfillment of prophecy, and we continue to live in the outworking of this sign in these last days. This was how the prophecy of Joel 2:28-32 was understood by the early church (Acts 2:16-21) and by our Pentecostal fathers and mothers at the turn of the 20th century.

Like the early disciples, today's Christians have been very curious about prophecy and the end of time. The disciples asked Jesus about the restoration of Israel, about times and dates. Jesus said it was not for them *to know* but *to receive*:

"But you will receive power when the Holy Spirit comes on you; and you will be my witnesses in Jerusalem, and in all Judea and Samaria, and to the ends of the earth" (Acts 1:8).

When Christians become as concerned about being witnesses to the ends of the earth as they are about the end of the earth, then the "forgotten sign of the times" will be faithfully carried out until all have heard or until He comes. Until that day there is no other option.

The church must be pushed from its isolation into a dynamic interaction with the world. This is the sentiment of the following lines from George MacLeod:

I simply argue that the cross be raised again.
At the center of the marketplace
As well as on the steeple of the church.
I am recovering the claim that
Jesus was not crucified in a cathedral
Between two candles
But on a cross between two thieves;
On the town garbage heap,
At a crossroad so cosmopolitan
That they had to write His title
In Latin and in Hebrew and in Greek;
At the kind of place where cynics talk smut
And thieves curse and soldiers gamble;
Because that is where He died
And that is what He died about
And that is where churchmen ought to be
And what church people ought to be about.[3]

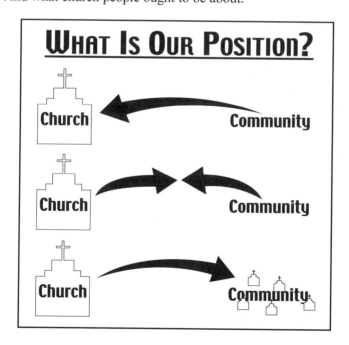

 Reflections

1. Look again at the section on "The Totality of Christ's Command." How would you apply lessons and actions from the five uses of the word "all" to your Christian living in your world?

2. How do you relate the section on "The Forgotten Sign of the Times" and other thoughts about the second coming of Jesus Christ to your global/local responsibility as a world Christian?

*Pause now for personal or group prayer before moving to Projections/Actions.

Projections

Today's date_____

By this time next year, next month, next week, I believe God for the following ministry goals to connect to God's work in my world (enter calendar dates for accountability):

1. Next year (date_____)
2. Next month (date_____)
3. Next week (date_____)

Actions

By this time tomorrow—in the next 24 hours—I will . . .

1.

2.

CHAPTER FOUR

EMPTY NETS—EMPTY TABLES

THE MISSIONARY SPIRIT IS THE SPIRIT OF
JESUS, THE SPIRIT OF THE INCARNATION
AND THE CROSS.
— J. HUDSON TAYLOR
MISSIONARY TO CHINA

What is the attitude of Jesus toward the harvest of unreached people? Throughout the Gospels (as listed below) we see the actions and teachings of our Lord which clearly demonstrate that He wants lost people to be found and His church to grow. This chapter will highlight evangelistic principles from two of the following events and teachings from the ministry of the Master. Our Lord is clearly not pleased with . . .

- Fishing without catching (Luke 5:4-11)

- An empty banquet table (Luke 14:15-24)

- Sowing without reaping (Matthew 13:3-9)

- A fig tree that bears no figs (Luke 13:6-9)

- Lost sheep that are not brought into the fold (Matthew 18:11-14)

- A lost coin that is sought but not found (Luke 15:8-10)

- Ripe harvests that are not reaped (Matthew 9:36-38)

- Proclamation without response (Matthew 10:14)

`

• Sons and daughters outside the Father's house (Luke 15:11-32).

Fishing Without Catching (Luke 5:4-11)

There seems to be a progression here (vv. 4-7):

One. "He said to Simon, '[You] put out into deep water, and [you all—plural] let down the nets for a catch'" (v. 4). Peter, the leader, had to obey the vision and lead others to the harvest of fish. Leaders receive the vision, the guidance and direction, and they, with others (their followers), begin to reap the harvest.

A few. "When they had done so, they caught such a large number of fish that their nets began to break" (v. 6). The vision begins with one and spreads to a few, a small group such as Peter's boat crew. This is probably where burnout occurs, when the vision comes to one and the one tries to do it all instead of imparting that vision to the others.

All. "So they signaled their partners in the other boat to come and help them, and they came and filled both boats so full that they began to sink" (v. 7). As with a concentric circle, there is a vision given to one, spreading to a few, and going out to all.

Observations

1. It takes a man or a woman with a vision from God. Obedience is required: "But because you say so, I will let down the nets" (Luke 5:5).

2. The vision involves a small circle of followers, coworkers, who will go with the leader and seek to win goal ownership among others.

3. When the harvest did come, the partners in the other boat came to help them (5:7: "They signaled their partners in the other boat to come and help them"). We need to learn to signal for help from our partners. We need to understand that the harvest is beyond

us. Like the man from Macedonia in Paul's vision (Acts 16), we need to be willing to say, "Come over and help us." If we become jealous of the harvest, we may lose it.

Applications

Examples of this partnering include:

1. *Within the local church.* We mobilize new workers and we help them into the harvest.

2. *Locally or within a geographic region.* We call others, perhaps a neighboring church, to participate as partners. Possibly a new church can be planted. We should never be jealous of the success of superchurches in our city. The principle is that when one church grows and flourishes, others will grow with it. It will raise the evangelical, gospel presence in the community for the good of all. Philippians 1:5 speaks of "your partnership in the gospel." If we are willing to share the harvest, God will send it.

3. *Internationally.* We need to be willing to partner internationally with other church movements and to call others "to come over and help us." In revival and church growth when there are more converts than we can effectively train, we need to be willing to admit that we require more help. Therefore, there will always be room for the "foreign" missionary to serve as helper, teacher, organizer, and administrator in cooperation with and under the supervision of national leadership. There is always a need for the "paraclete" missionary.

Jesus and the Harvest: Seven Lessons From Luke 5

1. *He instills direction from the Word.* Commission comes out of the context of teaching the Word of God, as demonstrated in 5:1. You cannot read the Word of God without seeing the vision of God, feeling the heart of God, and hearing the call of God.

2. *He sees potential we don't see.* "He saw at the water's edge two boats" (v. 2). Just as Moses failed to see the significance of the rod he held in his hand, and the disciples failed to see the potential of the little boy with the five loaves and two fish, we may fail to see as Jesus does. Jesus sees things we fail to see. This is why we need to keep looking to Him. He sees the personnel, the means, the methods, the churches available for the task. He is in the midst of His churches (Revelation 1:12, 13; 2:1). The harvest is His, not ours. Therefore, we ask the Lord of the harvest to send forth laborers into His harvest.

3. *He becomes personally involved in our lives, situations and ministries.* As He does this, our faith and our hope are inspired and built. He got into Simon's boat (5:3). Although this looks like a standard, physical move, it has tremendous symbolic significance. We can picture Jesus stepping into "our boat," our local church and ministry. In addition, Jesus progressively leads us from small things to larger things—Jesus "asked him [Peter] to put out a little from the shore" (v. 3). Peter had to be willing to do this before he was commissioned to greater fruitfulness.

4. *He speaks "out of" our personal experiences, even our failures and disappointments.* "Then he sat down and taught the people from the boat" (v. 3). Whose boat? Jesus was speaking out of Peter's boat. Peter was tired and fruitless. The boat that was supposed to be the symbol of his success as a fisherman was a reminder of his failure (v. 5). Was Jesus willing to identify Himself with tired, empty-handed, frustrated fishermen? Yes, because He wanted to teach these men a lesson about a greater harvest—the harvest of men's souls.

We are taught, then, that out of our own failures, weaknesses and disappointments, the call to missions and ministry comes. "But we have this treasure in jars of clay to show that this all-surpassing power is from God and not from us" (2 Corinthians 4:7). It has been said that "our efficiency without His sufficiency is only deficiency."

These fishermen had a well-organized and well-rehearsed routine. As always, they went through the regular course of searching for fish, spreading and gathering the nets, docking their boats on the shore, and washing their nets. But, there was no fish. Whether we gather fish or just wash the nets depends on whether or not Jesus is in the midst of the harvest.

5. *He leads into greater fruitfulness.* "Put out into deep water, and let down the nets for a catch" (Luke 5:4). God knows those who have receptive hearts. He stirs nations and peoples and makes them ready for His message. This miracle at the beginning of Peter's three-year discipleship would be repeated after the resurrection of Jesus. Peter, along with the other disappointed and disillusioned disciples, would be told by the Stranger on the shore to "throw your net on the right side of the boat and you will find some" (John 21:6).

6. *He is there, working with us, when the harvest comes.* I can imagine Jesus, with His sleeves rolled up, leaning over the edge of the boat, pulling in the nets full of fish. Consider the power of this realization: The Lord is working with us, and His presence goes with us in the harvest! This is the encouragement of the following scriptures:

> Then the disciples went out and preached everywhere, and the Lord worked with them and confirmed his word by the signs that accompanied it (Mark 16:20).

> Moses said to the Lord, "You have been telling me, `Lead these people,' but you have not let me know whom you will send with me. You have said, `I know you by name and you have found favor with me.' If you are pleased with me, teach me your ways so I may know you and continue to find favor with you. Remember that this nation is your people." The Lord replied, "My Presence will go with you, and I will give you rest." Then Moses said to him, "If your Presence does not go with us, do not send us up from here.

How will anyone know that you are pleased with me and with your people unless you go with us? What else will distinguish me and your people from all the other people on the face of the earth?" (Exodus 33:12-16).

What, after all, is Apollos? And what is Paul? Only servants, through whom you came to believe—as the Lord has assigned to each his task. I planted the seed, Apollos watered it, but God made it grow. So neither he who plants nor he who waters is anything, but only God, who makes things grow. The man who plants and the man who waters have one purpose, and each will be rewarded according to his own labor. For we are God's fellow workers; you are God's field, God's building (1 Corinthians 3:5-9).

"And surely I am with you always, to the very end of the age" (Matthew 28:20).

In my former book, Theophilus, I wrote about all that Jesus began to do and to teach until the day he was taken up to heaven (Acts 1:1).

If Luke was the Gospel of what Jesus "began to do and to teach," then Acts is a record of what Jesus *continues* to do in His church.

7. *He leads into a life of expanded fruitfulness through discipleship.*

When Simon Peter saw this, he fell at Jesus' knees and said, "Go away from me, Lord; I am a sinful man!" For he and all his companions were astonished [Amp.: "gripped with bewildering amazement"] at the catch of fish they had taken, and so were James and John, the sons of Zebedee, Simon's partners. Then Jesus said to Simon, "Don't be afraid; from now on you will catch men." So they pulled their boats up on shore, left everything and followed him" (5:8-11).

Why was Peter afraid? He feared when he was in the expressed presence of God. Here was an amazing sign, a revelation of God's power. It was much like the fear that gripped the heart of Isaiah when he saw a vision of Almighty God (Isaiah 6). He cried, "Woe to me! . . . I am ruined [literally, "I am cut off"]! For I am a man of unclean lips, and I live among a people of unclean lips, and my eyes have seen the King, the Lord Almighty" (v. 5).

Peter was afraid in the midst of success and productivity. Why are we afraid of success? It may be easier to continue in failure and mediocrity. Success may demand more of us. "What will happen if God blesses our church and we begin to grow?" The answer: "Don't be afraid . . . follow Jesus."

An Empty Banquet Table (Luke 14:15–24)

Key points:

- A great banquet was prepared (v. 16).

- Many guests were invited (v. 16).

- Timing was important; when all was ready, the host invited, "Come" (v. 17).

- There was resistance to the invitation (vv. 18-20).

- The host was angry and invited even others with urgency, "Go out quickly" (v. 21).

- The ultimate intention of the host—"that my house will be full" (v. 23).

Church Growth Applications

1. *The whole world has been given the general call of God (John 3:16).* In 2 Peter 3:9, we read, "The Lord is not slow in keeping his promise, as some understand slowness. He is patient with you, not wanting anyone to perish, but everyone to come to repentance."

We should do our best to reach all men everywhere with the message of the gospel because "now [God] commands all people everywhere to repent" (Acts 17:30). Peter stated this truth at the house of Cornelius after his vision in Joppa: "All the prophets testify about him that everyone who believes in him receives forgiveness of sins through his name" (10:43).

Paul stated, "I am obligated [KJV: "I am debtor"] both to Greeks and non-Greeks, both to the wise and the foolish. That is why I am so eager to preach the gospel also to you who are at Rome" (Romans 1:14, 15).

2. *Timing is important in the harvest.* "Come, for everything is now ready" (Luke 14:17). We must move with the Holy Spirit and say "Come" when He says "Come." The principle of receptivity states that we must get the harvest at the right moment. After World War II there was amazing receptivity in Japan and Germany. But within a few years those nations became resistant to the gospel.

3. *We must go to those who are receptive (14:18-21).* The original invitees were resistant and noncommittal. Each one was a person of means, self-sufficient and preoccupied:

- One had bought a field (v. 18).

- One had bought five yoke of oxen (v. 19).

- One was just married—and obviously financially able to provide the money for the marriage dowry and feast (v. 20).

Therefore the master went to the receptive—"the poor, the crippled, the blind and the lame" (v. 21). Donald McGavran would often speak of the "winnable masses" and noted that church growth often moves upward from the masses to the classes.

Keep in mind that each of those with excuses (vv. 18-20) could have become receptive in the event of a financial reversal or problem. The one with a field could have had it burned or it could have become unproductive for farming. The one with oxen could have seen them destroyed with illness or experienced a drop in the livestock market. The one with the new spouse could have seen the loved one become ill or die. It is important to minister to people when they become receptive. Watch for God's timing.

On a trip to Iowa in the mid-1980s, I learned from a pastor that a professional psychologist had been meeting with the local ministerial association. His purpose was to give the ministers special training in order to meet the rising need for counseling among the once prosperous farmers of that area. Faced with economic setbacks and the realities of recession, the once self-sufficient farmers were turning to God for help. The resistant had suddenly become receptive.

Clearly, the message of Jesus (sitting at the feast in the house of a prominent Pharisee) was that God would not be pleased with self-sufficient Israel (represented by the elite religious leadership), but would give the invitation to the Gentiles—the poor, the crippled, the blind and the lame. The challenge is to reach the receptive and win the winnable.

4. *There is an urgency in the harvest.* "Go out quickly" (14:21). Our mission must always be characterized by the example of our Lord, who said, "As long as it is day, we must do the work of him who sent me. Night is coming, when no one can work" (John 9:4).

5. *The direction of the harvest.* To the invited He says, "Come" (Luke 14:17); to the servants He says, "Go" (v. 21).

Ours is a message of dispersion . . . go where the people are . . . invite them on their own ground, in their own contexts.

6. *Go beyond barriers.*

- Go nearby—"Then the owner of the house became angry and ordered his servant, 'Go out quickly into the streets and alleys of the town and bring in the poor, the crippled, the blind and the lame'" (v. 21).

- Go beyond—"Go out to the roads and country lanes and make them come in" (v. 23).

There is a progression of geographical and cultural distances. Later, Peter would preach it like this on the Day of Pentecost: "The promise is for you and your children and for all who are far off—for all whom the Lord our God will call" (Acts 2:39).

As long as "there is still room" (Luke 14:22), we continue to go at home and beyond . . . both geographically and culturally. This was the heartbeat of Jesus, who spoke of "other sheep" and "other towns." This was the passion of Paul when he testified:

> It has always been my ambition to preach the gospel where Christ was not known, so that I would not be building on someone else's foundation. Rather, as it is written: "Those who were not told about him will see, and those who have not heard will understand" (Romans 15:20, 21).

7. *Persuasion and incorporation is the goal.*

- "Bring in" (Luke 14:21).

- "Make them come in" [KJV: "compel them"] (v. 23).

Our witness is more than just presence and proclamation. It also involves persuasion. We argue and persuade in the tradition and example of Paul and the early church:

> "Since, then, we know what it is to fear the Lord, we try to persuade men. . . . We are therefore Christ's ambassadors, as though God were making his appeal through us. We implore you on Christ's behalf: Be reconciled to God" (2 Corinthians 5:11, 20).

The end goal of our persuasion: "that my house will be full" (Luke 14:23).

Reflections

1. This chapter had some thoughts on two of the situations in the Gospels which did not please the Lord ("Fishing Without Catching" and "An Empty Banquet Table"). If you were to give a talk or teach a lesson (Sunday school class, Bible study/prayer group, etc.) on one of the others (such as "Sowing Without Reaping," "A Lost Coin Not Found," etc.), which one would it be and what are the main things you would say?

2. In the fishing story (Luke 5:4-11) Jesus stepped into Simon's boat—that is, into his life situation. Where do you see Jesus stepping into your local church and your personal life to get you putting out into deeper water and greater success?

*Pause now for personal or group prayer before moving to Projections/Actions.

Projections

Today's date_____

By this time next year, next month, next week, I believe God for the following ministry goals to connect to God's work in my world (enter calendar dates for accountability):

1. Next year (date_____)

2. Next month (date_____)

3. Next week (date_____)

Actions

By this time tomorrow—in the next 24 hours—I will . . .

1.

2.

THE FIRST
INFORMATION HIGHWAY

EXPECT GREAT THINGS FROM GOD.
ATTEMPT GREAT THINGS FOR GOD.
—WILLIAM CAREY
MISSIONARY TO INDIA
FATHER OF THE MODERN
PROTESTANT MISSIONS MOVEMENT

"Rome, we have a problem." The Roman centurion and his men were hopelessly lost somewhere in the northern corner of what we now call "the U.K." (United Kingdom). No doubt he was far beyond Hadrian's Wall or other Roman-built geographical markings. With a dispatch back to Rome, he sent his plea to his commander: "Send new orders. We've marched off the map!"

The first disciples were constantly marching off geographical, cultural, theological maps—"Therefore they that were scattered abroad went every where preaching the word" (Acts 8:4, KJV). When Peter was criticized about associating with the Gentiles, he explained, "The Spirit told me to have no hesitation about going with them" (Acts 11:12). The first "global believers" were "God's information highway"—ordinary people anointed with God's empowering presence, taking the gospel to the ends of the earth. "Global believers" throughout missions history have been men and women seized with a passion to know Christ and make Him known.

Europe's Moravians characterized that kind of love for Christ and His glory. Fleeing from anti-Reformation persecution in Bohemia and Moravia during the 17th century, they took shelter on the estate of a wealthy evangelical Lutheran nobleman named

Nicolas von Zinzendorf. Worship and love for Christ fueled the evangelistic passion of these young zealots who were deployed from their missions community to the uttermost frontiers of their world. Their worship and evangelistic commitment was expressed in the more than 2,000 hymns composed by Zinzendorf, who frequently stated, "I have one passion, and it is Him, only Him."

This passion caused two young Moravians to sell themselves into slavery in order to reach a remote island prison, carefully guarded by an agnostic and cruel prison master. In that unreached island prison were hundreds of lost men who had never heard the name of Jesus. On the day of their departure, friends and family gathered to say a final goodbye to these two brave believers. They would never see them again. As the boat sailed further and further from the dock, the last faint sound to be heard from the young missionaries was their singing. It was a song-turned-missionary motto carried across God's information highway by His faithful witnesses: "May the Lamb which was slain receive the reward of His suffering." The Moravians, and hundreds of missionary movements like them in missions history—all led by students and the laity—were following the "world Christian" heritage left to them in the marching orders of Jesus Christ to the first global believers.

How the Mission Movement Spread

Christianity began in Judea, an area that was no more than 50 miles wide and 100 miles long. At first it was basically an internal Jewish affair, but it began to spread with the activity of the disciples and the missionary journeys and letters of the apostle Paul. Note that when it began to spread, it moved in pockets. It grew in phases. The growth of the Christian movement was stronger in one part of the world at one time than it was in others, as opposed to being one massive wave growing over one mass of land. This is important to remember in terms of evangelistic strategy. The gospel grows according to the lines of family, relations, people groups, pockets, in various areas at various times.

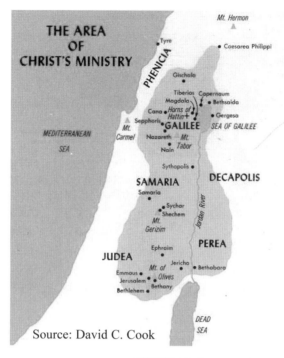

THE AREA OF CHRIST'S MINISTRY

Mt. Hermon

Tyre

Caesarea Philippi

PHENICIA

Gischala

Tiberios Capernaum
Magdala • Bethsaida
Cana Horns of
Hattin +
Sepphoris • Gergesa
Mt.
Carmel GALILEE
SEA OF GALILEE

MEDITERRANEAN

SEA

Nazareth Mt.
Tabor
Nain

Sythopolis •

SAMARIA DECAPOLIS
Samaria

• Sychar
• Shechem
Mt.
Gerizim

PEREA

Ephraim

JUDEA Jericho
Mt. of • Bethabara
Emmaus • Olives
Jerusalem • • Bethany
Bethlehem •

DEAD
SEA

Source: David C. Cook

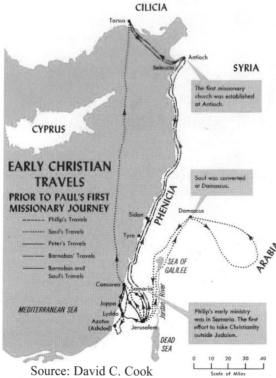

CILICIA

Tarsus

Antioch

SYRIA

The first missionary
church was established
at Antioch.

Seleucia

CYPRUS

EARLY CHRISTIAN TRAVELS
PRIOR TO PAUL'S FIRST MISSIONARY JOURNEY

------- Philip's Travels
.... Saul's Travels
——— Peter's Travels
——— Barnabas' Travels
——— Barnabas and
Saul's Travels

Saul was converted
at Damascus.

Sidon Damascus

PHENICIA

Tyre

ARABIA

SEA OF
GALILEE

Caesarea Samaria

MEDITERRANEAN SEA

Joppa
Lydda
Azotus
(Ashdod) Jerusalem

Jordan River

Philip's early ministry
was in Samaria. The first
effort to take Christianity
outside Judaism.

DEAD
SEA

0 10 20 30 40
Scale of Miles

Source: David C. Cook

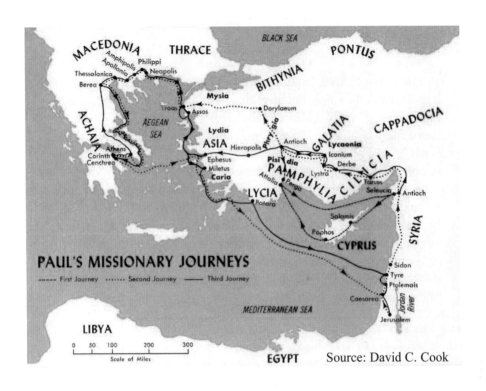

PAUL'S MISSIONARY JOURNEYS

----- First Journey ...... Second Journey ——— Third Journey

Source: David C. Cook

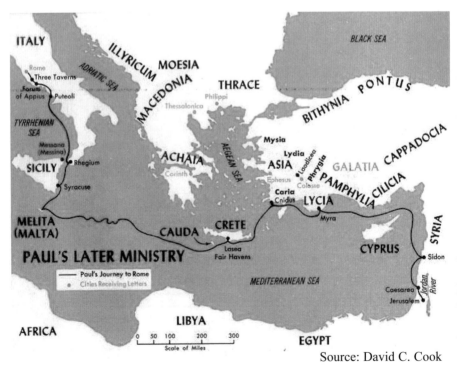

PAUL'S LATER MINISTRY

——— Paul's Journey to Rome
• Cities Receiving Letters

Source: David C. Cook

The early church expanded not only geographically but also culturally. Acts 1:8 is not speaking so much about geographical distances as it is cultural distances. When Jesus spoke of "Jerusalem," "Judea," "Samaria," and "the uttermost part of the earth" (KJV)—those are key words meaning different kinds of people in different cultural distances.

What is happening in the first seven chapters of Acts is the story of mono-cultural evangelism—the Jewish church working primarily among Hebraic, Palestinian-based Jewish people. In Acts 8, they began moving toward a similar culture—reaching out to their own surrounding culture (the Samaritans). The rest of the account in Acts 9—28 is the story of cross-cultural evangelism. The "uttermost part of the earth" is seen here as being synonymous with "Gentiles."

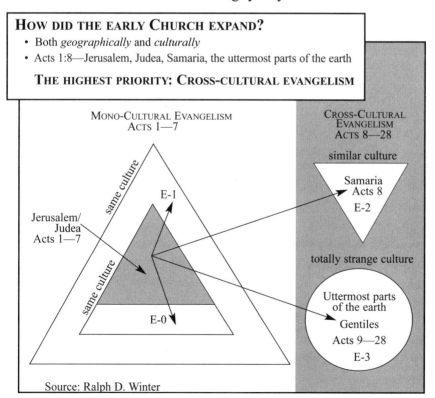

HOW DID THE EARLY CHURCH EXPAND?
- Both *geographically* and *culturally*
- Acts 1:8—Jerusalem, Judea, Samaria, the uttermost parts of the earth

THE HIGHEST PRIORITY: CROSS-CULTURAL EVANGELISM

MONO-CULTURAL EVANGELISM
ACTS 1—7

CROSS-CULTURAL EVANGELISM
ACTS 8—28

similar culture

same culture

E-1

Jerusalem/ Judea
Acts 1—7

Samaria
Acts 8
E-2

totally strange culture

same culture

E-0

Uttermost parts of the earth

Gentiles

Acts 9—28

E-3

Source: Ralph D. Winter

This is helpful when we begin to think of our task, whether we think of going to the other side of the world or whether we go across the street. We need to think in terms of cultural distance as well as geographical distance.

Two Structures in Missions History

Note: The idea origins of this section are with Ralph D. Winter in his provocative and strategic article, "The Two Structures of God's Redemptive Mission."

From the very beginning of its missionary expansion, the church has had two broad emphases—that of nurture (congregational model) and outreach (missionary form of expansion). This reality is vital in understanding how the church has expanded in a close relationship between the two structures of God's redemptive mission. At the outset of the Christian movement, the early church took their examples of church life and expansion from existing Jewish models.

The Jewish synagogue. The local church in the early church days took on the form of the Jewish synagogue. This was their only available model. They were Jewish people who met in synagogues and private homes. There were no Christian churches built for the first 100-200 years of the Christian expansion. The synagogue, therefore, became the model for the congregational form. The outreach model, during this time, was provided by the Jewish proselyting bands that had spread out across the Jewish diaspora during the intertestamental period.

The Roman world. As the church moved into the Roman world, the structure of the local church was formed along the Roman governmental pattern of the second and third centuries. Therefore, the local congregation took on the form of a diocese. This is not an original Catholic term; it was a Roman governmental term. The Catholic Church modeled itself after the Roman governmental form of the diocese. Unfortunately, connection and structure began to replace congregational life and vitality. The outreach expansional form followed the pattern of the Roman military orders. This led to the rise of the specialized communities in monasteries.

Medieval period (ca. A.D. 450-1500). As the church moved into the medieval period, following the breakup of the Roman Empire, the congregational model had begun to wane. The local church had adapted too much of the form of the Roman government. When the Roman government went under, the church was faced with serious problems. The congregational model fell into decline. The only thing that saved the Christian movement was the monastery.

The mission structure, on the other hand, had taken the form of the monastery after the Roman military orders. They actually maintained the Scripture and the life and vitality of the church. The expansion of the church was maintained not at the local level but through the monastery.

The Reformation (1500 and Beyond). Coming out of the medieval period, Martin Luther disregarded the option of using the monastery (he himself having been a part of it) and chose instead to concentrate on church reform through the congregational structure.

Unfortunately, the congregational structure was in decline. This left the newly emerging Protestant movement without any organized structure through which to be a blessing to the world. Because of this, there was no significant widespread Protestant expansion for approximately 300 years (1500-1800).

Protestantism did not have a vehicle, a structural methodology to expand the gospel into all the world. Therefore, all the advances that the Protestants made in Central Europe were lost to the Roman Catholics by the Counter-Reformation which they launched. The Roman Catholics won more people to the Roman Catholic Church in China, South America, and Africa than the Protestants ever won to Protestantism in central Europe. Why? Because they had a structure. They had an organization. They had a marching machine, like a military order, with religious orders such as the Jesuits, the Dominicans, and the Franciscans. The Protestants lacked this. Until they got a "missionary machine" in place, they floundered.

William Carey (1792). William Carey clearly saw the need for an organized missionary order. He wrote and preached about, and argued for a missions society. This is what he meant with the word *means* (or *methods*) in his famous essay "An Inquiry Into the Use of Means for the Propagation of the Gospel Among the Heathen." When he finally sailed for India in 1793 under the newly formed BMS (Baptist Missionary Society), his society was the first of 12 more societies organized over a period of 32 years. This ushered in "The Great Century of Missions" in the 1800s. During this time the great Protestant missionary stories of which we read occurred. This became the seedbed of our modern-day Pentecostal missionary effort and thrust.

From the early church to the modern time, we have had the need for two structures in God's redemptive mission.

Foundational Movements in Protestant Missionary History

The Puritans, the Pietists, the Moravians, and the Methodists all had four common elements they gave to us as a modern missionary heritage:

- They placed a high value on the role of Scripture.

- They emphasized personal faith and internal spiritual growth. The "Christ life" was placed over mere mental assent to creeds and doctrines.

- They emphasized purity.

- They focused upon lay participation in ministry.

The Puritans, for example, had an active ministry among American Indians in the New World (the American colonies).

They gave a theological push to the modern missionary movement, focusing on ecclesiastical purity as a check on the larger church systems. They also emphasized eschatology, stating the urgency in missions.

The Pietist contribution out of central Europe was spiritual-relational, searching for the "heart religion." This moved beyond Luther's emphasis that was more theological/political. It gave us one of the first modern models of small-group Bible studies and prayer groups that reached students and universities, and formed "churches within the church."

The Moravian contribution was structural. For the first time in history, perhaps since the early church, they were able to bring together the local church and mission outreach structures. They provided the structural integration of a local congregational form and a mission form that they brought together in a community-based missionary unit.

The genius and vitality of the Methodist missionary movement was that it combined two powerful components: a spiritual-gifts theology ("everyone has a ministry") and a structural organization. This combination brought the Methodists from being unheard of in America in 1776 to becoming the largest religious movement in this country by 1850, just 75 years later.

Three Periods of Modern Protestant Missions

Beginnings (1792-1945): "The William Carey Era." This was the period of colonial missionary expansion under the empires of Germany, Great Britain, France, and Spain in the New World. The advance of the missionary movement took place under the protection of the European colonial powers and, later, under the spreading military/economic influence of the United States. This was a period of massive recruitment of pioneer missionaries and financial support. The Western missionary was very much in charge.

Expansion (1945-1970): "The Nationals Will Do It." The emphasis during this period was upon indigenous, national expansion. Great growth occurred among Evangelicals and Pentecostals. The key focus during this time was the growth of the "younger church" in the "Southern World" (Asia, Africa, Latin America). The motto was "Let the nationals do it." In the '60s and '70s there was the liberal feeling in the mainline churches that said "The day of missions is over." There were calls for a "moratorium" on missions, and attempts were made to halt missionary expansion. Many of the churches in America during that time were calling their missionaries back home. With this came the rise of overseas, national churches and negative feelings toward the Western missionary. People had the impression that the church had expanded to the entire world, the Christian church was on all the continents of the world, and the sun never set on the kingdom of God.

A New Dawn (1970-): "The Final Frontiers." This mentality prevailed until people such as Ralph D. Winter and others made it evident that the job was not yet done. Winter pointed out that although there was a Christian presence in all regions in the world, there remained thousands of unreached people groups who had never heard the gospel. There remained many frontiers to penetrate. With this, "frontier missiology" came to the forefront.

The Contributions of Students and the Laity

Over the history of the expansion of Christianity, the most vital Christian movements have been initiated by students, young people and the laity. Mission movements in our Christian history have been from the "bottom up" from among the people. They have not been "top down." In fact, "top heavy" institutions, bureaucracies and structures tend to protect and propagate themselves, as opposed to creating new evangelistic movements. Efforts and resources tend to be turned inward instead of outward. When this has happened, God has inevitably raised up a new spiritual movement focused on mission.

There are numerous outstanding historical examples of students, young people and laity in mission. There was Philip Spener, author of *Pia Desideria* ("pious desires"), who influenced August Herman Francke, who subsequently started Bible study/prayer meetings for students at the University of Halle in Germany. This was the beginning of the Pietist movement, which greatly influenced young Nicolas von Zinzendorf. Zinzendorf's movement of young people and lay "tentmakers" became known as the Moravians. The Moravians deeply impacted John Wesley and young William Carey. Wesley and Carey's influence was felt in the opening years of the Pentecostal Movement, led and energized by the laity and young people.

There were notable lay movements in medieval history such as the Waldensians, a group which emerged around Peter Waldo, a young cloth merchant from Lyon, France. Waldo and his followers were disillusioned with corrupt practices among the Catholic ecclesiastical hierarchy.

Later there would be the prayer movements among students in England and North America. One of the movements originated with the so-called "Haystack Prayer Meeting." Caught in a thunderstorm, the students took refuge under a haystack and continued with their regular mission prayer meeting. Out of that prayer came a burden and a resolve to start a new missions society. That was the historical foundation for modern missions outreach from the United States. The Haystack Prayer Movement resulted in the first missionary society in North America and led to an international student missions movement.

Student Power

There is power in student-led evangelism. There is unlimited potential when students put their minds to do something as the Holy Spirit leads. Such is seen in these contributions:

- Theological: Student movements have tended to be theological, with the Word of God at the center. They have moved attention away from ecclesiastical power structures toward a fresh examination of God's commission. They have cried out to study the Bible, to pray and to hear God.

- Spiritual: Student movements have focused upon prayer, the inner life of renewal, and the life of discipleship. The Holy Club at Oxford's interest in spiritual life is an example of this.

- Structural: Student movements have also brought about the creation of missionary structures. The Haystack Prayer Movement led to the creation of missionary societies and denominational missions departments.

World Christian Students and Laity in the Future

Supporters. I believe there is going to be an increase in the number of people who will see themselves as supporters, with the gift of giving. They may not go, or be able to be involved directly on the front lines, but they will be active as giving participants. People are coming to the realization of what it means to self-sacrifice and to give. Being a supporter will be vitally important.

Ambassadors. These are world-traveling laity that work for the military or a multinational company.

Sojourners. These simply go. They go into "restricted access" nations. They realize, in the words of Brother Andrew, "No country is closed to the gospel if you're willing to go in and never come out."

Tentmakers. These individuals use their professions for their economic support while serving the mission of the church. Their expenses are paid by a company or they support themselves. The concept of tentmaking comes from Acts 18. Here, Paul came to Corinth, where he met Priscilla and Aquila. He partnered with these fellow tentmakers. He worked with them through the week in their professional occupation. On the Sabbath, he gave himself to preaching in the synagogue.

Planters. These are frontier missionaries, who sink into a culture and dedicate their lives to it. These long-term missionaries work to plant churches among the unreached groups.

Innovators. These students aid in the creation of new student movements, structures and initiatives.

Partners. These are individuals who see themselves as networkers, involved in the internationalization of missions with a spirit of partnership.

Disseminators. These are those who give themselves to propagate, teach and spread the vision (i.e. pastors, teachers, researchers, strategists, and those who move into missiology as an academic discipline).

Women in the Vanguard

The involvement of women in missions was another inherited feature of the great century of advance in the 1800s. Married missionary women had been the accepted norm in the early 1800s. The idea of a single woman going overseas was not yet popular. Yet, in the 1820s, there began a stream of single women going overseas. The first single American woman, not widowed, to serve as a foreign missionary was Betsy Stockton, a former slave who went to Hawaii in 1823.

For the first time in history, women outnumbered men in Protestant missions during the first decade of the 20th century. Mission records from Baptist and Presbyterians working in the Sheng Teng province of China in 1910 show 79 women missionaries in comparison to 46 men. Helen Barrett Montgomery reported in 1910:

> It is indeed a wonderful story. We began in weakness. We stand in power. In 1861 there was a single missionary in the

87

field, Miss Marston, in Burma. In 1909 there were 4,710 unmarried women in the field, 1,948 from the United States. In 1861, there was one organized women's society in the country. In 1910 there were forty-four.[2]

By 1914, about 21,500 Protestant missionaries served overseas. Women constituted half of this number. One-fourth of these were single women.

A large part of the dynamic success of Pentecostal missions is due to the effective leadership of committed women who were accepted as equal partners in ministry. Early Pentecostals simply believed the promise of Joel 2:28, 29, that sons and *daughters* would prophesy. This was particularly true at Azusa Street, where seven of the 12 members of the credentials committee were women. This committee selected and approved candidates for licensing.

In 1910 the following Pentecostal women entered missionary work:

- Ida Evans (Church of God missionary) and her husband, R.M., went to the Bahamas.

- Aimee Semple McPherson, founder of the International Church of the Foursquare Gospel, began missions work with her husband in China.

- Lillian Trasher sailed to Egypt, where she began her world-famous orphanage.

- Also in 1910, Miss Clyde Cotton from Boaz, Alabama, preached a revival where one of the best-known Church of God evangelists, J.W. Buckalew, received the Pentecostal experience.

Missions historian Gary McGee reveals that "throughout most, if not all, of the history of Pentecostal missions, married and single women missionaries have constituted a majority." He notes, however, that in the latter half of the 20th century, a number of single women in denominational missions agencies steadily declined. He says:

> Other prominent women, including Elizabeth V. Baker, Marie Burgess Brown, Florence L. Crawford, Minnie T. Draper, Christine Gibson, Aimee Semple McPherson, Carrie Judd Montgomery, Virginia E. Moss, and Avis Swiger, while not serving as missionaries (with the exception of McPherson), impacted Pentecostal missions through the institutions that they founded (schools, missions agencies, denominations) or served.[3]

In more than any other arena of ministry, Pentecostal missions has demonstrated that on the Day of Pentecost the Pentecostal experience broke the last barrier of separation. This was the contention of David duPlessis, who said shortly before his death, "Jesus baptized the women exactly like the men, and I say for the exact same purpose as the men are baptized so the women are baptized."[4]

Reflections

1. What are three special things from missions history which you would like to see repeated/continued in the future?

2. What role do you see for students, laity and women in missions outreach (past, present, future)?

*Pause now for personal or group prayer before moving to Projections/Actions.

Projections

Today's date _____

By this time next year, next month, next week, I believe God for the following ministry goals to connect to God's work in my world (enter calendar dates for accountability):

1. Next year (date_____)
2. Next month (date_____)
3. Next week (date_____)

Actions

By this time tomorrow—in the next 24 hours—I will . . .

1.

2.

Part One Resource Connections

1. Find out more (from your local church, your association or denomination) about your church's missions history). *For example:* Pathway Press can help you order Charles W. Conn's books, *Like a Mighty Army: A History of the Church of God* and *Where the Saints Have Trod: A History of Church of God Missions* (1-800-553-8506; *www.pathwaypress.org*).

Ask Church of God World Missions about their new missions history project, *Until All Have Heard* (1-800-345-7492).

2. Check out the following contact information. Ask about Bible studies, books and other resources, and catalogs.

U.S. Center for World Mission
1605 Elizabeth St., Suite #107
Pasadena, CA 91004

Web sites:

www.USCWM.org
www.MissionFrontiers.org
www.Perspectives.org

Ask about a free copy of *Mission Frontiers* magazine and how to order *Perspectives on the World Christian Movement.*

Evangelism and Missions Information Service (EMIS),
P.O. Box 794,
Wheaton, IL 60189,
(630) 752-7158.
Web site: *www.wheaton.edu/bgc/emis.*
E-mail: *emis@wheaton.edu*

Ask for *World Pulse* newsletter and *Evangelical Missions Quarterly* journal.

3. Contact your area or international office for your association or denomination. Ask them for prayer/support/ministry involvement information:

For example:
Church of God World Missions
P.O. Box 8016
Cleveland, TN 37320-8016
(800) 345-7492
Web site: *www.cogwm.org*

Cross-Cultural Ministries
Church of God International Offices
P.O. Box 2430
Cleveland, TN 37320-2430
(423) 472-3361
Web site: *www.churchofgod.cc*

Advancing Churches in Missions Commitment (ACMC)
4201 N. Peachtree Road, Suite 300
Peachtree City, GA 30341-1207
1-800-747-7346
Web site: *www.acmc.org*

Great Commission Handbook
P.O. Box 3550
Barrington, IL 60011-3550
Web site: *www.GoYe.com*

Youth With a Mission
Web site: www.missionadventures.net

Women of the Harvest
P.O. Box 151297
Lakewood, CO 80215-9297
877-789-7778
Web site: *www.womenoftheharvest.com*
E-mail: *harvestmag@aol.com*

Men/Women of Action
P.O. Box 2430
Cleveland, TN 37320-2430
423-478-7955

Master's Commission
P.O. Box 2430
Cleveland, TN 37320-2430
423-478-7225

Women's Ministries
P.O. Box 2430
Cleveland, TN 37320-2430
423-478-7170

PART TWO

GOING TO
GLOBAL
WINDOWS

Preview

Part II shows the missions challenge of our current world scene. It includes an explanation of the "unreached peoples" concept and gives special attention to the world of Islam and the world of the city.

Globalbeliever.Compassion—"The Great Compassion"

When he saw the crowds, he had compassion on them, because they were harassed and helpless, like sheep without a shepherd. Then he said to his disciples, "The harvest is plentiful but the workers are few. Ask the Lord of the harvest, therefore, to send out workers into his harvest field" (Matthew 9:36-38).

Globalbeliever.Companion—"The Great Companion"

And surely I am with you always, to the very end of the age (Matthew 28:20b).

Then the disciples went out and preached everywhere, and the Lord worked with them and confirmed his word by the signs that accompanied it (Mark 16:20).

Just before the opening chorus in the singles Sunday school class, Rick and Steve are at the coffeepot discussing the latest computer operating systems. Karen sees her chance to seize the moment with, "Oh, you guys do Windows? Have you heard about 'Global Windows 2000'?" Karen was connecting with the guys' interest in computer "windows" to help them see through God's windows to the world and to catch a vision for global challenges, especially in an area of the world called the "10/40 Window."

Veteran missionary Robert Cary related a story about a little boy excitedly looking through a toy-store window. His grandfather thought he saw the youngster looking at the different types of world globes. A few days later he waited anxiously as his grandson opened his birthday present. Choosing one of the world globes, Grandpa just knew his grandson would be overjoyed, but the little fellow was visibly disappointed.

"What's the matter?" asked Grandpa. "I thought you wanted the world globe—the one we saw at the toy store."

"Oh, I did," responded the boy, "but I wanted the one with the lamp in the middle, the one that lights the world at night."

"We'll go to the store," promised the grandfather, "and we will get you the special globe with the lamp in the middle. But never forget that it is much more expensive. It costs more to light up the world!"

It cost God everything He had to light our world with the gospel. Looking through His windows to our world and walking through His open doors of opportunity will also cost today's global believer a price to be a world Christian disciple.

Yes, God has some windows, but He also has some doors. The first global believers had the assurance that every new opportunity to connect to God's work in their world was the result of the initiative of their proactive God opening the door for them (Acts 14:27; 1 Corinthians 16:9; 2 Corinthians 2:12; Colossians 4:3).

After you look through the window in this section, then step through God's open door for you: "See, I have placed before you an open door that no one can shut" (Revelation 3:8).

CHAPTER SIX

PEOPLE IN A WINDOW

I HAVE SEEN THE SMOKE OF A THOUSAND VILLAGES
— VILLAGES WHOSE PEOPLE ARE WITHOUT CHRIST,
WITHOUT HOPE IN THE WORLD.
—ROBERT MOFFAT
MISSIONARY TO SOUTH AFRICA

We are facing a world population that has surpassed the 6 billion mark. One demographer has traced the world population from the time of Adam to 1830. It required thousands of years between these dates for the world population to reach the 1 billion mark. By comparison, it only took 100 years (from 1830-1930) for the world population to reach 2 billion. Then, it only took 30 additional years (1930-1960) for the world population to reach 3 billion. Within a short 15 years (1960-1975) the world population moved to 4 billion. From 1975-1987 it surpassed the 5 billion mark. By 1999 it had moved to an excess of 6 billion.

	BILLIONS
Adam—1830	1
1830—1930	2
1930—1960	3
1960—1975	4
1975—1987	5
1987—1999	6

If the world were a town of 1,000 people, it would include:

565 Asians
210 Europeans
85 Africans
80 Latin Americans
60 North Americans

It's religions would include:

300 Christians
175 Muslims
128 Hindus
55 Buddhists
47 Animists

How do we reach people in this world of staggering statistics? Over the past 20-25 years, since the initiation of the "people group" concept, many feel that the "people approach" to evangelization is the most strategic and effective.

Understanding "Unreached People"

A *people group* is a significantly large sociological grouping of individuals who perceive themselves to have a common affinity for one another or "groupness" due to their shared language, religion, ethnicity, residence, occupation, class or caste, situation, and so forth. For example:

- Urdu-speaking Muslim farmers of the Punjab

- Cantonese-speaking Chinese refugees from Vietnam living in France

- Vietnamese refugees in Orange County, Southern California

- Polish refugees in Vienna, Austria

- Latino immigrants in Los Angeles

An unreached people group represents a group in which there are either no believers or there is not a large enough group to carry the message throughout the rest of the unevangelized group. Statisticians and missiologists estimate that there are thousands of unreached people groups, accounting for approximately 3 billion yet unreached people in the world.

India 1987

PEOPLE
PROFILE

Lambadi of India (Banjaras)

The Lambadi are a sturdy, well built, ambitious people and have a light complexion. The Lambadi were historically nomadic, keeping cattle, trading salt and transporting goods. Most of these people have now settled down to farming and various types of wage-labor. Their habit of living in isolated groups away from others, which was a characteristic of their nomadic days, still persists.

The Lambadi are now experiencing rapid changes, and their traditional customs, practices and institutions are undergoing far-reaching transformations.

Location : The Lambadi are located throughout much of south-central India. Over one million live in the state of Andra Pradesh. Many others are located in the states of Madhya Pradesh, Himachal Pradesh, Gujarat, Maharashtra, and Orissa. Much of this area is within the wet and dry tropical climate of India.

Religion :
Animism

Population :
3,000,000+

Status :
.5% Christian

Global Mapping Project Inc.   (818) 794-7688   1605 Elizabeth Street, Pasadena, California 91

P E O P L E
P R O F I L E

Sherpa of Nepal

Living high in the valleys flanking Mt. Everest, the Sherpas were
traditionally traders into Tibet. But when China seized Tibet in the
1950's it's borders became closed to trading traffic. At the same
time Nepal was opening her own borders to an increasing influx of
tourists. At first they came only tro scale the 8000-meter peaks, later
they came to go trekking - a form of extended backpacking complete
with a quide, cook and porters. Today, the vast majority of Sherpa
income comes from acting as guides and porters for these trekking
and climbing expeditions. They also run the lodges where the
trekkers stop for meals and rooms, as well as owning and managing
many of the trekking companies.

The Sherpas are a society that has undergone tremendous social and
economic changes in the past 20 years. Although they are still
staunch Tibetan Buddhist, they are showing signs of becoming more
receptive to change.

Location : The Sherpa live in the Bagmati,Janakpur, and Sagar-
matha zones of Nepal. They reside mostly in four distinct regions just
south of Mt. Everest : Solu, Pharak, Khumbu, and Rolwaling.These
regions go from 8,500 feet to 17,000 feet above sea level. Some
reside in the Helambu region north of Kathmandu.

Religion :
Tibetan Buddhism

Population :
25 ,000 - 35,000

Status : less than
0.1% Christian

East Asia

P E O P L E
P R O F I L E

Pakistan 1988
Also in:
Iran, Afghanistan

Baloch of Pakistan

A sturdy, traditionally nomadic people whose origins trace back to the high plateaus east of the Caspian Sea. The Baloch migrated to the borderlands of Iran, Afghanistan and present-day Baluchistan. In past centuries, Baloch princes ruled from Kalat over much of southern Afghanistan and S.E. Iran and the Talpur clan ruled from Hyderabad over much of the southern Indus River valley, but these principalities fell under British rule in the mid-19th century and the Baloch were forcibly incorporated into Pakistan in 1947. Due to poverty-stricken conditions in the arid interior of Baluchistan, hundreds of thousands of Baloch have migrated to the urban ghettos of Karachi and additional thousands have settled in the fertile plains of the Sind.

Location: The Baloch inhabit the Baluchistan province of western Pakistan and the Baluchestan va Sistan province of southeastern Iran. Many live along the coast of the Arabian Sea eastwards from the Strait of Hormuz to the city of Karachi. Others inhabit the Nimruz province in southwestern Afghanistan and approximately 40,000 are found in the Soviet Republic of Turkmenistan near the oasis of Merv. Considerable numbers of Baloch also live in the Sind province of Pakistan, in Oman, the Gulf States and along the coasts of Kenya and Tanzania. * See Appendix A & B for additional details.

Religion:
Islam (Sunni)

Population:
5,000,000

Status: less than 0.0001% Christian

Iran

Afghanistan

Pakistan

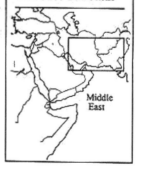

Middle East

GMI

103

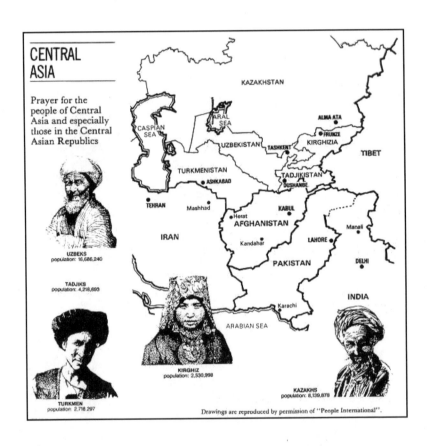

CENTRAL ASIA

Prayer for the people of Central Asia and especially those in the Central Asian Republics

UZBEKS
population: 16,686,240

TADJIKS
population: 4,218,693

TURKMEN
population: 2,718,297

KIRGHIZ
population: 2,530,998

KAZAKHS
population: 8,139,878

KAZAKHSTAN

ARAL SEA

CASPIAN SEA

ALMA ATA

FRUNZE

UZBEKISTAN   TASHKENT   KIRGHIZIA

TIBET

TURKMENISTAN   ASHKABAD   TADJIKISTAN   DUSHANBE

TEHRAN   Mashhad   KABUL

Herat   AFGHANISTAN   Manali

IRAN   Kandahar   LAHORE

PAKISTAN   DELHI

INDIA

Karachi

ARABIAN SEA

Drawings are reproduced by permission of "People International".

104

Taking the "people-group approach" to world evangelization is better for the following five reasons:

1. It is Biblical and historical—this is the way we see the gospel spreading in the Bible and throughout church history.

2. It recognizes the cultural reality that people in most parts of the world make decisions as an entire group.

3. It helps us approach the task systematically and allows for frequent evaluation of how we are doing.

4. It takes into account the holistic needs of a people that can be satisfied by the combination of works, words and wonders.

5. It helps keep us focused on the remaining unevangelized people groups of the world as an intentional, not accidental, strategy.

Church of God People Movements

The Church of God has been blessed in our growth by capitalizing on this reality of people groups. In fact, in a number of areas we have witnessed significant "people movements." Here are a few examples:

1. *Southwest Germany.* In 1936 Herman Lauster returned to his native Germany after having been converted as an immigrant in the United States. Lauster came from the farm country of southwest Germany, an area known as Schwabia, where people speak a special form of the German language. Back in Germany, Lauster evangelized his own people, and the Church of God grew among rural, Schwabian-speaking working class laborers and farmers.

2. *Urban West Indian England.* Reverend O.A. Lyseight and other church leaders immigrated to England from the Caribbean in the early 1950s. Lyseight began churches among the immigrants. Today, our strength in Great Britain is still among the West Indian population—a specialized people group.

3. *Indian South Africa.* A similar process developed among the Asian Indian immigrants in South Africa. Missionary J.F. Rowlands saw this as a particular "unreached people group." After a period of discouragement with meager results, a land-slide revival came. Today, the "Bethesda" movement of Asian Indian churches stands as a monument to the vision of a pioneer who understood "people group" thinking.

4. *Indonesia (Ethnic Chinese).* The growth of our work in Indonesia has been primarily among the ethnic Chinese population in that country. Our leaders have recognized that evangelism takes place along the lines of family, language, friendship and associations. The presence of over 1 million members is testimony to this reality.

5. *Indonesians in Holland.* This work grew as Indonesians (primarily ethnic Chinese) immigrated to Holland. Church of God believers in Indonesia simply followed their families and friends in Holland to set up connections that would lead to the establishment of churches.

6. *French-speaking Africans in Brussels, Belgium.* Historically, Belgium is the former colonial "mother" of what was once called the "Belgian Congo" in central Africa. Later, we knew it as "Zaire." Today that country is called the Democratic Republic of Congo, and because of the colonial connections, citizens travel freely to Belgium. One of the immigrants to Belgium, when asked why he came to Europe, said, "We are here because you were there."

By the mid-1980s there were more than 15,000 Zairians living in Brussels. Many of them brought a vital Christian experience with them (there are 15 believers in the Democratic Republic of Congo to every 1 in Belgium). One of them was Martin Mutyebele, an engineer with a Belgian copper mining company operating in central Africa. Mutyebele joined the Church of God and eventually developed an African congregation in Brussels.

By 2000, the church was ministering to more than 2,000 people weekly—the largest Protestant congregation in Belgium.

7. *Upper/Middle Class Filipinos in Manila.* When Gerald Holloway returned from his Stateside missionary furlough to the Philippines in the early 1980s, he had a strong burden from the Lord to penetrate the Catholic professional class in Manila. Before that, he worked among the rural poor where the Church of God had ministered for a generation.

Holloway understood the special qualities of these people which made them unique—they would not be reached through traditional Protestant evangelistic methods. His home Bible study exploded into a burgeoning megachurch in Manila's financial district. Eventually, scores of satellite congregations across the urban centers began to emerge among the unreached professional class. Today, the exciting story told in Holloway's book, *Maximizing Opportunities* (Pathway Press), relates how this "people movement" has followed the Filipino diaspora with thriving congregations in such places as Hong Kong, Singapore, Sydney, Los Angeles, San Francisco, and the United Arab Emirates.

The "People Approach" to World Evangelization

Eleven men gathered on the Mount of Olives some 2,000 years ago to wait for their Master. Jesus had instructed them to be there. After three years of following Christ, through the tumultuous days of His trial and death, and then 40 days of instruction in the kingdom of God, they knew it was important to obey Him and be there as He said.

When He arrived they worshiped Him (while some still doubted). At that pre-Ascension encounter He gave them a command that would ensure the continuation of His kingdom and the expansion of His church. He said to them:

"All authority in heaven and on earth has been given to me. Therefore go and make disciples of all nations, baptizing them in the name of the Father and of the Son and of the Holy Spirit, and teaching them to obey everything I have commanded you. And surely I am with you always, to the very end of the age" (Matthew 28:18-20).

With that, He was taken out of their sight. That commission was completed with the empowerment for ministry 10 days later on the Day of Pentecost.

Since that day, Christians have been involved in this business of world evangelization. How true have we remained to the commands and patterns of Scripture? How effective have we been in reaping the harvest and fulfilling His command to disciple the nations? Briefly, let's consider those questions in the framework of three perspectives: Historical Precedents, Biblical Patterns, and Strategic Prospects.

Historical Precedents

The legacy of colonialism. The modern missionary movement had to do mission under the political structures of colonialism. The European colonial empires tended to view the world in terms of large regions and countries. As people came under the influence of colonialism, they were pressed into the molds of "sameness." For example, in the British colonial areas of Africa and India, English was enforced as the official "national" language for purposes of trade, education and government. Peoples of various tribes and languages were not seen so much as distinct but as being "British" in culture and language.

Tribal and cultural differences were also not clearly recognized when the League of Nations and the United Nations emerged in their respective historical eras. In 1994, the United Nations, for example, recognized more than 225 political entities as "nations" (based upon geographical and political boundaries) despite the existence of more than 20,000 different tribal, cultural and language groups in the world.

The pattern of Western missions. Western missions followed the precedent set by colonialism. Their missions and denominations tended to draw up strategies and send forth personnel to general geographical regions and specific political entities known as "countries." Thus, some mission boards sent only one missionary team to a country or region regardless of how many subgroupings of people groups were there. This was a "country approach to world evangelization."

Biblical Patterns

The testimony of Scripture. The Scripture indicates a wide variety of names for various groups of people, even those living within the same political borders. The Old Testament has a number of different names to designate differences in language, residence and culture. Likewise, in the New Testament, there is a rich variety of terms to express the diversity of different groups of people. For example, consider the use of the following Greek terms and their specific emphasis or meaning:

ethne—nations

phule—tribe

glossa—tongue, language

laos—people

demos—residents, citizens

Thus, when Jesus gave His command in Matthew 28:18-20 to make disciples, He spoke of *panta ta ethne* ("all the nations"). Notice that *ethne* is very close to our English spelling of *ethnic* and denotes a variety of cultures, languages, tribes, even those living within a geopolitical boundary.

Obviously, since neither European colonialism nor the United Nations existed in those days, Jesus had something other than political and geographical "countries" in mind. He was speaking of the kaleidoscope of various cultures, languages and ethnic groups that made up the New Testament world of His day. It was into this world that Jesus said, "You are to go and make disciples"—the world of *all the peoples* (*panta ta ethne*).

Early Christian expansion. The record of the Book of Acts, and subsequent records, reveals that the New Testament church expanded not only across geopolitical borders but across cross-cultural frontiers. Using the outline of Acts 1:8 we can see how the church moved into new cultural areas in evangelization of a multitude of people groups. The distance involved in evangelism was as much, or more, cultural than geographical.

Clearly, the Biblical pattern has been a people-centered, not a region or country-centered, approach. In addition, the Biblical pattern has shown us a movement of whole peoples, not just individuals, to Christ. This was articulated by Donald A. McGavran in *The Bridges of God* and *Understanding Church Growth*. The Bible indicates that whole groups of people, even whole cities, moved to Christ in conversion movements (Acts 9:32-35; 14:8-20). Missiologists refer to these as "people movements."[1]

As the New Testament church spread, three distinct cultural expressions of the church emerged: Palestinian Jewish Christianity (Acts 1—6); Hellenistic Jewish Christianity (Acts 7—9); and Hellenistic Gentile Christianity (Acts 10—28). Paul recognized cultural and language differences as he spoke of becoming "all things to all men" (1 Corinthians 9:20-22).

Unfortunately, much of our present evangelistic strategy has been built upon the historical precedent of Western colonial missions to regions, countries and individuals, rather than upon the Biblical pattern of evangelization among the distinct people groups of *panta ta ethne* which resulted in burgeoning people movements and the phenomenal growth of the early church.

Strategic Prospects

The Lausanne legacy. In the years following the International Congress on World Evangelization (ICOWE) at Lausanne, the Lausanne Committee for World Evangelization (LCWE) teamed with its strategy working group to develop new approaches toward fulfilling the Great Commission. Heavily influenced by the writings of McGavran and others, the seminal address at ICOWE by Ralph Winter, as well as the active strategy thinking of Peter Wagner, a new approach to world evangelization began to emerge.

In answering the question "How do we reach them?" it was discovered that the best approach would not be "one country at a time," or even "one person at a time," but "one people at a time."

A people-centered approach. The "people-centered approach" was crystallized in Edward Dayton and David Fraser's *Planning Strategies for World Evangelization.* Called a "missiological *tour de force*" by Peter Wagner, the text is one of the best statements on people-centered evangelization available.[2]

The book takes the LCWE definition of *a people* as a "significant sociological grouping of persons who perceive themselves to be different due to common characteristics in language, religion, occupation, residence, ethnicity, et cetera, or any combination of the above."

Using the metaphor of fishing, Dayton and Fraser point out that there are some 22,000 varieties of fish; that seven of the 12 disciples were fishermen; that just as different ways of fishing are needed for different kinds of fish, so are different strategies required for different kinds of people (for example, a large 200-foot net for tuna, but a rod and line for brook trout).

They show the weakness of the "standard approach" to world evangelization, which assumes that any evangelistic strategy is applicable to any cultural situation. One methodology may work well in one city or culture but fail in another. Their evangelistic maxim is that there is no universal evangelistic strategy. Evangelistic strategies must be customized to reach specific target audiences.

The "people approach to world evangelization" realizes this and seeks to find specialized strategies for each of the major blocs of remaining unreached people groups in the world today. This approach is more culturally sensitive to the felt needs of the receptor audience and ensures that the gospel is not only preached but "heard" (according to Romans 10). For a people approach to world evangelization, "hearing the gospel" means that the gospel has been heard and understood in ways that allow them to make an intelligent and meaningful response to the message within their own language and cultural realities.

As Jesus commissioned His disciples, He thought of the myriads of tribes, tongues and peoples who comprised the cultural variety of the first-century world. To each new generation His commission has been repeated. His approach is "the people approach" to world evangelization.

Where Are These Unreached People Groups?

The majority of our unreached world is located within a rectangular band that has been called "the 10/40 Window." This area, formerly called "the Resistance Belt" (with many so-called Restricted Access Nations) lies between 10 degrees and 40 degrees north of the equator and stretches from the west coast of Africa to East Asia.

The 10/40 Window concept was first introduced to the Evangelical world by Luis Bush at the 1989 International Congress on World Evangelization in Manila, Philippines.

The importance of the 10/40 Window is related to seven important realities:

1. This part of the world has historical and Biblical significance. Here is the region where Christianity began—where Jesus was born, died and rose again. Much of God's dealings with mankind took place here, making it a truly significant area.

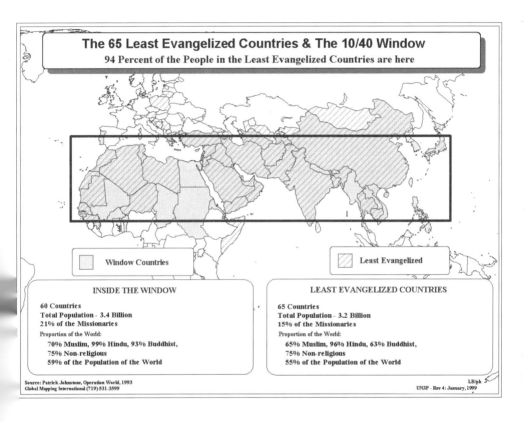

2. Most of the unevangelized people and countries of the world are here in the 10/40 Window. Almost two-thirds of the world's population live here.

3. The heart of Islam, the religion of the world's 1 billion Muslims, is in the 10/40 Window. Twenty-eight Muslim-dominated countries are in this region.

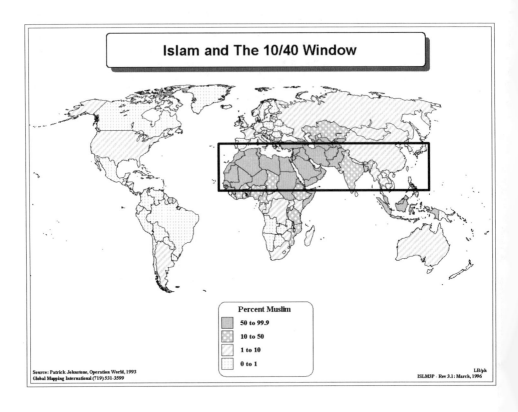

Islam and The 10/40 Window

Percent Muslim

50 to 99.9

10 to 50

1 to 10

0 to 1

Source: Patrick Johnstone, Operation World, 1993
Global Mapping International (719) 531-3599

LB/pk
ISLM3P - Rev 3.1: March, 1996

4. Here is where three main religious blocs are located: Islam, Hinduism and Buddhism.

5. We need to focus our attention on the 10/40 Window because the poor are there, most earning less than $500 per year. It has been said by Bryant Myers of World Vision, "The poor are lost and the lost are poor."

6. There the variables determining quality of life and human development—life expectancy, infant mortality and literacy—measure very low.

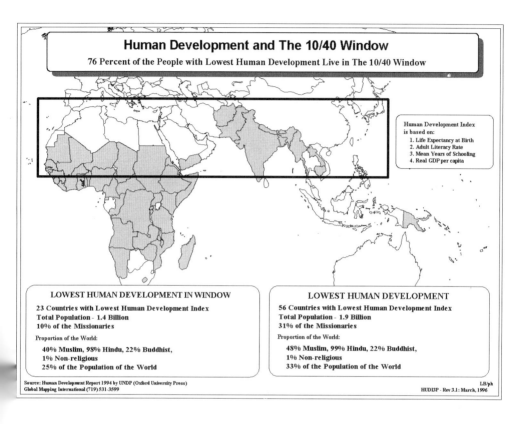

Human Development and The 10/40 Window

76 Percent of the People with Lowest Human Development Live in The 10/40 Window

Human Development Index is based on:
1. Life Expectancy at Birth
2. Adult Literacy Rate
3. Mean Years of Schooling
4. Real GDP per capita

LOWEST HUMAN DEVELOPMENT IN WINDOW

23 Countries with Lowest Human Development Index
Total Population - 1.4 Billion
10% of the Missionaries

Proportion of the World:
40% Muslim, 98% Hindu, 22% Buddhist,
1% Non-religious
25% of the Population of the World

LOWEST HUMAN DEVELOPMENT

56 Countries with Lowest Human Development Index
Total Population - 1.9 Billion
31% of the Missionaries

Proportion of the World:
48% Muslim, 99% Hindu, 22% Buddhist,
1% Non-religious
33% of the Population of the World

Source: Human Development Report 1994 by UNDP (Oxford University Press)
Global Mapping International (719) 531-3599

LB/ph
HUDI3P - Rev 3.1 : March, 1996

7. The 10/40 Window is presently a stronghold of Satan, a very strategic region.

STRONGHOLDS OF THE 10/40 WINDOW

NATIONAL MINI-PROFILES FOR INTERCESSORS

A Publication Of
The SENTINEL GROUP

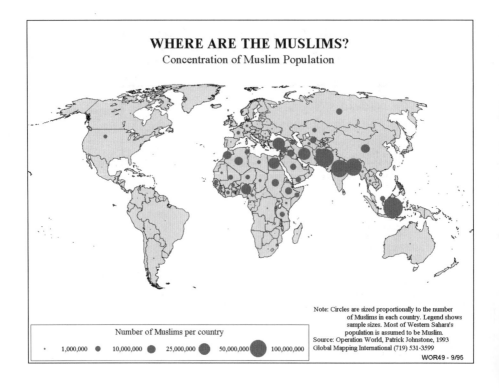

WHERE ARE THE MUSLIMS?
Concentration of Muslim Population

Number of Muslims per country

1,000,000   10,000,000   25,000,000   50,000,000   100,000,000

Note: Circles are sized proportionally to the number of Muslims in each country. Legend shows sample sizes. Most of Western Sahara's population is assumed to be Muslim.
Source: Operation World, Patrick Johnstone, 1993
Global Mapping International (719) 531-3599

WOR49 - 9/95

Lines to a Rickshaw Puller
Chandran D.S. Devanesen

I pass you every morning
on my way to the station.
The light is raw and the wind is keen.
All around you the city is stretching its limbs
and wiping the sleep from its eyes.
The raucous voice of the crow is everywhere.
But you hear nothing, you see nothing,
You lie curled up in your rickshaw
with sprawling limbs and inert body
like some tired animal.

Some mother must have cradled you
pressing you against the soft comfort
of her warm breast.
But now you shape your body
to fit the wooden embrace
of the hard sides of your rickshaw
for its walls are your home, your rented home.
Your intimacy with it is very great.
Your worldly possessions are in the box
under the seat with its torn fibre cushion
keeping company with your oil lamps,
the battered old *topee*
you wear on rainy days,
and a few *beedis*.
The shafts are worn smooth
by the contact of your forearms.
The rickshaw and you—
you belong together.
I have passed you by at other times—
when you were not asleep
and something of your life
has trailed after me.
I remember the laughter of your fellows
as you twitted the grain seller
who sits by the rickshaw stand
until the old hag exposed her gums
in a toothless grin . . .
I have watched you fight with your creditors
with the ferocity of a trapped beast
over pitiful sums, the price of a packet of fags.
I have heard you whine for a fare
when the day's earnings were poor.
I have seen you resentful and bitter
when you spat on the ground
and talked unconscious communism
I pass you by like a hundred others

who also pass you by—
and the road may be the road
from Jerusalem to Jericho for all we know.
I would like to put my hand on your shoulder
and say to you "Comrade,
there is One who died for us
and dying made us blood brothers."
But I am filled with the cowardice of the well-dressed—
for clothes are by no means flimsy
when it comes to erecting barriers
between man and man.
I am afraid you will wake with a start
and betray resentment in your eyes
as you see in me what I really am—
your well-dressed enemy.
And then you will acknowledge defeat
and put on your mask of patient stupidity.
You will jump up and dust the seat
and grin and point to it with a flourish of your hand.
You will want us to sell our brotherhood
for eight annas.

Day after day I pass you by,
you the man by the roadside
and I the priest and the Levite rolled into one,
passing you by.

The late Dr. Devanesen was Director for the Institute for Development Education, Madras, India. He was formerly Principal of Madras Christian College, Madras, and Vice Chancellor of North East Hill University, Shillong, Assam.

Reflections

1. You have looked through some global windows at your current world scene. What are three new things you have seen?

2. In Lamentations 3:51 Jeremiah said, "Mine eye affecteth mine heart"(KJV). The *NIV* reads, "What I see brings grief to my soul." What is God speaking to your heart through what you have read in this chapter and through what you see in your world today?

*Pause now for personal or group prayer before moving to Projections/Actions.

Projections

Today's date _____

By this time next year, next month, next week, I believe God for the following ministry goals to connect to God's work in my world (enter calendar dates for accountability):

1. Next year (date_____)
2. Next month (date_____)
3. Next week (date_____)

Actions

By this time tomorrow—in the next 24 hours—I will . . .

1.

2.

CHAPTER SEVEN

MUHAMMAD'S MOVEMENT

> He that lives by the life [Christ's life] cannot die.
>
> —Raymond Lull
> First missionary to the Muslims

In A.D. 570 a married couple by the name of Abdullah and Aminah gave birth to a child who grew as a strong, entrepreneurial, resourceful man. He was married at the age of 25 to Khadijah and began to work as a caravan manager. This young man, who had grown up in the home of a chief of a pagan deity, began receiving "revelations" and having contacts with Christians and Jews. Later, he would incorporate some of their teachings into his. At the age of 40, this man, known to us as Muhammad, continued to receive revelations which he recorded. A movement came into being around this man that swept across his side of the world, dominating Jerusalem and the Christian cities of North Africa, despite their former Christian influence. It would have controlled all of Western Europe had the advancement of Islam not been stopped by Charles Martel in A.D. 732. At one time Islam controlled the part of the world from Spain to India. Today, at more than 1 billion strong, it is one of the world's fastest-growing movements, predicted to double in size by the year 2020. One out of every six people in our world today is a Muslim.

Where are the Muslims? Islam is not a movement confined to the Middle East. North Africa is also dominated by Islam. This is a geographical area larger than the continental United States. Asia and the former Soviet Union also have a sizeable Islamic population. The movement is strong in Southeast Asia. Indonesia is the largest Muslim country in the world. In the United States alone there are an estimated 8 to 10 million Muslims (data from 2000).

Who are the Muslims? Evidently the most sizeable group are

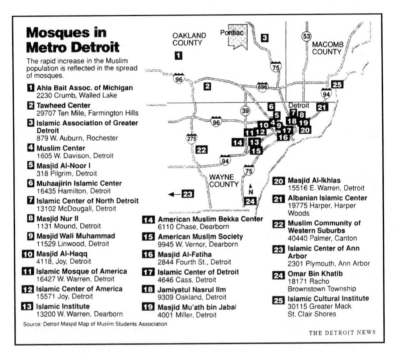

Mosques in Metro Detroit

The rapid increase in the Muslim population is reflected in the spread of mosques.

1 **Ahla Bait Assoc. of Michigan**
2230 Crumb, Walled Lake

2 **Tawheed Center**
29707 Ten Mile, Farmington Hills

3 **Islamic Association of Greater Detroit**
879 W. Auburn, Rochester

4 **Muslim Center**
1605 W. Davison, Detroit

5 **Masjid Al-Noor I**
318 Pilgrim, Detroit

6 **Muhaajirin Islamic Center**
16435 Hamilton, Detroit

7 **Islamic Center of North Detroit**
13102 McDougall, Detroit

8 **Masjid Nur II**
1131 Mound, Detroit

9 **Masjid Wali Muhammad**
11529 Linwood, Detroit

10 **Masjid Al-Haqq**
4118, Joy, Detroit

11 **Islamic Mosque of America**
16427 W. Warren, Detroit

12 **Islamic Center of America**
15571 Joy, Detroit

13 **Islamic Institute**
13200 W. Warren, Dearborn

Source: Detroit Masjid Map of Muslim Students Association

14 **American Muslim Bekka Center**
6110 Chase, Dearborn

15 **American Muslim Society**
9945 W. Vernor, Dearborn

16 **Masjid Al-Fatiha**
2844 Fourth St., Detroit

17 **Islamic Center of Detroit**
4646 Cass, Detroit

18 **Jamiyatul Nasrul Ilm**
9309 Oakland, Detroit

19 **Masjid Mu'ath bin Jabal**
4001 Miller, Detroit

20 **Masjid Al-Ikhlas**
15516 E. Warren, Detroit

21 **Albanian Islamic Center**
19775 Harper, Harper Woods

22 **Muslim Community of Western Suburbs**
40440 Palmer, Canton

23 **Islamic Center of Ann Arbor**
2301 Plymouth, Ann Arbor

24 **Omar Bin Khatib**
18171 Racho Brownstown Township

25 **Islamic Cultural Institute**
30115 Greater Mack St. Clair Shores

OAKLAND COUNTY · Pontiac · MACOMB COUNTY · Detroit · WAYNE COUNTY

THE DETROIT NEWS

the Arabs, followed by the Bengalis, Javanese, Punjabis, Central Asian Turks, Urdu speakers, Anatolian and Rumelian Turks, Sudanese, Hausas, Persians, Malays, and Kurds. One-sixth of mankind is Muslim. Sadly, only 2 percent of Christian missionaries are working among this sizeable, unreached block.

Many Christians know very little about Muslims. Test your knowledge of the world of Islam in the following quiz (more than one answer can be correct):

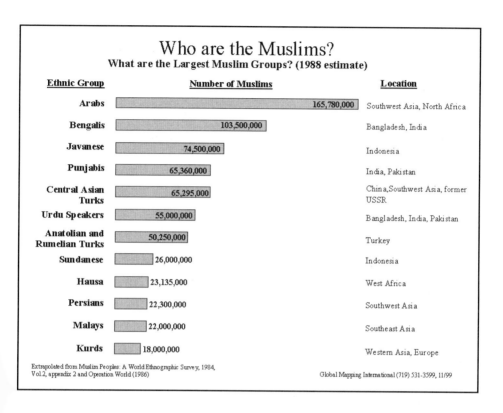

Who are the Muslims?
What are the Largest Muslim Groups? (1988 estimate)

Ethnic Group	Number of Muslims	Location
Arabs	165,780,000	Southwest Asia, North Africa
Bengalis	103,500,000	Bangladesh, India
Javanese	74,500,000	Indonesia
Punjabis	65,360,000	India, Pakistan
Central Asian Turks	65,295,000	China, Southwest Asia, former USSR
Urdu Speakers	55,000,000	Bangladesh, India, Pakistan
Anatolian and Rumelian Turks	50,250,000	Turkey
Sundanese	26,000,000	Indonesia
Hausa	23,135,000	West Africa
Persians	22,300,000	Southwest Asia
Malays	22,000,000	Southeast Asia
Kurds	18,000,000	Western Asia, Europe

Extrapolated from Muslim Peoples: A World Ethnographic Survey, 1984,
Vol.2, appendix 2 and Operation World (1986)

Global Mapping International (719) 531-3599, 11/99

1. Missionaries to Muslims
   a. are crazy
   b. are one in a million
   c. love sand, heat and camels

2. The largest major bloc of people unreached by the gospel of Jesus Christ are
   a. Buddhists
   b. Hindus
   c. Chinese
   d. Muslims
   e. Animists

3. Most Muslims live in
   a. Asia
   b. Middle East & North Africa
   c. West Africa
   d. United States

4. The number of Muslims in the U.S. is approximately equal to the population of
   a. France and Germany
   b. Des Moines
   c. Kuwait and Oman
   d. Houston

5. The Koran
   a. is the Muslims' holy book
   b. is read by all Muslims
   c. is memorized by some Muslims in its entirety
   d. mentions Jesus and other Biblical prophets
   e. is also sometimes spelled Quran

6. To get from place to place, all Muslims
   a. drive Cadillacs
   b. ride camels
   c. walk
   d. use public transportation

7. Arabic
   a. is the only language in which the Koran can be accurately read
   b. is the language of heaven
   c. uses the same alphabet as English, French and Spanish
   d. is spoken by all Muslims

8. For Muslims to come to know Jesus
   a. more Christians will have to pray for their salvation
   b. many more Christians will have to befriend them to tell them about Isa (the Arabic name for Jesus)
   c. they'll have to learn English so they can read the Bible

9. Most Muslims
   a. drive fast
   b. speak fast
   c. fast

10. The country with largest population of Muslims is
   a. Saudi Arabia
   b. India
   c. Iran
   d. Indonesia

11. Muslims worship
   a. Muhammad
   b. Jesus
   c. Allah
   d. money and oil

12. Great Britain today has more Muslims than
   a. Baptists
   b. Anglicans
   c. Pizza parlors
   d. cab drivers

13. The European country with the most Muslims is
   a. Spain
   b. Belgium
   c. France
   d. Britain

14. The Muslim world
   a. has few cities
   b. has a number of megacities
   c. has shrinking cities
   d. has more tents than cities

15. Muslims are divided into
   a. 315 people groups
   b. 14,500 people groups
   c. 741 people groups
   d. 930 people groups

16. Most Muslims in the United States are
   a. students
   b. African-American converts
   c. tourists
   d. immigrants

17. The South American country with the most Muslims is
   a. Brazil
   b. Surinam
   c. Venezuela
   d. Argentina
   e. Guyana

18. The Church of God has a strong ministry among Muslims in
   a. Detroit
   b. Sao Paulo
   c. Surabaya
   d. Hong Kong
   e. Nairobi

19. The largest Muslim city in the world is
   a. Daccab
   b. Shanghai
   c. Cairo
   d. Istanbul
   e. Jakarta

20. The largest number of Muslims in America are found in
   a. Denver
   b. Detroit
   c. Washington, D.C.
   d. Los Angeles

ANSWER KEY
1-b; 2-d; 3-a; 4-c; 5-a, b, c, d, e; 6-c; 7-a; 8-a, b; 9-c; 10-d; 11-c; 12-a; 13-c; 14-b; 15-c; 16-d; 17-b; 18-c; 19-c; 20-b, c, d.

The Five Pillars of Islam:

1. Recitation of the creed: This creed, which is repeated daily around the world, consists of only eight Arabic words. It means "There is no god but God, and Muhammad is the apostle of God."

2. Ritual prayer five times a day: Prayer times include early morning at dawn, soon after midday, two hours before sunset, just after sunset, and two hours after sunset.

3. Almsgiving

4. Fasting: This includes the monthlong fast of Ramadan.

5. The pilgrimage to Mecca: Annually, people make this trip from all over the world. It is televised globally by satellite in at least 14 major world languages.

Church of God Ministry Among Muslims

This survey of Church of God ministry among Muslims is not the final word on the subject. Our research is continually being updated. The nature of this overview is to present a challenge, to ask what has been happening among us as a worldwide movement, and to follow the guidance of the Holy Spirit for tomorrow. Since this ministry focus is only now beginning to be highlighted in a broader way in our denomination, much more needs to be written.

Looking back. We need a detailed chronological investigation of our first contacts as a church with the Muslim world. In a sermon written, but never preached, L. Howard Juillerat wrote of masses of humanity coming into the major cities of America. He also referred to "Mohammedans," one of the earlier terms used for Muslim people. This was in his manuscript on "The Spirit of Missions." He never preached that sermon because he died in the flu epidemic of 1918, the same plague that canceled the General Assembly that year. The sermon was preserved by Juillerat's widow in "Gems of Religious Truth" *(Church of God Evangel Press*, 1919) and kept alive in a centennial collection called *A Treasury of Pentecostal Classics: Writings From the First Century of the Church of God.*[1]

Research is also needed to determine if there were any significant ministries to Muslims in the ministries of pioneers like Robert Cook and J.H. Ingram. Certainly the story of Lillian Trasher's orphanage ministry among the Arab children of Cairo, Egypt, would need to be cited. Leaving for Egypt in 1910, Trasher would no doubt be among the first Church of God members to have contact with the Muslims.

The stories of Josephine Planter and Margaret Gaines are well known. Church of God historian Charles W. Conn believes that Planter, who went to Tunisia in 1912, was the first Pentecostal missionary to that country. Her message at Lee College in 1946 recruited young Margaret Gaines, who began her missionary ministry in that North African country.

Other scattered contacts with the Muslim world have been made over the last 25 years through Church of God laity involved in military service and private business. My hunch is that there are scores of other stories and testimonies like this in our churches, not only in the United States, but also from other countries. As our common interest in this ministry is publicized, numerous reports of additional outreaches in our denomination will surface.

Revival in the 1990s

During the 1990s there were two wonderful revivals and stories of church growth in the heart of the Muslim world. These countries will be the leaders in Muslim ministry in coming years. From 1989-1991, more than 30,000 new believers came to Christ in our churches in these two countries alone (Indonesia and Bulgaria).

Indonesia. There are more than 1 million Church of God members in Indonesia, the world's largest Muslim country, and the fourth largest in overall population (200 million). Our church is active in all of Indonesia's 27 provinces. We operate Bethel Seminary in the capital city of Jakarta and 10 regional Bible schools across the country. In Jakarta alone we have over 200 local congregations with a combined membership of more than 100,000. There are some 2,400 ministers, 5 percent of whom are former Muslims (data from 2000).

Until 1993, the main seminary had only one course in "Islamology." This was expanded as they began building a missiology faculty and curriculum the same year. Special courses are also offered in a training program developed by our large congregation in the city of Surabaya.

The Surabaya church, in east Java, was started with seven people in a garage in 1977. By early 1994 they had a weekly attendance of 30,000 in multiple services and had planted more than 30 other congregations, most of them averaging over 1,000 in attendance. In 1993, the main church began construction on a 20,000-seat auditorium.

The church is baptizing 500 disciples per month, after each one has completed a required "School of Ministry." There is a network of 1,200 small Bible study/prayer groups—70 percent led by women. The pastor estimates that 60 percent of the church's membership are former Muslims, 30 percent former Buddhists and 10 percent "mixed." He attributes the interest in Christ to the social involvement of the church in the community (the church has an extensive social welfare ministry), a preaching focus upon successful family life, intercessory prayer, and the convincing power of God through signs and wonders. His ultimate church growth maxim is, "We grow because we pray. Prayer produces faith."

The church, and many of our churches across that country, experienced some dark days of resistance and persecution in the latter half of the 1990s and at the outset of 2000. They need our continual prayers and human rights advocacy.

Bulgaria. Bulgaria, at the eastern perimeter of Europe on the Black Sea, holds special significance in the history of contacts between Christians and Muslims. It is a "crossroads nation" at the convergence point between Europe and Asia. The country is bordered on the east by the predominantly Muslim country of Turkey.

There are historical reasons for the presence of more than 2 million Muslims in this country of 9 million (22 percent Muslim, or every fourth person). Researcher Daniela Gaydarova-Augustine explains that more than 500 years of Muslim domination of Bulgaria under the Ottoman Empire produced four distinct Muslim groups in the country.

The more recent historical situation is better understood by remembering the Marxist control of the country after World War II. From 1945 to 1989 the country was subjugated to communist totalitarianism. Religious groups, including Muslims, were suppressed. Turkish Muslims were forced to take Bulgarian names. Our own church was aggressively persecuted during this time. Following the political changes initiated in November 1989, Muslims, like other groups, demanded restoration of political, social and cultural rights, including the return of original ethnic Turkish names.

One of the most alarming developments for Christians (of three traditions: Orthodox, Catholic, Evangelical) was the Muslim plan to build the largest Muslim center in Europe—the third largest in the world—in the capital city of Sofia at a cost of $10 million. The development was published in the daily newspaper *Duma* April 11, 1991. Fearing a renewed Islamization of the population, the plan was defeated in a public outcry. It led to favorable discussions among the three Christian traditions for a united "Christian Center."

Capitalizing on the new changes in the country in 1989, the Church of God experienced explosive growth from 5,000 members to more than 20,000 in two years. The largest single congregation in Bulgaria is the Sofia Church of God. This local church has 3,000 members in regular attendance with six daughter churches scattered across the city.

Augustine estimates that as much as 50 percent of the national Church of God membership are former Muslims from the Gypsies and Turks. These groups were being won to the Lord by a threefold strategy for three kinds of Muslim subcultures:

1. To reach the Muslim intellectuals, trained groups of students should form friendships in the universities and take an approach using apologetics.

2. Fundamentalist Muslims among the lower classes are reached through social services, mercy ministries, and medical care. Women in particular suffer oppression in these groupings.

3. Gypsies, being socially ostracized yet spiritually sensitive, respond well to social ministry and to signs and wonders.

The trends reported by Church of God missionaries were matched by a World Pulse report from the Evangelical Missions Information Service early in 1992. Stan Guthrie's article, "Conversions Among Turks Suggest Gospel Lift Off Near," showed how God's kairos moment in Bulgaria had the potential of spreading into neighboring Turkey. Guthrie interviewed Steve Hagerman, director of "Friends of Turkey" in Grand Junction, Colorado. Hagerman's encouraging report described the rise from three known believers in Turkey in 1968 to 1,000 by 1990. "You know, we worked over 22 years to see 1,000 converts in Turkey," Hagerman said of evangelical efforts in general, "and yet in the last three years, more than 2,000 Turks have come to faith in Christ in Bulgaria."[2]

Following a survey trip to the area, one missions observer stated, "The news is exciting, if only as a confirmation that God's day for the Turkish people is coming. Pray with us that the spiritual awakening in Bulgaria will continue and spill over into Turkey."

Regional Highlights

Middle East. Faithful missionaries and national churches have labored for decades in such places as Israel and Egypt. Most of our growth in these areas has come through the conversion of individuals from nominal Christian backgrounds or by transfer growth from other evangelical groups. Few of our members there came from a strictly Muslim background, but significant opportunities have developed to reach out in friendship to Muslim neighbors.

More recently there has been growth among immigrants to Israel, Lebanon and the Persian Gulf countries. Hundreds of thousands of immigrants and foreign guest workers have come to those countries from Romania, Russia, India, Pakistan and the Philippines. Many have brought with them their Pentecostal faith and have been gathered into Church of God congregations.

Far East. Indonesia is certainly the bright spot for the Church of God in this part of the world. Continued research will no doubt reveal varied stories from places such as Mindanao (southern Philippines), Malaysia, India and Pakistan. Missionary Chuck Quinley recently told the amazing story of Mansour Shayestehpour, a former Iranian Muslim converted in the Philippines through a series of miraculous divine interventions, including visions of Jesus.

Europe. Shortly after the dramatic political changes of the early 1990s, a heartwarming report came from the leadership of the "Samaritan Ministry" of the Church of God in Germany. In September 9, 1991, a "mercy/evangelism" team left Germany with two tractor trailer loads of relief supplies for Albania, where 75 percent of the population is Muslim. Upon their arrival in the capital city of Tirana, they met up with a Dutch missionary and were joined the next day by an Asian Indian evangelist from England.

The team reported the successful delivery of tons of supplies, along with the blessing of seeing many Muslims turn to Christ through the viewing of the *Jesus* film. They reported that while watching the film, "grown men cried openly," and at the end of the evangelistic message many believed in Christ! They were invited by a Muslim leader to preach the gospel to a cluster of three villages where some 600 families (about 9,000 people) lived. Here they distributed 16 tons of goods and hundreds of New Testaments.

Another "testimony point" in Europe is in the southern frontier where Spain looks across to the continent of Africa. On an isthmus in northwest Africa is the Spanish-controlled city of Ceuta, a military installation city of some 70,000 people. Since Ceuta is 30 percent Muslim and borders the Muslim country of Morocco, the Church of God established a ministry center there, responding to the vision of an Argentinean medical doctor, Luis Solis.

Dr. Solis secured the government documents to work as a foreign doctor in the local Red Cross Hospital. The hospital had only 200 beds and was the only medical center to serve a vast area. There was, therefore, government sympathy with Dr. Solis's plan to start a medical clinic. The clinic was placed in a center that also houses a Muslim Ministries Training Center and a sanctuary for the growing local Church of God congregation pastored by Alfonso Medina.

This was a significant move for North Africa and also for Spain. Many parts of that country were under Islamic rule between the eighth and 15th centuries. In July 1989 the Spanish government granted Islam official recognition. The same year the largest mosque in Europe (financed with a $17 million grant from Saudi Arabia's King Fahd) was opened in Madrid on an 8,000-square-meter piece of real estate donated by the Spanish government (reported by *World Christian News*, Youth With A Mission, November 1989).[3]

Latin America. The missionary vision of Luis Solis characterizes a groundswell evangelical missions movement in Latin America that is focused on Europe (Spain and Portugal in particular) and the Muslim world. An interdenominational missions thrust is coming from COMIBAM (a Spanish acronym: "Congresso Missionero Ibero-Americano," the Ibero-American Missionary Congress). The initial COMIBAM event was an exciting missions congress in Sao

Paulo, Brazil, in November 1987. The movement is now an inter-denominational association. One of the early leaders was a Guatemalan Church of God pastor, Rodolfo Giron (a graduate of the Church of God Theological Seminary) who was chosen as the president of COMIBAM. In the early 1990s he reported that Church of God "hot spots" for cross-cultural missions vision were in Argentina, Guatemala and Costa Rica.

It was my privilege to attend the COMIBAM Congress in Sao Paulo as one of the 300 invited North American observers. More than 3,000 participants were involved. Probably 75 percent of the attendees were students, laity and young professionals. Within two months following COMIBAM, I also witnessed a record attendance at "El Salvador '88," the first Central American Church of God Youth Conference on World Evangelism in San Salvador, El Salvador. One of the highlights of that same trip was a historic moment in Guatemala City, Guatemala, where I preached the commissioning service for Juan José and Marta Lima. Juan José, a Guatemalan Church of God evangelist, and his wife, Marta, were being sent to Ecuador as the first fully sponsored missionaries from the Church of God in Guatemala. Latin America is moving from a mission field to a missions force and will figure prominently in our future work among Muslims!

Declaration on Christian Attitudes Toward Muslims

Current statistics describe Western contributions to Christian work among Muslims as less than two percent of total Western mission resources. This uneven distribution appears to be the result of general misconceptions about the Muslim world. These misconceptions are particularly intensified in Western countries due to the Gulf War, hostage crises, and terrorist attacks. Popular imagery, within both national media and religious circles, can lead to conclusions suggesting Muslims to be "enemies" and "people unable to receive the gospel of

Jesus Christ." Part of this image is caused by Western media attention to pro-Israel issues without due consideration being given to the other side of the same issues.

We are commanded by Scripture to love all people, including Muslims. As followers of Jesus Christ, we are obligated by the Great Commission mandate in Matthew 28 to effectively communicate the gospel of Christ to all peoples, without exception or criteria.

Regardless of how much effort we have contributed to world mission, we have failed to provide the necessary resources to adequately communicate the gospel of Jesus Christ to the Muslim world. In the future, we will endeavor to assure that our view of the Muslim demonstrates the same love Jesus Christ displayed for all humanity on the Cross of Calvary.

We, the undersigned, as followers of Jesus Christ, believing that it is our primary responsibility to share the good news of Jesus Christ with all the peoples of the world, confess that:
- we have failed to understand the significance of the many emotional issues of Muslim peoples, especially in regard to the nation of Israel;
- we have allowed our false perceptions and lack of understanding to result in wrong attitudes and a lack of compassion for Muslim peoples and, therefore, not sought to alleviate suffering among them;
- we are guilty of believing and perpetuating misconceptions, prejudice and, in some instances, hostility and outright hatred toward Muslim peoples; and,
- we have not recognized the timing of the Lord when the Holy Spirit has moved on the hearts of Muslims and given these nations a hunger for an understanding of true Christianity.

In spite of our attitudes, the Holy Spirit is working among Muslim peoples through Christian witness and direct revelation.

We repent of attitudes of apathy and hostility we have borne toward Muslims. Repentance is a decision that results in a change of mind, which in turn leads to a change of purpose and action. Reconciliation is the goal of our repentance. In an effort toward reconciliation, we pledge to:
- earnestly pray on a committed basis for the acceptance of the gospel of Jesus Christ by Muslim peoples;
- earnestly pray on a committed basis for followers of Jesus Christ to develop attitudes of compassion, love, and forgiveness toward Muslims;
- act within our individual spheres of influence to rebuke sinful attitudes that we encounter within the Christian community;
- earnestly advocate prayer and relief and development assistance for

Muslim peoples, some of whom are the poorest, least educated, least medically provided for, and most victimized by violence;

• support on a committed basis our brothers and sisters already working in Muslim world through prayer and financial support; and,

• earnestly pray and seek God's will to determine our individual role in ensuring that all Muslims have an opportunity to understand and respond to the good news of Jesus Christ. One clear way is by developing relationships and sharing our faith with Muslims who live in our communities and around the world.

Published by the Association of International Mission Services (AIMS) in cooperation with AIMS member agencies focusing on the Islamic world

Reflections

1. Most Christians misunderstand or have little knowledge of the Muslim world. What are three new things you have learned about Muslims from this chapter?

2. What are some special ways we can be available to God to reach out to and minister to Muslim people?

*Pause now for personal or group prayer before moving to Projections/Actions.

Projections

Today's date _____

By this time next year, next month, next week, I believe God for the following ministry goals to connect to God's work in my world (enter calendar dates for accountability):

1. Next year (date_____)
2. Next month (date_____)
3. Next week (date_____)

Actions

By this time tomorrow—in the next 24 hours—I will . . .

1.

2.

CHAPTER EIGHT

YOUR URBAN WORLD

THE BIBLE MAY BEGIN IN A GARDEN BUT
IT ENDS IN A CITY.
                    —RAYMOND BAKKE
               URBAN PASTOR/URBANOLOGIST

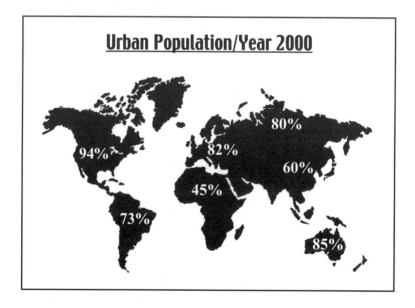

Urban Population/Year 2000

94%
82%
80%
60%
45%
73%
85%

We are facing an urban future. Those who are serious about reaching our world today and tomorrow must engage the powers of the city, and move decisively into the city. It is here that we desperately need the incarnation of the gospel.

137

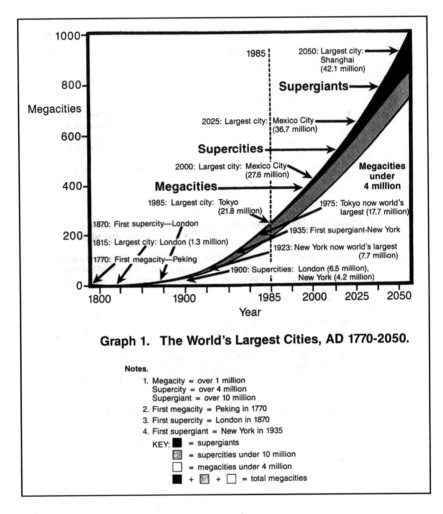

Graph 1. The World's Largest Cities, AD 1770-2050.

Notes.
1. Megacity = over 1 million
   Supercity = over 4 million
   Supergiant = over 10 million
2. First megacity = Peking in 1770
3. First supercity = London in 1870
4. First supergiant = New York in 1935
KEY: ■ = supergiants
     ▨ = supercities under 10 million
     □ = megacities under 4 million
     ■ + ▨ + □ = total megacities

One writer said that the city will drive you to the gospel. Unfortunately, this cannot be said conversely. Although it could and should, the gospel does not always drive Christians to the city. We tend to read the Word of God with a filter that allows us to see only what we want to see. If we would really read, hear and obey the Word of God and allow the gospel to motivate us, it would compel us to the city.

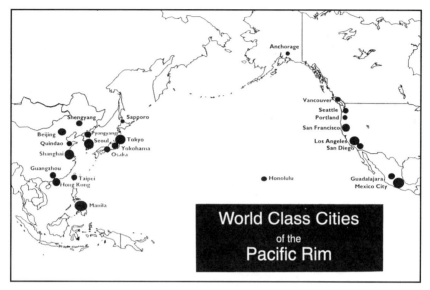

World Class Cities
of the
Pacific Rim

A glance through a typical Evangelical or Pentecostal church hymnal bears little mention of the city or the streets. On the contrary, you would find in those pages many songs about nature, the God of the valleys, the God of the mountains and fields, and the God of the streams. We tend to enjoy our evangelical retreats—"out, away from it all," where we can find "true spirituality and communion with God." What is needed, however, is a new generation of thinkers, theologians, technologists, researchers and writers who will form their views of Christian living and the mission of the church out of the context of the city.

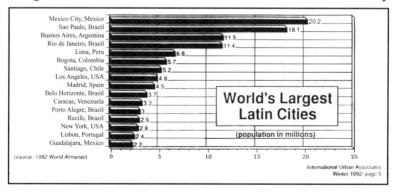

World's Largest Latin Cities

(population in millions)

We have an anti-urban bias, especially those who come from a small-town, rural, holiness, Pentecostal background. Common thought has contributed to this anti-urban feeling, picturing the city as a place of depravity and sin where we and our children will get lost. We are told to stay away from the city. Common thinking points to God's creation of gardens versus man's creation of cities. It reasons that after Cain's rebellious departure the first thing he did was establish a city.

The truth is that God loves the city and its inhabitants. The Bible, in actuality, is an urban book. In his article, "Towards a Biblical Urban Theology," Robert Linthicum, former director of Urban Advance for World Vision International, writes:

> The Bible is an urban book. It is hard for us to appreciate that the world of Moses and David and Daniel and Jesus was decisively more urban than was the world of A.D.1000.
>
> The world in which the Bible was written was dominated by cities. Ancient Nineveh was so large that it took four days to cross it on foot. Babylon had a city water and irrigation system so advanced that it was unequaled until the 19th century. The Rome of the apostle Paul's day had a population exceeding one million.
>
> The Biblical people of God were themselves urban people. David was king of Jerusalem as well as an empire. Isaiah and Jeremiah were prophets committed to Jerusalem. Daniel was appointed mayor of the city of Babylon by King Nebuchadnezzar.
>
> Nehemiah was a city planner, a community organizer and governor over Jerusalem. Paul was Christianity's premier evangelist to the major cities of the Roman Empire.
>
> If the Bible is such an urban book, why do we not see it that way? Why then do we approach the Bible with a rural theological mind-set?[1]

Over the last 2,000 years of history, Christians and theologians have developed a rural village mentality. Actually, the Bible was written with an urban theological mind-set.

There are over 1,400 references to cities in the Bible, either by specific name or general reference. There are approximately 119 cities mentioned by name. When the people of God went into Babylonian captivity, the Lord, through the prophet Jeremiah, told them to seek the welfare of the city. God wants His people to evangelize the cities.

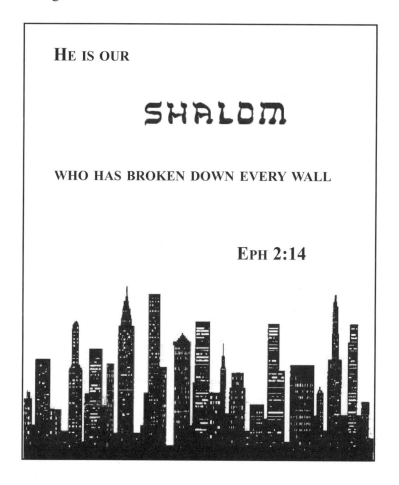

HE IS OUR

SHALOM

WHO HAS BROKEN DOWN EVERY WALL

EPH 2:14

Ray Bakke, an evangelical urban expert and former inner-city pastor, has noted God's desires for the city, as found in Isaiah 65. From a premillenial standpoint we understand these to be future events, when the fully realized kingdom of God is established on earth. But consider this: If God is the same yesterday, today and forever, surely He would be pleased with our striving to bring about His ultimate design (outlined in Isaiah 65) in our world today. This is what God wants in our cities today:

1. A *happy* city (vv. 18, 19)—rather than sadness and heartache, God wants urban happiness. The words *delight* and *joy* are used. God says He will "rejoice over Jerusalem."

2. A *healthy* city (v. 20)—consider today's infant mortality and the plight of the elderly in urban centers of misery. Contrast that to the health of infants and older people promised in this verse.

3. A city with adequate, fair *housing* (v. 21)—God is concerned with the problems of homelessness and promises a dwelling with vineyards and gardens. We should be working on God's housing agenda.

4. A city with *honorable* business/economy (v. 22)—a careful look at this verse reveals unfair exploitation and wrong business practices. God's kingdom agenda calls for justice and economic equity.

5. A city with the *humanization* of work, family and neighborhood (v. 23)—rather than the oppressiveness of "toil in vain," God's city provides a place of refuge where work is holy unto the Lord, where family and neighborhoods are fostered.

6. A city of *harmony* (v. 25)—"violence" is the defining word of urban life today. God's city is a place where violence is absent and people live together in harmony.

This is "God's urban agenda," not that of any political program. As we work primarily for the personal reconciliation of people to God, we also seek the welfare of the city under the guidelines of this value system. We listen to God's heart for the city, in the following poetic expression:

The Streets I Feared to See

I said: "Let me walk in the field."
God said: "Nay, walk in the town."
I said: "There are no flowers there."
He said: "No flowers, but a crown."

I said: "But the sky is black,
There is nothing there but noise and din."
But He wept as He sent me back,
"There is more," He said, "there is sin."

I said: "But the air is thick,
And fogs are veiling the sun."
He answered: "Yet souls are sick,
And souls in the dark undone."

I said: "I shall miss the light,
And friends will miss me, they say."
He answered me, "Choose tonight,
If I am to miss you, or they."

I pleaded for time to be given;
He said: "Is it hard to decide?
It will not seem hard in heaven
To have followed the steps of your Guide."

I cast one look at the fields,
Then set my face to the town.
He said: "My child, do you yield?
Will you leave the flowers for the crown?"

Then into His hand went mine,
And into my heart came He;
And I walk in a light divine,
The streets I had feared to see.

—George MacDonald (1824-1905)[2]

143

SECTORS OF AN URBAN WORLD
Implications for Ministry

Points of Entry

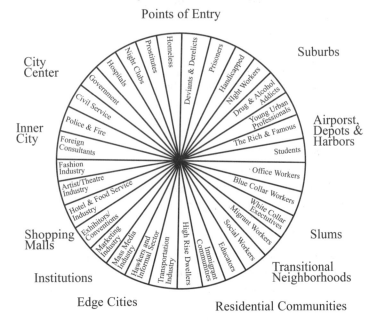

Church and Mission Issues:
1. How do we locate these groups and enter their subcultures?
2. How do we define needs and communicate the gospel?
3. How do we disciple Christians within these communities?
4. How do we plant or renew churches in these contexts?
5. How do we prepare pastors or mission workers for effective ministry in these urban worlds?

An Urban Cross-Cultural Role Model

Today's urban witnesses need a refresher course in the Biblical models for their personal role in the task of urban mission. Great Commission missions must continue to be informed by Biblical examples if exegesis and evangelization are to remain welded together. That is why Paul's self-understanding of his place in God's work provides inspiration and information for our calling to urban ministry.

144

Nine Self-Images

From the standpoint of the "theology of biography," Paul's personal case study is one of the finest exhibits of an urban cross-cultural church planter. Likewise, the one book that serves as a model missionary treatise from the pen of this masterful apostle is his letter to the Romans. From Romans 1—16, nine specific roles or self-portraits of Paul emerge:

1. Servant (1:1)
2. Called apostle (1:1)
3. Separated (1:1)
4. Debtor (1:14-16)
5. Intercessor (9:1-3; 10:1)
6. Minister/priest (15:16)
7. Pioneer (15:19-21, 23, 24)
8. Peacemaker/mediator (15:25-28, 31)
9. Brother/companion (7:4; 12:1; 15:14)

How did Paul understand these in relation to his calling to major cities? How can they shape our personal growth as urban witnesses?

1. *Paul the servant*—"a servant of Christ Jesus . . ." (1:1). Paul had no difficulty in communicating his intense self-description as a *doulos Christou Iesou* (literally, "a slave of Christ Jesus"). Five other Greek words indicating servitude were at his disposal. He deliberately chose the strongest. Karl Barth said, "The essential theme of his mission is not within him but above him." *Doulos* expressed total dependence, absolute subordination, and complete obedience. Kenneth Wuest notes that *doulos*, "slave of the emperor," was a common term used in the Roman world. He believes that Paul used *doulos* purposely to show Christians in Rome the "imperialistic challenge" of Christianity coming to the city. The kingdom of Paul's Master would someday displace the imperialism of Rome.

Lessons: Today's urban witnesses are not primarily servants of the city or any of its occupants (regardless how poor, displaced or oppressed). They are not servants of a church or a mission. They are servants of Jesus Christ, and their allegiance to Him will bring them into confrontation with idols and powers that seek to intimidate, seduce, or buy them into a substitute allegiance.

2. *Paul the called apostle*—"called to be an apostle . . ." (1:1). Paul actually said he was "called an apostle." The "to be" has been added to make a smoother translation, but it should not change or weaken the meaning. In other words, Paul was not in the process of becoming an apostle as if he were anticipating a future role. He was an apostle the moment God called him.

The term *apostle* is from a Hebrew concept (the Old Testament *shaliach*—messenger). The messenger derived his authority from the one who sent (in Paul's case, from Jesus Christ himself). Paul needed no other authority or credentials. He was possessed by and sent by Jesus Christ, the Lord of the harvest.

Lessons: Today's urban witnesses are given significant apostolic authority that proceeds from their position of servanthood in Jesus Christ. Since the call and commission for today's harvest in the city comes from the Lord of the harvest, let us call on Him to send laborers into His harvest (Matthew 9:38).

3. *Paul the separated*—"set apart for the gospel of God" (1:1). Paul was not on a trial run in the cities. There was no probationary period to see if he wanted to go through with this commitment that began on the Damascus road. The idea carried in the text is that of being set apart permanently for the work of God. He was separated *from* the world and its power of attraction, and he was separated *to* the specific purpose of God. His mind was made up. He was committed to the gospel of God before entering Rome.

This is important since *Rome* was not a friendly word to Christians. This powerful city was synonymous with raw power, maliciousness, greed, sin, corruption. Therefore, each mention of this word (carrying in itself a challenge to Christians) is followed in the text by the counterbalancing effects of the gospel to which Paul was set apart.

Lessons: Against the backdrop of aggressive intolerance and growing hostility, today's urban witnesses must remind themselves that they have been set apart for the gospel of God. Inherent in that revealed gospel is God's divine protection, presence and power for His people in the midst of today's cities.

4. *Paul the debtor* (1:14-16)—"I am obligated both to Greeks and non-Greeks, both to the wise and the foolish. That is why I am so eager to preach the gospel also to you who are at Rome. I am not ashamed of the gospel, because it is the power of God for the salvation of everyone who believes: first for the Jew, then for the Gentile."

Paul saw himself indebted to the city, seeking its welfare. He longed to take this city for God by entering into its hopes, dreams, hurts and aspirations. He was not ashamed of the power of the gospel to address every need in the city. The "ashamed" of verse 16 is *epaischunomai*, which expresses "a feeling of fear or shame which prevents a person from doing a thing."

Why would even the idea of shame or fear arise? John Sanday suggests a one-word answer: *Rome.* He gives this expanded translation of verse 16:

> Even there, in the imperial city itself, I am not ashamed of my message, repellent and humiliating as some of its features may seem. For it is a mighty agency, set in motion by God himself, and sweeping on with it towards the haven of messianic security for every believer—first in order of precedence the Jew, and after him the Gentile.

"The apostle knew," says Ralph Earle, "that he had a great gospel worthy of being preached in the capital city of the greatest empire the world had ever seen. Rome boasted of her power which consisted of military might. But Paul declares that this gospel is the 'power of God.' It is more than human might."[3]

Lessons: The self-identity of today's urban witness must be identified with the powerful gospel of Jesus Christ ("I am . . . it is"). The grace inherent in that gospel propels us with resolute courage and passion to extend God's light into the urban night.

5. *Paul the intercessor*—"I speak the truth in Christ—I am not lying, my conscience confirms it in the Holy Spirit—I have great sorrow and unceasing anguish in my heart. For I could wish that I myself were cursed and cut off from Christ for the sake of my brothers, those of my own race" (9:1-3). "Brothers, my heart's desire and prayer to God for the Israelites is that they may be saved" (10:1).

The passage (9:1-3) has to be conditioned by the fact that he speaks "in Christ" (*lego en Christo*, "I say in Christ"—a popular Pauline phrase). Paul's grief (*lupe*) is seen as a state of mind, but his anguish (*odune*) has strong physical associations. Here is the language of strong emotions.

His wish, "that I myself were cursed," is literally, "I was wishing." It is in the imperfect tense, says Marvin Vincent, and carries a tentative idea, implying that the wish was begun but stopped at the outset by a prior consideration which renders it impossible. John Bengel believes that although the prayer was pious and solid, the thing which Paul wished could not have been done. It was impossible in the light of what Paul had just stated in Romans 8:38, 39 (that nothing in heaven or earth could separate him from the love of Christ). It is easier to reconcile the passage, says Sanday, when one notes that the passage is the language of feeling, not of reasoning and reflection.[4]

"This "language of feeling," the *affective* element in mission, is missing in some Christian circles today. There is a need to recapture the same sense of passion, zeal and consecration that characterized our first love for Christ and His original call upon our lives. There is a desperate need to move beyond the sometimes cold and calculated projections, so carefully and professionally articulated in our board rooms, conferences and strategy sessions. Let there be impassioned cries from our altars of prayer, "Give us souls . . . give us this city . . . or we will die." Let there be feeling and weeping as Jesus wept over the lost city of Jerusalem.

Lessons: Urban mission cannot remain a cognitive exercise— it must touch our hearts. Let us intercede with God for a new wave of impassioned urban intercessors, raised up as salt and light. Let there be pleading with God for His mercy and salvation to bring deliverance and freedom.

6. *Paul, the minister/priest* (15:16)—"To be a minister of Christ Jesus to the Gentiles with the priestly duty of proclaiming the gospel of God, so that the Gentiles might become an offering acceptable to God, sanctified by the Holy Spirit."

Paul saw a priestly function in preaching the gospel. His preaching was a means to an end— his acceptable sacrifice-offering to God. Henry Alford says that the Greek construction shows that the Gentiles themselves were the offering. Paul is "the sacrificing priest of the gospel of God." The "proclaiming" of verse 16 is the form of the verb *hierourgeo* (literally "sacrificing"), signifying "to perform sacred rites, to minister in priestly service." Another translation of the phrase reads, "serve the gospel as a priest."

Paul applied this unique term, which is found only once here in the New Testament. The verb is based on *hieros*, which means "holy, sacred, consecrated." A form of this word is used to signify the whole Temple area at Jerusalem.

Lessons: Urban witnesses must not see their work as another humanitarian service or philanthropy. Urban mission is a divine calling—a priestly service—building a new temple, a people consecrated to God. The conversion of people in today's cities brings glory to God, "an offering acceptable to [Him], sanctified by the Holy Spirit."

7. *Paul the pioneer* (15:19, 20, 23, 24)—"So from Jerusalem all the way around to Illyricum, I have fully proclaimed the

gospel of Christ. It has always been my ambition to preach the gospel where Christ was not known, so that I would not be building on someone else's foundation. . . . There is no more place for me to work in these regions. . . I plan to . . . go to Spain."

For Paul there was more. He had run out of room (v. 23). Paul the pioneer was revealed. He spoke not of villages, towns, or even cities, but of *klimasi* ("regions"). This term goes beyond the mere tribal political divisions of the world to reflect a broad visionary perspective. John Bengel notes that *klimasi* expresses "the supposed sloping of the earth, the equator towards the poles, a zone." The word was used only two other times in the New Testament (2 Corinthians 11:10; Galatians 1:21). Paul was standing as a visionary pioneer—not content to be successful in one region, envisioning other spheres, regions—with a global desire to reach more and more into the farthest limits of the known world.

Lessons: Once urban church planters have developed, strengthened, and consolidated new churches, it is time to appoint leaders and move on. Urban church-planting teams, while keeping their hands to the plow (the present task), will be needed continually in *new* places. Urban witnesses in world-class cities will need to continually remember that cities are connected to surrounding regions and cities in other regions and to keep their vision focused beyond.

8. *Paul the peacemaker/mediator* (15:25-28, 31)—"Pray . . . that my service in Jerusalem may be acceptable to the saints there" (v. 31). There was still tension and misunderstandings between the Jewish and Gentile churches, and Paul had to fit the role of peacemaker/mediator. In verse 28 he uses the picture of "sealing" (see KJV), which was taken from the agricultural world of tenant farming. A producer would deliver his harvest to the owner with a seal for identification.

"Fruit" (*karpon*, v. 28) signified results in Paul's mission (cf. Romans 1:13; Philippians 1:22; 4:17). He was hoping for the acceptance of Gentile believers by Jewish Christians as the seal and fruits of his labors and evidence of God's approval (Romans 15:30, 31). The commission to the Gentiles, begun in Jerusalem (Acts 22:21), would now come "full circle" to the "mother church." In this action, Paul wanted to demonstrate (to Gentiles and Jews) his solidarity with Jerusalem.

It is also believed that Paul was helping to dispel rumors from the Judaizers that he was preaching a new gospel and starting a new movement. Paul demonstrated his submission in love and identification with the leadership of the church. He was a real churchman, a mediator concerned for the unity of the Body as opposed to his own personal gain.

Lessons: Urban witnesses must not become "detached" in the city. For their own growth, and the blessing they can be to others, they must demonstrate traits of loyalty, accountability, reliability and communication. They will often be called upon to be agents of reconciliation and bridges of communication.

9. *Paul the brother/companion in the gospel* (7:4; 12:1; 15:14)—"my brothers" (15:14). Paul used *adelphos* ("brother") 18 times in the 16 chapters of Romans. The first nine occur in chapters 1-12, but the last nine are concentrated in the three final chapters (14-16). He was driving home the point as he drew his letter to a close. His use of "brothers" was an affectionate expression of interest.

In 15:30 he urged his brothers to join in his struggle. Here is the language of interdependence, an appeal for personal support. "So that by God's will I may come to you with joy and together with you be refreshed" (v. 32). The Greek expression for "refreshed" is used metaphorically of lying down together to rest (see Septuagint reference of Isaiah 11:6). Pictured here as weary, needing emotional and spiritual support from his brothers, Paul was open and transparent. He was not afraid to express his need and knew that they would not disappoint him.

Paul's concern was exhibited for his friends in Rome. He called them "my brothers" (7:4; 15:14) and instructed them about the care for a fellow brother (14:10, 13, 15, 21). His relationship was personal—he mentioned 35 individual people by name in the final 27 verses of the book (ch. 16).

Lessons: Regardless of rank or position in their mission, denomination or church circles, today's urban witnesses should remember that in the final sense, they are simply "a brother," or "a sister." For their own spiritual survival, urban witnesses must exercise a spirit of interdependence, transparency and affection. Their greatest resource, after God's enabling grace and power, will be the people of God.

Reflection: Paul began and concluded this great book with the lordship of Jesus Christ (compare Romans 1:1 and 16:27). He was not as impressed (or overwhelmed) by Rome as he was by Jesus Christ the Lord. He opened and closed his letters with the Word of God (compare 1:2 and 16:26). Paul doesn't begin by seeing the city or seeing the people of the city. He begins, and ends, by seeing his God and seeing himself in the light of the calling and work of God in his life.

Reflections

1. From what we see in the Bible, what does God want for the city and how does He want to use you and your church to reach out to your city?

2. In the Bible study from Romans, we learned that Paul saw himself in nine special ministry roles. How could you apply some or all of these as examples for your own ministry involvement in the world?

*Pause now for personal or group prayer before moving to Projections/Actions.

 ## Projections

Today's date _____

By this time next year, next month, next week, I believe God for the following ministry goals to connect to God's work in my world (enter calendar dates for accountability):

1. Next year (date_____)
2. Next month (date_____)
3. Next week (date_____)

 ## Actions

By this time tomorrow—in the next 24 hours—I will . . .

1.

2.

Part Two Resource Connections

1. Contact the following resources for excellent information on involvement in the 10/40 Window and reaching unreached people groups:

Christian Information Network
11005 State Highway 83 N., Suite 159
Colorado Springs, CO 80921
(719) 522-1040; fax (719) 277-7148
Web site: *www.christian-info.com*
E-mail: *CIN@cin1040.net*

Bethany World Prayer Center
13855 Plank Road
Baker, LA 70714
(504) 774-2002
Web site: *www.bethany-wpc.org/profiles/home.html*

2. Check with your association or denomination about prayer/support/ministry opportunities among unreached peoples in major cities and in the 10/40 Window:
Church of God World Missions
P.O. Box 8016
Cleveland, TN 37320-8016
(800) 354-7492
Web site: *www.cogwm.org*

PART THREE

ACCESSING A "WIN/WIN" SITUATION

Preview
Part III defines and discusses terms such as evangelism, evangelists, and church growth. It gives practical ideas and strategies for local church growth and church planting.

Globalbeliever.Comforter—"The Great Comforter"

But the Comforter, which is the Holy Ghost, whom the Father will send in my name, he shall teach you all things, and bring all things to your remembrance, whatsoever I have said unto you (John 14:26, KJV).

Globalbeliever.Company—"The Great Company"

The Lord announced the word, and great was the company of those who proclaimed it (Psalm 68:11).

June 1967, on a hot, dusty road near Hermosillo, Mexico, a wide-eyed teenager drops Spanish-language copies of the "Way of Salvation" tract out the rear window of the van. He is the youngest member of a witnessing group called "Pioneers For Christ," led by professor David Bishop on a "missionary orientation" trip from West Coast Bible College in Fresno, California.

With pious satisfaction, this young missionary watches as the poor peasants stop to pick up the "good news" announcements. It hasn't occurred to him that the people may not know how to read. He hasn't learned about cross-cultural communication, missions strategy, or the practice of contextualization of the message. All he knows in his youthful innocence and zeal is God's promise that "the fruit of the righteous is a tree of life, and he who wins souls is wise" (Proverbs 11:30). The consecration chorus from a recent chapel service is fresh on his mind:

Lord, lay some soul upon my heart,
And love that soul through me.
And may I ever do my part
To win that soul for Thee.

To win that soul for thee, dear Lord,
To win that soul for Thee.
And may I ever do my part
To win that soul for Thee.

That young man on the way to Hermosillo was me. Two weeks in Mexico changed my life forever and set me on a path toward becoming a global believer. Later, it translated into a missionary ministry for me and my young family.

Now, I'm a part of an international denomination which has revival and evangelism in its heart and soul. In fact, the Church of God (Cleveland, Tennessee) introduced a campaign called *WIN Challenge* in the year 2000: "A bold soulwinning initiative designed to involve dedicated Christians in an all-out effort to win 1 million new converts in the year 2000." *WIN* is an acronym that captures the phrases **W**itnessing to the lost, **I**nstructing them in the Word, and **N**urturing them in the faith. *WIN* is an admirable and attainable goal. There is no doubt that any sizable church movement can win 1 million new people to Christ every year. For me (and I pray for you, individually), I want to win at least one. It's a "Win/Win" situation.

CHAPTER NINE

PEOPLE OF PERSUASION

> SOULS ARE CRYING, MEN ARE DYING, WON'T YOU
> LEAD THEM TO THE CROSS? GO AND FIND THEM,
> HELP TO WIN THEM, WIN THE LOST AT ANY COST.
> —FROM *WIN THE LOST AT ANY COST*
> LEON H. ELLIS, PENTECOSTAL SONGWRITER

Evangelism has been a priority among Pentecostals throughout our history. The historical self-image of the major Pentecostal church bodies is that we were raised up to be an instrument of evangelism in the world. Traditionally, therefore, it has been felt that to be a Pentecostal is to be an evangelistic witness. Pentecostals see aggressive evangelism in the pages of the New Testament, and due to our high regard for the Bible and our literal interpretation of Scripture, we interpret the Pentecostal experience as a mandate for evangelism in its various forms and methods.

Definition and Nature of Evangelism

There is a multitude of explanations and definitions for the term *evangelism*. Many years ago the Madras Conference of the International Missionary Council came up with some 31 definitions! The word's history from the New Testament reveals a twofold usage—as a noun and as a verb. The noun is *euangelion,* meaning "good news," and occurs 75 times. The verb is *euangelizo,* meaning "to publish good news," and occurs 24 times. The gospel is the evangel, the good news. For Pentecostals, *evangelism* is defined as the act of proclaiming the good news of Jesus Christ in the power and anointing of the Holy Spirit with the intention that individuals will come to put their trust in Christ for salvation and serve Him in the fellowship of His church.

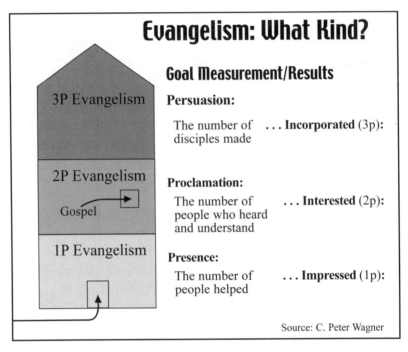

Evangelism: What Kind?

Goal Measurement/Results

Persuasion:

The number of disciples made   ... **Incorporated (3p):**

Proclamation:

The number of people who heard and understand   ... **Interested (2p):**

Presence:

The number of people helped   ... **Impressed (1p):**

3P Evangelism

2P Evangelism

Gospel

1P Evangelism

Source: C. Peter Wagner

For Pentecostals, evangelism involves much more than simply proclaiming the gospel. Evangelistic proclamation is not an end in itself but a means to an end—the persuasion of sinners to accept Christ as Lord and to follow Him as responsible, reproducing members of a local church. Pentecostal evangelism rejects the liberal tenets of universalism that say the work of evangelism is simply to inform people that they are *already* saved. Neither do Pentecostals believe that proclaiming only for the sake of giving objective information is sufficient. Pentecostal evangelism involves the good news of deliverance over against the bad news that humanity is dead and bound in the oppression of sin. Pentecostal evangelism therefore calls for a confrontation; it is the conveyance of truth-as-encounter. The Pentecostal witness preaches for a verdict and expects results.

This is the sense in which Jesus announces His mission of evangelism under the anointing of the Holy Spirit:

The Spirit of the Lord is on me, because he has anointed me to preach good news to the poor. He has sent me to proclaim freedom for prisoners and recovery of sight for the blind, to release the oppressed, to proclaim the year of the Lord's favor (Luke 4:18, 19).

There is, therefore, a persuasiveness and aggressiveness in Pentecostal evangelism characterized by the preaching of the apostle Paul as he seeks to persuade King Agrippa to become a believer. Paul indicates that he has been rescued in order to rescue others through evangelism. God's commission to him is central to his evangelistic testimony:

"I will rescue you from your own people and from the Gentiles. I am sending you to them to open their eyes and turn them from darkness to light, and from the power of Satan to God, so that they may receive forgiveness of sins and a place among those who are sanctified by faith in me" (Acts 26:17, 18).

THE FIVE-PS OF EVANGELISM

1. PRESENCE—HOW TO:
   Learn the culture.
   Build relationships.
   Identify, serve.
2. PROCLAMATION—HOW TO:
   Build a bi-cultural bridge.
   Communicate the gospel to
      the entire group.
   Contextualize the message.
   Listen to and understand
      world view, beliefs, and
      needs.
   Translate scripture.
3. PERSUASION—HOW TO:
   Lead family groups (or
   individuals) to the point of
   decision for Christ.
   Make disciples in culture.
4. PLANTING—HOW TO:
   Plant the first church.
   Produce a cluster of churches.
   Train leadership.
5. PROPAGATION—HOW TO:
   See churches multiply.
   See an evangelising force
      reach the culture people
      group.
   See an evangelizing force
      reach beyond its own
      people.

Source: Ralph D. Winter

Social Action or Evangelism?

Expression of Christian commitment does not need to be reduced just to one ministry or another. There must be a holistic balance. The same New Testament that has Matthew 28 also has Matthew 25. To put it another way, as John Stott has stated, Jesus not only gave us the Great Commission but also the Great Commandment (to love God supremely and to love our neighbors as ourselves).

There does not have to be a choice between doing good and making disciples. I read a very helpful clarification of this relationship between social action and evangelism a few years ago in a *World Vision* magazine article by an African church leader, Gottfried Osai-Mensah of Kenya. He said four words could show the different opinions held by Christians on this matter— *is, or, for, and*—and stated the possibilities like this:

1. Social action *is* evangelism. This is a very liberal understanding of evangelism. It would mean that anything and everything done as a social action would be called "evangelism." This is not acceptable.

2. Social action *or* evangelism. In this case, one has to make a choice to take one or the other. Some people may press you to do this, but God does not. It is clear that *both* social action and evangelism are advocated in the Scripture.

Most Evangelical and Pentecostal Christians would choose the third or fourth opinion:

3. Social action *for* evangelism. Social action is seen as a channel or a methodology in order to open up an opportunity to witness. This seems to work on a practical level, but what happens if there are good works in social action and people still reject the gospel? Some people also criticize this approach as a way to manipulate people into religious commitment.

4. Social action *and* evangelism. Many Christians are coming to understand that the Bible teaches and demonstrates *both* social action and evangelism. Though this be true, we must always give

a priority to evangelism in light of each individual's eternal destiny. What will it profit individuals to have received help and not to have given their lives to Jesus Christ?[1]

After relating these options in classes over the years, students also pointed out to me that there could be a fifth understanding:

5. Social action *in* evangelism. That is, evangelism in and of itself is a social action. If you evangelize someone whose activity has disrupted the social harmony of a neighborhood and peace returns to that people, haven't you contributed a positive social action *through* and *in* evangelism?

Another insight on this balance between social action and evangelism is provided by British Pentecostal pastor Roger Forster, whose church is among the poor in London's East End. He uses the three-way comparison of *works, words* and *wonders* to show how different denominations and groupings of Christians have been falsely categorized.

The *works* people, he says, are mainline Christians (Protestant and Catholic) who provide food and clothing, shelters for the homeless, and march against abortion and other social ills. The *words* people, he explains, are the Evangelicals who place emphasis on great Bible exposition. The *wonders* group, as you might suspect, are the Pentecostals and Charismatics who are busy getting people saved, healed and delivered. These separations into categories, says Forster, are foreign to the Bible. What the Bible teaches is the integration of all three. Each Christian and each local church should be concerned to demonstrate a balanced involvement in works, words and wonders.

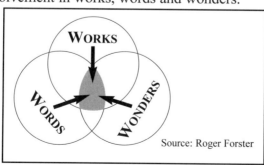

Source: Roger Forster

Biblical/Theological Foundations for Evangelism

Pentecostals have seen their evangelistic outreach as more than the mere extension of a religious movement or recruitment to a particular ideology or experience. From the outset of the modern Pentecostal Movement there was a sense of "divine destiny," the participation with God in a new work for the last days. The theological mood and atmosphere set by premillennialism and the actualization of the experiences and promises of Scripture (particularly the "outpouring" passages such as Joel 2:28-32 and Acts 2:16-21) caused Pentecostals to view evangelism as an extension of the purposes of God for them in the world.

Pentecostals have seen redemption as the central purpose of God in Scripture and evangelism as the comprehensive method for fulfilling that purpose. Their literal Biblicism has caused them to be aggressively obedient to the Great Commission passages in the Gospels. Acts 1:8 could be claimed as the golden text for their style of evangelism: "But you will receive power when the Holy Spirit comes on you; and you will be my witnesses in Jerusalem, and in all Judea and Samaria, and to the ends of the earth."

For Pentecostals, the connection of the "power" to the evangelistic task is quite clear: only the coming of the power of the Holy Spirit to those who are witnesses for Christ makes the work of evangelism possible. In this light the "power" passages of Acts 1:8 and 2:1-4, as well as the "enduement" passage of Luke 24:49 have been central to Pentecostal preaching and teaching on evangelism.

Therefore, evangelism—not other spiritual gifts or manifestations—should be seen as the primary result of the baptism of the Holy Spirit and the operation of spiritual gifts (though speaking in tongues is the initial evidence of the baptism in the Holy Spirit). Evangelism occupies the central place in the growth of Pentecostal churches. Other supernatural manifestations revolve around it.

Motivation for Evangelism

A sense of participation in what is central to the nature and heart of God motivates Pentecostals toward evangelism. Emerging from this central desire of God for evangelism come additional facets of the Pentecostals' motivation for reaching the unconverted.

First, Pentecostals have understood one of the primary steps of obedience in Christian discipleship is an obedience to evangelize. Therefore, evangelism is not an end within itself once a person is reached and led to a personal belief in Christ. Immediately this new convert is urged to testify to others and to begin preaching. He is "saved to serve."

In early Pentecostalism in particular, we find many accounts of people who started preaching within a few days of their conversion. C. Peter Wagner's study of the dynamic growth in Latin American Pentecostalism indicates that personal witnessing and street evangelism by the newly converted have been the central marks of its outstanding expansion.

Second, it is clear in the theology of Pentecostal evangelism that humankind is lost, under the judgment of eternal punishment, unless they are reached with the good news of the gospel (Ezekiel 18:4; Luke 13:3-5; Romans 2:12; 3:23; 5:12; 6:23; 2 Thessalonians 1:7-9; James 1:15; 2 Peter 3:9). The doctrinal confessions of all major Pentecostal organizations reflect their belief in "eternal life for the righteous and eternal punishment for the wicked," with no liberation nor annihilation (in terms of "second chance" salvation).

This is related to a third motivation for evangelism: the imminent return of Christ and the end of all things. There is an "eschatological urgency" inherent in the evangelistic theology and practice of Pentecostals. Thomas F. Zimmerman, former general superintendent of the Assemblies of God, has stated the surety of impending doom and judgment that hangs over the world in a coming retribution that will be both universal and final. Out of this reality he says, "Men must be told!"

Supernatural Evangelism

The "telling" in Pentecostal evangelism, however, has involved more than verbal proclamation. Pentecostals have understood miraculous signs and wonders to be demonstrations of "the Lord working with them, and confirming the word with signs following" (Mark 16:20, KJV). This was clearly the strategy of the early Christians (Romans 15:19; 1 Corinthians 2:1-5).

This makes Pentecostal evangelism distinctive since it proceeds from a worldview of power leading to what Ray H. Hughes calls "supernatural evangelism." Divine healing, for example, has been an evangelistic door opener that leads to verbal proclamation (Acts 3). For Pentecostals, every healing and miracle and every spiritual manifestation or "power encounter" in exorcism becomes an "earnest" of the kingdom of God and the means whereby the message and dominion of this Kingdom are actualized in the lives of people who are delivered. Pentecostal evangelists and missionaries would identify with the report of one missionary from England to Le Havre, France, in 1930: "Every new work is opened on the ministry of divine healing; for without the supernatural it would be impossible to get any interest created in the gospel message."[2]

This conviction of "God among us and working with us" is a key factor in the persuasive attraction of Pentecostal-Charismatic worship. That Pentecostal worship is a key evangelistic factor has been agreed upon by both inside interpreters and outside observers of Pentecostal church growth. Central to Pentecostal worship is the unique style of preaching in Pentecostal evangelism. It is "Spirit-endowed preaching which is pungent and penetrating," says Hughes, who claims that there is a "miracle element" present in Pentecostal preaching, making it a powerful evangelistic force.

Supernatural evangelism has also been called "power evangelism," a concept first articulated in the Fuller Theological Seminary School of World Mission and popularized by Pastor John Wimber, in his book *Power Evangelism*:

By power evangelism I mean a presentation of the gospel that is rational but that also transcends the rational. The explanation of the gospel comes with a demonstration of God's power through signs and wonders. Power evangelism is a spontaneous, Spirit-inspired, empowered presentation of the gospel. Power evangelism is evangelism that is preceded and undergirded by supernatural demonstrations of God's presence.[3]

Evangelism and the Media

Aggressive Pentecostals in their attempt to evangelize every available person, have made extensive use of radio and television. Pentecostal radio preachers began blanketing the United States with gospel broadcasts in the 1920s and 1930s. Leading denominations established departments of radio and television as they moved into the electronic age.

One of the earliest television pioneers was Rex Humbard—founder of the Cathedral of Tomorrow in Akron, Ohio. He televised a weekly worship service into America's living rooms. Moving from the tent to the tube, Oral Roberts expertly telecast his healing campaigns and television specials. By 1985, he commanded an audience of 2.5 million households.

Later the pioneers of televangelism were joined by a new breed of television evangelists.

- Pat Robertson founded the Christian Broadcasting Network (CBN) and its popular 700 Club, which eventually drew 4.4 million viewers daily.

- Jim Bakker began his broadcast career under Robertson's tutelage and later founded the PTL Network ("Praise the Lord").

- Jimmy Swaggart began with the radio broadcast "The Campmeeting Hour," and eventually moved to television. By mid-1987, Swaggart attracted 3.6 million viewers per day and received 40,000 letters weekly at his headquarters in Baton Rouge, Louisiana.

Robertson's ministry pioneered televangelism as a two-way medium with the establishment of phone-in prayer lines. Annually, CBN and the PTL Networks were recording hundreds of thousands of conversions and miraculous healings. This was also the pattern established in the televangelism ministry of Paul and Jan Crouch through the Trinity Broadcasting Network in Southern California.

Eventually, televangelism was to make a wider contribution to humanitarian ministries and higher Christian education. Oral Roberts established Oral Roberts University and the City of Faith Medical Center. Swaggart funneled some $12 million annually into the foreign missions enterprises of the Assemblies of God and funded an international child-care program to feed, clothe, educate and heal some 250,000 children in Third World countries. In addition, he founded a Bible college to train evangelists, pastors and missionaries. Robertson funded "Operation Blessing," providing food and medical attention to needy people in the United States and abroad. Bakker's PTL Ministry opened a home for handicapped children and another for unwed mothers. Pentecostals have effectively used the media as a channel to preach the gospel of salvation.

The Future of Evangelism

As Pentecostals and Charismatics move into the future, there does not appear to be any departure from their aggressive stance of evangelism. There is continued commitment toward training and deploying evangelists. There have been congresses and consultations held on the strategy of evangelism, particularly in the great urban centers of the world. Two statements, "A Declaration at St. Louis" (1968) by the Assemblies of God and "A Covenant on World Evangelism" (1983) by the Church of God, reveal strong sentiments of self-identity as agencies for evangelism.

Evangelists

The term *evangelist*, though briefly mentioned in the Bible, is not specifically defined. The term originates from the Greek word *euangelistes*, "one who proclaims good news." Traditionally, Pentecostal evangelists were distinguished as those who devoted their lives to full-time itinerant ministry of preaching the gospel, especially the message of salvation and deliverance. In this regard, an evangelist is one with a specialized ministry that involves more than being a witness for Christ, which is a duty expected of all believers in the Pentecostal-Charismatic heritage.

Biblical Descriptions and Models

The word *evangelist* is used only three times in the New Testament (Acts 21:8; Ephesians 4:11; 2 Timothy 4:5). Although Philip is the only person specifically called an evangelist (Acts 21:8), other workers may have functioned in the same role: Timothy (2 Timothy 4:5), Luke (2 Corinthians 8:18, 19), Clement (Philippians 4:3), and Epaphras (Colossians 1:7; 4:12). Evangelists are seen as a gift to the church from the ascended Christ (Ephesians 4:11). They have been classed with apostles and prophets as itinerant workers in contrast to pastors and teachers, who are more related to a local assembly (though this may be an imposition from church history more than an interpretation of the Scripture itself). Many Pentecostal pastors, in the spirit of the young pastor Timothy, have seen themselves in a dual role of pastor-evangelist (2 Timothy 4:5). Indeed, in the history of the Pentecostal tradition, an itinerant evangelist often established a local congregation, continued to pastor it as founding pastor, and conducted occasional revival/evangelistic crusades away from the local church base.

The composite picture of a Pentecostal evangelist would identify with the lessons emerging from Philip, a New Testament evangelist (Acts 8).

1. *One who is from among the people, chosen as a deacon but gifted with a preaching ministry* (Acts 6:5; 8:5). The roots of most early Pentecostal evangelists were from the common people of the poorer class. Most were lay preachers who were later ordained to the clergy.

2. *Miracles typically follow the evangelist's preaching* (8:6). Divine healing and miracles of deliverance have been emphasized in the preaching of Pentecostal evangelists as inclusive in the salvation message.

3. *The evangelist crosses cultural, racial and economic barriers to preach Christ* (v. 5). The crowds attending the crusades of itinerant evangelists are typically racially integrated.

4. *The evangelist baptizes converts* (vv. 12, 38). Evangelists have not always left this to local pastors (a source of tension).

5. *The evangelist is flexible, preaching from city to city, ready to follow the leading of the Holy Spirit to another place or person* (vv. 26, 29, 40). The leading of the Holy Spirit, even to another country, has been a hallmark of traveling evangelists. Many would not limit themselves to a calendar of specific dates for a crusade but would leave the conclusion of evangelistic crusades open-ended, depending on the work of the Holy Spirit and the response of the crowds.

The Evangelist in Christian Tradition

Stephen Neill has traced three main types of evangelists in the expansion of Christianity:

1. A person called by God to perform evangelistic ministry in a specified geographic area among a designated group of people

2. A paid agent representing a missions society in itinerant evangelism to areas where the church or missions society has not yet been firmly established

3. A lay preacher or pastor entrusted with the care and oversight of an existing church.

Evangelists in the Pentecostal Tradition

Pentecostal evangelists fit into all three of Neill's classifications but are not necessarily bound by them, particularly those among independent "healing" evangelists with large, visible ministries. William W. Menzies indicates that the Pentecostal evangelists of the 1920s and 1930s had ministries that were far-reaching in their influence. In *All Things Are Possible*, David Harrell traces the self-sustaining and extensive ministries of evangelists in what he calls "the healing revival (1947-1958)," and "the Charismatic revival (1958-1974)." His bibliographic essay is a valuable resource for researchers on Pentecostal evangelists.

A complete history of Pentecostal evangelists is not possible in this overview. No one evangelist could be said to be the prototype of all modern Pentecostal evangelists. Nevertheless, a survey of the literature of Pentecostalism suggests that many outstanding figures made an impact during various eras. Gordon Atter had "Biographical Sketches of Pentecostal Pioneers" as a separate chapter in his review of Pentecostal history. He includes individuals such as Frank Bartleman, W.T. Gaston, Howard A. Goss, C.H. Mason, Claude A. McKinney, Charles F. Parham, W.W. Simpson, A.H. Argue, Charles E. Baker, Marion Keller, Alexander Boddy, Stephen and George Jeffreys, and Lewi Pethrus in his review of some 45 Pentecostal pioneers from the United States, Canada and Great Britain. Others of note are Aimee Semple McPherson, Charles S. Price, Smith Wigglesworth, William F.P. Burton, Teddy Hodgson, J.W. Buckalew, A.J. Tomlinson, J.F. Rowlands, Edith Mae Pennington, Mary C. Moise and Maria B. Woodworth-Etter. Harrell's study highlights the more recent figures of William M. Branham, Oral Roberts, Gordon Lindsay, Jack Coe, T.L. Osborn, A.A. Allen, W.V. Grant, Don Stewart and Morris Cerullo.

Pentecostal evangelists typically incorporate the following methodologies in their mass crusades: music, testimonies, prayer for the sick, and the extensive use of publishing (tracts, magazines, paperback pamphlets and books). Many of the early evangelists

173

combined an itinerant preaching schedule with the planting of new churches, often "preaching them out" and turning them over to associates or an organized denomination. A number of them began as children, and the phenomenon of the child evangelist (or "boy preacher") was popularized in Pentecostalism. "Little David" Walker and Marjoe Gortner are notable examples.

The message of Pentecostal evangelists focused on salvation and deliverance, with a popular highlighting of divine healing. Prayer lines for the sick have been common as well as confrontations with spiritual oppression resulting in exorcisms. In addition, evangelists have prayed for seekers to be baptized in the Holy Spirit. Eventually, the ministries of North American healing evangelists extended to the international arena.

Many evangelists have remained independent, not allowing themselves to be "tamed" or controlled by any denomination. This has been a source of tension and has caused contempt for the ministry of the evangelist in denominational circles. On the other hand, nonaffiliated evangelists have often seen their work as interdependent with the missions outreaches of established church departments of home and foreign missions. Harrell notes that there has been isolation and fragmentation among the healing evangelists themselves, although some efforts have been made to form networks and associations. Many early independent evangelists, however, were incorporated into the polity and structure of newly formed denominations.

Pentecostal Evangelists and the Future

Pentecostal-Charismatic trends indicate that the ministry of the itinerant evangelist will continue into the 21st century with more attention being given to integrity and accountability.

Major Pentecostal denominations encourage the ministry of evangelists, holding conferences for mutual exchange and providing training for evangelistic ministry. Pentecostals have participated in interdenominational conferences designed for itinerant evangelists, such as the gathering of 4,000 evangelists at the International Conference for Itinerant Evangelists in Amsterdam, Netherlands, in July 1983 (followed up by a similar gathering in July 2000 in Amsterdam). In addition, there continues to be an emphasis on the development of lay evangelists in the Charismatic Movement, and new Pentecostal-Charismatic evangelists are becoming prominent in the non-Western world.

Reflections

1. After reading about evangelism, what are some new ideas you have about connecting to unreached people in your community, especially through social action?

2. What is the ministry of the evangelist and how can this ministry be encouraged and multiplied in our churches today?

*Pause now for personal or group prayer before moving to Projections/Actions.

Projections

Today's date _____

By this time next year, next month, next week, I believe God for the following ministry goals to connect to God's work in my world (enter calendar dates for accountability):

1. Next year (date_____)
2. Next month (date_____)
3. Next week (date_____)

Actions

By this time tomorrow—in the next 24 hours—I will . . .

1.

2.

CHAPTER TEN

GOING MEANS GROWING

> THE CHURCH EXISTS BY MISSION, JUST AS
> FIRE EXISTS BY BURNING.
> —H. EMIL BRUNNER
> SWISS THEOLOGIAN

Pick up any popular evangelical magazine or specialized journal for Christian workers. Analyze the ads. Peruse the propaganda. You'll find church growth seminars, books, "experts," services, even "guaranteed church growth or your money back." Everybody talks about this special term, church growth. It is used often in conversation but seldom understood.

The purpose of this section is to answer some fundamental questions about church growth (and the modern Church Growth Movement) and point out additional resources for those who are serious about the growth of their church. Here are four common questions about the Church Growth Movement mentioned in church growth classes and conferences:

- What do we mean by church growth?

- Where did it come from?

- What are its chief characteristics?

- How do Pentecostals fit in?

Misconceptions

Before discussing what church growth *is*, we must be reminded about what church growth is *not*.

177

1. *Church growth is not a special program from a denominational office or outside resource agency.* Specialized programs and enlargement campaigns are necessary, commendable, and may figure into the overall picture; but church growth cannot be limited to a specialized package administered by an individual or a resource company.

2. *Church growth is not another method.* Any father who has tried to assemble a Christmas toy "by the book" will tell you it is not always simple to use someone else's method. Unlike Sunday school busing, small groups, Christian day schools or cassette ministry, church growth is much more than a wholesale adoption of methodologies.

The adage is true: "Methods are many, principles few; methods don't last, principles do." Church growth proponents seek for guiding principles and leave the selection of methods to a variety of factors and variables. One of their observational principles states, "Church growth is complex." It cannot be reduced to methods or steps, regardless of how few or how many.

3. *Church growth is not a shortcut to success.* Church people have become success-oriented. "Bigger is better" and "the bigger, the better." Though church growth advocates believe in quantity (and believe God wants many people saved), they should not be falsely accused of asserting a fill-your-church-quick mentality. Church growth comes when the pastor and people are willing to pay the price for growth and to work with God for results.

In this regard it is significant that the pastor of the world's largest church, Dr. David Yonggi Cho, has written a church growth book titled *More Than Numbers.* If anybody could talk about numbers and quantity, Pastor Cho could! He reminds us, however, of the *spiritual* dynamics of growth, quality growth, the kingdom of God and other factors that are more than numbers.

There was no shortcut to success for Pastor Cho, no slick seminar with a "bag of tricks," no instant methods. Many components were at work in the amazing growth of the Yoido Full

Gospel Church in Seoul, Korea—much of it long, hard hours and years of faith and determination.

4. *Church growth is not another happening or event.* I've been in parts of the world where *evangelization* had become a noun instead of a verb (somewhere you go instead of something you do). In other words, churches sponsored their annual two-week evangelization (like a revival) as if church growth took place only during an annual outreach or membership emphasis.

Unlike golf, baseball or duck hunting, church growth cannot be relegated to a seasonal emphasis. It is an ongoing process, a continual burden of the local church. It should be emphasized with regularity just like tithing, worship, attendance, prayer and Bible reading. Church growth is a process.

5. *Church growth is not a fad or trend.* Let's get church growth out of the gimmicks-and-popularity syndrome. It is a bona fide movement with over one-third century's experience in field observation, practice, research and publication. After hundreds of theses and dissertations, entire book lines and publishing houses, departments of church growth in denominations, seminaries and Bible colleges, church growth has survived the flak and furor of myopic critics. It is a movement of the Holy Spirit because the heartthrob and passion of the Church Growth Movement is to see people won to Christ and discipled in responsible, reproducing congregations. Church growth is here to stay.

What Do We Mean by Church Growth?

C. Peter Wagner put it this way:

Simply stated, church growth means all that is involved in bringing men and women who do not have a personal relationship to Jesus Christ into fellowship with Him and into responsible church membership.[1]

The constitution of the North American Society for Church Growth defines church growth as follows:

Church growth is that discipline which investigates the nature, expansion, planting, multiplication, function, and health of Christian churches as they relate to the effective implementation of God's commission to "make disciples of all people [nations]" (Matthew 28:19, 20). Students of church growth strive to integrate the eternal theological principles of God's Word concerning the expansion of the church with the best insights of contemporary social and behavioral sciences, employing as the initial frame of reference the foundational work done by Donald McGavran.[2]

Where Did It Come From?

Though modern historians in this century point back to Donald A. McGavran, the growth of the church has a longer tradition. It is a central theme of Scripture—the story of the seeking and finding God who calls to Himself a people out of the world and builds His church through the self-giving love of His only begotten Son.

That's why McGavran, and a host of missionary colleagues, went to the far-flung corners of the globe early in the 20th century to disciple the nations and to see the growth of the body of Christ. This was what was supposed to have happened in McGavran's field of India.

He was frustrated, however, with meager results. In 1934 he was the executive officer of a large mission agency of 70 missionaries. They had hospitals, leprosy homes, orphanages, boarding schools, agricultural centers and evangelistic workers—but they had no growth. With less than 2,000 members, the mission work was stationary, having grown very little in the preceding 10 years.

McGavran tells the rest of the story in *Effective Evangelism: A Theological Mandate.*[3] The book provides an excellent Biblical foundation and historical overview of the church growth school of thought.

The term *church growth* is a true McGavranism. Terms like *missions* and *evangelism* had been redefined completely out of a Biblical context by the theological and missiological liberals of the 1930s. Disgusted with this loss of vision and meaning, McGavran began using the term *church growth* to recapture the Biblical priority on soulwinning, church planting and evangelistic preaching.

He eventually distilled years of experience, field research on growing churches, and interdenominational interviews from around the world into his first major statement of church growth principles titled *The Bridges of God.* Although research and observation had begun 20 years prior, the contemporary Church Growth Movement was technically set in motion with this book.[4]

McGavran furthered his ideas through the establishment of the Institute of Church Growth (1961) and its accompanying popular journal, *Church Growth Bulletin* (1964). The bulletin's name was later changed to *Global Church Growth.* Now, the revised title, *Strategies for Today's Leader*, continues to serve as the official literary representative of the Church Growth Movement. In 1965, the institute was moved to the campus of Fuller Theological Seminary in Pasadena, California, where it became known as the School of World Mission and Institute of Church Growth.

Most of the researchers in those early days of the institute were career missionaries and overseas national leaders (church growth should not be labeled "Made in the U.S.A."; it draws from a wide scope of evangelistic experience among international sources). Eventually, many experienced missionaries and church planters began to call for insights from McGavran, C. Peter Wagner and their colleagues to be shared with North American pastors. This is probably where the personal acquaintance with church growth of many begins.

Wagner calls 1972 "a pivotal year" since he and McGavran team-taught a course on church growth especially designed for American pastors and church executives that year. Church growth had come to the North American scene.

One of the students in that first class was Win Arn, who subsequently resigned his denominational leadership post and pioneered the Institute for American Church Growth. Not long after Arn's move, a department of church growth, called the Charles E. Fuller Institute for Evangelism and Church Growth, was established in the Fuller Evangelistic Association.

Church growth book clubs and publishing lines were formed, denominational authors began customizing church growth principles for their constituencies, schools began courses and seminars on the subject, and the movement became well integrated into the North American evangelical world. Lyle E. Schaller, veteran church consultant to hundreds of U.S.-based denominations, reviewed the previous decade of Church Growth Movement in 1980 and said that church growth was the most influential development on the American religious scene of the 1970s (see the Foreword to *Church Growth: Strategies That Work*, by Donald McGavran and George G. Hunter III).[5]

What Are Its Chief Characteristics?

Among a variety of descriptions of the church growth school of thought, I offer four basic observations:

1. *It is Biblically and theologically based.* Though critics would point to the use of scientific research methods and the social sciences evident in church growth thinking, the basic convictions behind the teachings of the Church Growth Movement are from the heart of Scripture itself. Along these lines, McGavran criticized an impotent "search theology" among his opponents that emphasized seed sowing over actual harvesting.

He reminds his students in *Understanding Church Growth* that the living God of the Bible is a searching, saving God—the God who finds. He asserts that evangelistic proclamation should be done with the intention of harvesting. He called this a "theology of harvest." Many Biblical expositions from the theologians of church growth thinking demonstrate that it is God's will for the church to grow.[6]

ACTS 2: CHURCH GROWTH TEACHES:

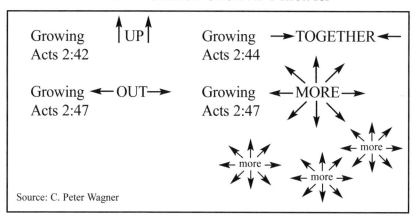

Growing UP
Acts 2:42

Growing →TOGETHER←
Acts 2:44

Growing ←OUT→
Acts 2:47

Growing ←MORE→
Acts 2:47

Source: C. Peter Wagner

2. *It is propagated as a movement.* The Church Growth Movement has all the marks and characteristics of a movement:

- History

- Ideology

- Special language

- Literature

- Proponents and opponents

- An academic base

What distinguishes the Church Growth Movement from being just another sociological movement, however, is that it has Biblical roots and has been raised up by God in this century to call attention to the priority of the Great Commission in this generation. The Holy Spirit propels the movement.

3. *It is solidified as a field of study.* Under the umbrella of the wider field of missiology, church growth is recognized as an academic discipline. By the fall of 1985, for example, Fuller

Seminary's School of World Mission had some 300 students from 72 nations. In the 20-year interval from the transition of the Institute of Church Growth to Fuller's campus in 1965, 22 doctor of philosophy degrees in missiology had been given, along with 151 professional doctorates in missiology and large numbers of master of theology and master of arts degrees.

"By 1986," McGavran recalls, "five shelves, 12 feet long, were filled with more than 600 researches done in the past 21 years."[7] In Fuller's School of Theology, hundreds of pastors have been trained in the principles of church growth through the doctor of ministry program.

In a 1984 lecture, C. Peter Wagner (the first incumbent of the Donald A. McGavran Chair of Church Growth) reviewed the following six kinds of church growth research being conducted:

- Local churches

- Denominations (general or regional/district)

- Geographical areas (country analyses)

- Cultural or socioeconomic groups

- Growth of churches in a given theology or philosophy of ministry

- Particular church growth issues or teachings

The ongoing academic research and field studies in church growth have now spread to a number of worldwide centers, institutes and theological schools.

4. *It is part of a wider stream of worldwide revival and evangelism.* It should not be thought that church growth people are the only ones emphasizing effective evangelism and the discipling of the nations. Wagner recognized this with the title of his 1973 *Christianity Today* article introducing church growth thinking to the North American scene, "Church Growth: More Than a Man, a Magazine, a School, a Book."

Of course, the man referred to was Donald A. McGavran; the magazine, *Church Growth Bulletin* (now *Strategies for Today's Leader*); the school, Fuller School of World Mission; the book, *Understanding Church Growth*.

The Billy Graham organization, for example, has done much to foster efforts toward evangelism and church growth. Graham and his colleagues were the motivators toward three strategic world congresses in the 20th century: the Berlin Congress on World Evangelism in 1966 and the International Congresses on World Evangelization at Lausanne, Switzerland, in 1974 and in Manila, Philippines, in 1989.

Out of the Lausanne meeting came the Lausanne Covenant, the Lausanne Movement (an evangelical network/association committed to world evangelization), and an ongoing Lausanne Committee for World Evangelization that has sponsored dozens of regional conferences, consultations, and publications on Great Commission missions and evangelism.

Most of the leaders in the Church Growth Movement are actively involved in Lausanne. A follow-up meeting, "Lausanne II," was held in Manila in July 1989, bringing together some 4,000 international delegates, over half of them representing leadership that is younger, female, and from the "Southern World" (Africa, Asia, Latin America).

Church growth practitioners, strategists and researchers recognize the broad field of contribution from many corners of the world's harvest fields, especially from the Pentecostal Movement.

How Do Pentecostals Fit In?

This question was one I needed to deal with as a Pentecostal when I first studied with McGavran, Wagner and company at Fuller, where much of the spotlight on international church growth was on the influence of Pentecostals and Charismatics. Finding a lack of clearly stated reasons for church growth from a Pentecostal perspective, that is, the "insiders" view, I gathered writings and reflections written about Pentecostals by Pentecostals.

The resulting study was *Azusa Street and Beyond: Pentecostal Missions and Church Growth in the Twentieth Century*. An entire section of *Azusa Street* (Part Four: *Pentecostals and the Church Growth Movement*) reviews the close relationship and differences between the two movements over the years.[8]

Space doesn't permit a complete narrative of that relationship, but it should be mentioned that Pentecostals were doing the job of world evangelization and church growth before coming into the stream of the church growth school of thought. This is basically the assertion of Donald McGavran in a September 1976 interview in the *Church Growth Bulletin*.

In his January 1977 article in the same publication, "What Makes Pentecostal Churches Grow?," McGavran said, "The question underlined above has animated my mind since the early sixties."[9] Pentecostals were among the earliest research associates at the original Institute of Church Growth in 1961.

In his writing for *The Pentecostal Minister* on the "Characteristics of Pentecostal Church Growth," C. Peter Wagner made the following remark:

> Through the years I have become very close to Pentecostals. Why? Primarily because I am a student of church growth: and, no matter where I look around the globe, I find that Pentecostal churches are leading the way in rates of increase.[10]

After the publication of Wagner's original research on Pentecostal growth, some observers might have spoken of the "Pentecostalization" of church growth thinking and methodology. His research was first published as *Look Out! The Pentecostals Are Coming!* and has been most recently revised and updated as *Spiritual Power and Church Growth*.[11] In addition, Wagner has an extensive section on Pentecostal church growth in an exhaustive new resource edited by Pentecostals, *Dictionary of Pentecostal and Charismatic Movements* (Zondervan, 1988).

One of the contributions church growth research has made to Pentecostal churches, however, is the discovery that many Pentecostal churches don't grow. Research conducted in Latin America and published in *Latin American Church Growth* demonstrated that some Pentecostal congregations and denominations on that continent had reached a plateau or were declining.[12]

In short, the two movements have been fellow sojourners with identical dedication to the Great Commission and church growth. Church growth proponents have learned from the Pentecostal dynamics of the Holy Spirit. Pentecostals have been blessed by the research and principles brought to light in church growth strategy. May the leaders in both movements continue their forward thrust in advancing the growth of the church and the evangelization of the world.

Eight Barriers to Effective Church Growth

The young advertising whiz kid sits across the table from the chief executive officer with the greatest plan since the discovery of mashed potatoes. With one cynical line the veteran disarms him, "What are you gonna do when it doesn't work?" Frustrated pastors or Sunday school superintendents on the brink of burnout have second-guessed their calling when the long-awaited growth of the church seemed slow or distant in coming. In the lean years of church life we pray, plan, push and promote with little results. What do we do when "it doesn't work"? When it comes to church life, it is painful to admit that growth barriers exist.

From my travels, research, classes and interviews, it seems there are at least eight barriers to overcome in order to see revitalization and new life.

1. *The theological barrier.* I grew up in a Pentecostal church on a steady diet of hard-core evangelistic preaching and passionate songs like "Rescue the Perishing," "Throw Out the Lifeline," and "Win the Lost at Any Cost." I was president of our local evangelistic outreach and witnessed wherever I could. I understood

personal evangelism as a necessary part of Christian discipleship and was motivated to seek the baptism of the Holy Spirit as the indispensable enduement of power for service. Nobody told me that evangelism and the growth of the church was optional!

I hope that the theological convictions characterizing the evangelistic fervor of Pentecostals and Charismatics are not slipping. Do we really believe God is "not wanting anyone to perish, but everyone to come to repentance" (2 Peter 3:9)? Do we really believe that man is inherently sinful, depraved in his nature, and, apart from God, will spend eternity in hell?

What things are nonnegotiables in our theology? Does God really mean it when He commands us to make disciples of all men everywhere? Does God want the lost to be saved and the church to grow? Answers to such questions as these may reveal theological barriers that need to be removed in order to believe that God wants His church to grow.

Starting Points:

- Reexamine your basic belief system on the nature of man and the expectations of God.

- Assemble your congregation around God's Word for a fresh examination of the Great Commission and the story of redemption throughout the Bible.

- Preach and teach church growth from the pulpit, integrating it into the discipleship curriculums (Sunday school, Family Training Hour, home cell groups, etc.).

2. *The knowledge barrier.* "Church growth" as a specialized term and as a specific movement is stereotyped with myths and misconceptions. For that reason this topic may be a "turnoff" for some because of the sour taste left by wrong ideas about church growth. Many associate the term with gimmicks, methods, and less-than-ethical schemes to knock the top off the growth charts. They see church growth as the glorification of numbers and

crowds and the idealization of the "superchurch." Nothing could be further from the truth.

Any pastor or lay church leader who researches church growth principles and observations comes away with a solid conviction regarding the value of church growth.

Starting Points:

- Review and study books on church growth such as Donald McGavran's *Understanding Church Growth* and C. Peter Wagner's *Your Church Can Grow.*

- Make use of church growth resources from resource agencies.

3. *The commitment barrier.* C. Peter Wagner's bold claim is that any church can grow if it is willing to pay the price for growth. Furthermore, he states the two most widely demonstrated signs of local church growth: (1) The pastor is a possibility thinker who can lead his or her church to growth. (2) The people want to grow and are willing to pay the price for growth. Some churches (pastor and people combined) will not grow because they have simply decided that they are not willing to put in the time, energy, money, prayer and other resources for the sake of God's work.

Many will not have problems with their theology or even their knowledge of some elementary growth principles, but their basic problem is an issue of the will. They have not made the conscious choice to aim for growth. They have come up against the commitment barrier and are too lazy to push through it.

Starting Points:

- Take inventory of your church's commitment level.

- Carefully analyze your church's priorities by detailing where peoples' time, money and energy are spent in the church.

- Begin planning now for a "growth commitment" campaign.

Profile of a Church Growth Congregation

1. Loving
2. Open
3. Committed

4. Flexible
5. Willing to change
6. Big in attitude

4. *The risk barrier.* This generation could very well be described as a "generation of caution." Everything must be carefully calculated before a move is made. Where is the daring, risking dimension of faith exhibited in Scripture and characteristic of early pioneers? Church growth stretches your faith into a visionary faith. It goes beyond the rational dimension of strategic planning and logical steps . . . outside your personal "comfort zone."

Rick Warren, a highly successful church planter and pastor of a growing church says, "When I die I would like this statement put on my gravestone: 'At Least He Tried.'" Church growth pastors like Rick Warren are characterized with the spiritual gifts of faith and leadership. The absence of visionary faith and sanctified risk taking will keep the church from growing.

Starting Points:

- Consciously ask God to increase your faith and the faith of your church.

- Carefully consider hard, bold plans for church growth.

- State your growth goals (long-term and short-term) in measurable terms within a certain time frame (C. Peter

Wagner provides additional insights on goal setting in *Leading Your Church to Growth*).

- Set up a way to hold yourself accountable for the accomplishment of your goals.

5. *The diagnostic barrier.* Getting past the diagnostic barrier involves a willingness to go beneath the surface of church life to do intensive research, ask probing questions, make tough adjustments, and implement new models and policies. Some churches will not grow because they are too content to keep placing Band-Aids over serious diseases that require in-depth surgery.

In the final analysis, church growth for many of our churches will require change. Many do not want to change and therefore do not want to grow because they know growth will inevitably bring change. Church growth is unlikely where deep diagnosis is not allowed.

Starting Points:

- Study the dynamics of change through such writers as Lyle Schaller (*The Change Agent*; *Hey, That's My Church*; *Assimilating New Members*; etc.).

- Lead your church through careful, consecrated introspection with such tools as the *The Church Growth Survey Handbook* (Wagner/Waymire) and other diagnostic tools from church growth agencies.

- Ask for outside help through church growth consultants.

6. *The structural barrier.* Many churches are hindered by outdated systems or ineffective ways their ministries are structured. Must the Sunday school, Family Training Hour, youth programs, worship services, and so forth, be the same as they always have been? Are there adjustments that need to be made in time, location, personnel, format and the order of worship service? Are people finding a place to "plug in" to your church through existing structures? Is the church physically accessible (with practical

things like parking, directional signs and adequate lighting)? Are people coming for a while and not staying? If so, why?

Starting Points: Attack the assimilation problem with a four-fold approach to incorporation:

- Incorporation sensitivity—helping people develop attitudes of watchfulness, openness, and flexibility with newcomers.

- Incorporation strategy—focusing the overall planning and goal setting of every church department on reaching and holding new people. If Ford can say "Quality is job 1," then let our people say "Incorporation is job 1!"

- Incorporation structure—designing the format, arrangement, accessibility, and even physical appearance of our church to let people know they are welcome and they belong.

- Incorporation study—reviewing and evaluating our progress so we can continue to be the church for others.

The church is the only institution on earth that exists solely for the benefit of its nonmembers. Breaking down the structural barriers will help us focus on reaching the unreached.

7. *The leadership barrier.* Very few studies relating leadership to church growth had been done until C. Peter Wagner's popular book *Leading Your Church to Growth* appeared in 1984. Now, strong pastoral leadership is recognized as a dynamic component in the growth process. The will to grow begins with the pastor and the leadership team of the local congregation. Church growth doesn't just happen accidentally. Show me a church that is growing and I'll show you a pastor who is effectively finding the goals God wants for that church and equipping the people to do the work of the ministry.

Starting Points:

- Examine the leadership style and effectiveness of the pastor and leadership team (numbers of leadership resources are now available).

- Determine (through evaluation instruments, questionnaires of spiritual gifts, etc.) the ministry capability of the congregation to ensure that believers discover, develop and use their spiritual gift.

- Help the pastor and selected lay leaders attend special training conferences and workshops on church growth.

8. *The invisible barrier.* Growing a church means much more than strong, charismatic leadership, competent management of ministries, and effective training. We are engaged in a *spiritual* undertaking. Jesus said He would build His church and the gates of hell would not prevent it (Matthew 16:18). This does not mean, however, that there won't be a struggle.

When the church grows, the kingdom of God advances into new territory controlled (though temporarily) by the kingdom of darkness. This ground will not be surrendered without a fight. A spiritual breakthrough is necessary. Could this be a big part of the secret that early Pentecostal pioneers knew when they spoke of "praying through" and "digging out a church"?

Starting Points:

- Help your people understand the meaning of spiritual warfare (many resources are now available).

- Set your heart and mind on periods of prayer and fasting.

- Mobilize the congregation to aggressive intercessory praying and spiritual warfare.

- Declare war on Satan and begin to see intentional church growth as an advancement of the kingdom of God.

Church growth barriers are real, but not insurmountable. Recognize them, deal with them, and let them only be a temporary challenge to effective and continuous growth in the power of the Holy Spirit.

Reflections

1. List three new ideas you learned from this chapter's discussion of church growth, along with how these new insights may change the way you and your local church look at church growth challenges and possibilities.

2. This chapter discussed eight barriers to effective church growth ("What Will Keep Your Church From Growing"). In a positive way, identify some barriers that may be affecting your church and think about ways to move beyond them.

*Pause now for personal or group prayer before moving to Projections/Actions.

Projections

Today's date _____

By this time next year, next month, next week, I believe God for the following ministry goals to connect to God's work in my world (enter calendar dates for accountability):

1. Next year (date_____)
2. Next month (date_____)
3. Next week (date_____)

Actions

By this time tomorrow—in the next 24 hours—I will . . .

1.

2.

CHAPTER ELEVEN

OUTSIDE STAINED-GLASS WINDOWS

AMONG OTHER DESIRES OF GOD-IN-CHRIST, HE
BEYOND QUESTION WILLS THAT LOST PERSONS BE
FOUND. WE SERVE A GOD WHO FINDS PERSONS.
—DONALD A. MCGAVRAN
FOUNDER OF THE CHURCH GROWTH MOVEMENT

Donald A. McGavran was the founding dean and senior professor of missions at the School of World Mission and Institute of Church Growth at Fuller Theological Seminary in Pasadena, California. He was a former missionary who served 32 years in India under the United Christian Missionary Society (1923-1955) and the author of numerous articles and books, including *The Bridges of God, Understanding Church Growth,* and *How Churches Grow.* The following conversation with Dr. McGavran took place when I studied with him and Peter Wagner at Fuller.

Analysis of Growth: An Interview With Dr. Donald A. McGavran.

McClung: Dr. McGavran, in speaking about church growth, we often make the mistake of starting with the practical issues of methodology. What would you say is the primary beginning point when we discuss church growth?

McGavran: One thing we must say is that the growth of the church is fundamentally, basically a theological business. We must hear Christ saying, "All authority has been given unto me in heaven and on earth. Go therefore and disciple all the peoples of the earth." Now, it's not all the individuals: it's the peoples (*panta ta ethne*), the tribes, the castes, the segments of society. It is the university professors, the coal miners. All these segments of society must be won to Christ. That's not optional. It's not that some Christians play golf and some go in for missions. Missions is absolutely essential.

McClung: In *Understanding Church Growth*[1] you spoke of the three ways a church grows—biological, transfer, conversion. You said that even though our children grow up in Christian families, are converted, and join the church (biological growth), which is good and necessary, "biological growth will never win the world for Christ." Could you comment on the necessary balance in the three ways a church grows?

McGavran: When I was in Eugene, Oregon (at the original Institute of Church Growth), I spoke to a group of pastors. One of them said, "Oh, we've had good growth at our church. We had 54 additions last year." And I said, "How many were biological, how many were transfer, and how many were conversion?" He said, "What did you say?" I repeated the question and he replied, "I don't know what you mean." So I explained. He said, "I don't know the answer to that, but I'll find out." A couple of weeks later he came back and said, "Of our 54 additions last year, 44 were transfer, eight were biological, and two were first-time converts."

That's the picture in many churches. There tends to be mainly biological and transfer growth in America. The amount of conversion growth is rather small. Even the greatly growing churches experiencing the most growth are mostly from transfers. We've got to say to our ministers, "Let's make a special effort, brethren, to win those who are not believers."

We need to emphasize conversion growth here in America. First of all, conversion growth is needed among the segments of society that find themselves in nominal Christianity, but are not believers. We have a responsibility to them. Then, we must reach out to the masses of people who are not even touched by existing churches.

McClung: Regarding transfer growth, I remember your quoting a discerning Filipino leader in *How Churches Grow* who said, "Western evangelism is little more than well-organized gathering in of existing friends; but the kind of evangelism we need must convince. . . . " Do you think that the Pentecostal emphasis on the ministry of the Holy Spirit in signs and wonders should be emphasized in order to convince the lost and thereby produce more conversion growth?

McGavran: Yes. Signs, wonders and healings are coming back to the scene. When I first started the Institute in Eugene, I had a Pentecostal from Trinidad who said that in Trinidad very few among the large Indian population had become Christians. But, then, in his church there were some "power encounters;" there were healings and exorcism of demons. And he said that immediately he began to see a considerable number of conversions from among the Indians.

McClung: At Fuller we are hearing a lot about these kinds of happenings outside the United States. How does this relate to the American pastor?

McGavran: Such happenings can occur more frequently right here. But the difference is that in the United States we have a form of religion that not too many people mention, although it is very widespread—secularism. In secularism, people do not really believe God does anything. Americans struggle with signs and wonders because of secularism. This is not the case overseas where people believe, maybe on an animistic basis, that miracles do happen.

We've got to say that every man and woman in North America makes a "leap of faith." Either he leaps to a belief that God is real—He made the laws and can change them—or he makes the leap of faith which says, "All we have is law. There is no God." It is here that the Pentecostal church—with its tremendous emphasis on God the Holy Spirit acting right now in society—is needed.

McClung: Placing this in the context of a local community, what are some signs a pastor can look for indicating that people are ready to make that "leap of faith"? It seems that some of the receptivity factors you mention in *Understanding Church Growth* are occurring right now on the world scene (high mobility, crises, economic instability, for example).

McGavran: Yes, the pastors in North America must see—must train themselves to see, must educate themselves to see—that there are large groups of receptive people, people who can be won, that most churches are overlooking. Most church growth thinking says that there are many ways to find the receptive people who have recently moved into the community. The question is, "How can we make people really welcome, and how can we make sure they fit into some of the smaller organizations of the local church?"

McClung: By this, do you mean small groups?

McGavran: Yes, you've got to get them into a small group where they know everybody and everybody knows them. They become a part of a loving, caring, smaller community.

McClung: It seems that people in North America in particular are looking for that right now.

McGavran: Yes. In addition, there are dozens of these factors in church growth. That's what the Church Growth Movement has contributed to the American scene—an awareness of the many different ways in any denomination that a church grows.

McClung: If you were pastoring the "church on the corner" in North America, what would you change? What would you do differently in really aiming at conversion growth? How do we reach the "secular man" who has no heritage of a church background, no memory of Sunday school Bible stories, no thought of God?

McGavran: Our greatest resource is the power of the gospel in changed lives. I would emphasize the testimony of new Christians who have been where these people are, who have believed, and who have found a totally new form of life. That's the essential resource.

McClung: What about changes in our styles of worship? Are there forms or styles of worship that need to be changed without being "lifted" away from their effectiveness?

McGavran: I'm very pragmatic. If God is blessing what you are doing, the church will be growing. If the church isn't growing, then ask yourself, "Is there something here we need to change? Do distinctly Pentecostal forms of worship pull people or do they alienate them?" One of the big factors in church growth is that it says "measure progress" and then determine what God wants you to do in the light of what God is blessing. There are things our denomination has always done. We must ask whether God blesses them or not. Those things God is not blessing to the winning of souls should be laid aside.

McClung: You often speak of "priorities" and "church growth thinking." What do you mean by this?

McGavran: Church growth thinking means the following:

- You accept the fact that God wants His lost children to be found. He doesn't just want us out there searching for them. He wants to see them walk back across the Father's threshold and say, "Father, I have sinned. Accept me back into the fellowship." That's the basic thing.

- It also means that we must be accurate in our counting. How many have we found? What are the growth patterns of our church? We've got to act in the light of what is actually happening. We've got to be realistic.

- It means being aware of the many facets of church growth. There are scores, maybe hundreds, of things we can do. There are exceedingly diverse environments in which we can do them.

McClung: This would also involve the whole area of "faith thinking," goal setting, making faith projections.

McGavran: Yes, faith projections and goal setting in the light of what we have in our situation.

McClung: What are some other key priorities a local church should be stressing?

199

McGavran: One key priority that has often been stressed is the Sunday school. To say, "If you want to grow, have a good Sunday school" is both true and untrue. There are many places that emphasize a good Sunday school and do not grow. But if you emphasize an intensely evangelistic Sunday school so that every teacher asks himself or herself, "Are my pupils saved? How can I win their families?" then it boosts church growth. If it is simply educationally perfect, with the right number of square feet per child, good surroundings, and lettered lessons, then you can have an excellent Sunday school and your church will not grow.

And then there are the ethnics. Over 10 years ago, I was speaking in Toronto on church growth. There were about 1,000 people there—English-speaking, fairly well-to-do Canadians. I said to them, "You really ought to be winning French Canadians. You ought to be starting French Canadian churches." And I got a pretty chilly reception! But after it was over, a dark-haired man came up to me with a smile on his face. He said, "I'm so glad you said that. I'm a French Canadian, and we want to join churches where you can advocate a separate nation for French Canadians without being considered traitors." Later, I found out that some denominations were starting to plant those kind of French Canadian churches successfully.

McClung: Do you think the Pentecostals have something unique to offer the ethnic groups?

McGavran: The Pentecostals do a wonderful job among the ethnics coming into this country. They come over here, and they are not secularized. When they come, they believe in miracles. They confront secularism, and there is a vacuum there. I am inclined to think that if the Pentecostals would stress signs and wonders in the ethnic community, they could win them in a big way.

McClung: There has been an increasing focus on the inherent power and potential in the laity. Should not the training of local church leaders be one of the main items on our agenda?

McGavran: One of the biggest contributions of the Church Growth Movement has been the emphasis upon finding people to train for church growth. When I began, the first thing I did was establish an Institute of Church Growth for career missionaries and give them insights that would enable them to see some of these things we are talking about. In church growth thinking all across America—and now into many parts of the world—what we have been emphasizing is the training of our lay leaders. Churches grow *chiefly* when the lay leaders are involved.

McClung: Not just any laymen, but lay *leaders*.

McGavran: *Lay leaders.* You've got to involve people who will give their time and who are willing to learn. *Evangelism Explosion* teaches us a great deal along that line. James Kennedy took his leaders and trained them how to talk to other people. I consider this approach one of the big thrusts in church growth.

This leads to something else. There are a lot of these "thrusts" in church growth. Some emphasize this kind of evangelism and some that kind of evangelism. I say that all evangelism that brings sinners to God is church growth.

McClung: A balance is necessary for church growth, isn't it? We tend to jump on one idea or method and say, "This is the answer."

McGavran: That is quite right. We must keep our eyes open and see what God is blessing, realizing that God has many servants who will be discovering many different things that work. Sometimes it's signs and wonders; sometimes it's teaching people how to talk to others in effective evangelism; sometimes it's teaching others how to recognize receptive units; sometimes it's emphasizing an evangelistic Sunday school. The church growth mind welcomes all of these things and prays to God for enough hours in the day to do them!

McClung: We have discussed a number of important issues that are particularly relevant to the North American local church. Let me ask you about the Church Growth Movement as a whole. Where do you think it is heading?

McGavran: The danger is that the Church Growth Movement will be perceived as a fad and that it will eventually fade out. I hope that we can avoid that idea, because church growth is fundamental to the church. Whether it's called the "Church Growth Movement" or something else, this activity— this search, this hunger, this obedience—is fundamental to the church. What I hope and expect is that the Church Growth Movement will continue and that we will see some denominations—maybe the Church of God—practice it so effectively that it will expand more rapidly. Then other churches will say, "Hey, I think we can do that ourselves."

I look forward to church growth institutes, church growth seminaries, church growth organizations, and church growth magazines being founded—all focused on the thought, "God wants His lost children found."

McClung: Dr. McGavran, as a closing challenge to Pentecostals, and particularly to Church of God leadership, what would you say to us? If you, for example, stood at our General Assembly and faced our people, what would be your admonition?

McGavran: I would urgently stress the following priorities for the Church of God:

1. Thank God for what He has done and is doing by giving you remarkable growth.

2. Fear—even as you fear death—getting "sealed off" into respectable churches that grow only by biological and transfer growth. This is the "kiss of death" for a church.

3. Spend 2 percent of your annual income to research church planting and development. The most effective way any local church or denomination grows is through the planting of new congregations.

4. When you find an open field, throw in your resources, plant churches, and reap the harvest!

5. Double the number of your missionaries, because the need of the world is desperate.

CHURCH PLANTING: The Mother-Church Concept

During the 1980s "church planting" became a familiar addition to our vocabulary, although the idea behind this term was at the very foundation of the history and growth dynamics of many denominations. Referred to as "church planting" or "church extension," this phenomenon traditionally was referred to as "new field evangelism." Basically, it is the ministry of starting new churches.

Recently the emphasis on church planting is becoming more widely known at the local level. The way to help a local church grow larger and faster is not only in *adding* new members to the church, but also in *multiplying* the church by planting new churches. How is this done? Three steps are necessary:

1. Developing a vision

2. Defining the Biblical foundations

3. Determining a strategy.

Developing a vision. Church growth research reveals that the greatest percentage of church growth occurs through church planting. It is natural for a church to grow, and it is also natural for a church to "mother" yet another church or churches. With the growing world population and the increasing challenge to reach as many souls as possible, it is impossible to evangelize our world and our community through existing churches. In order to reach an increasingly varied and complex society, multiple groups of new churches for many kinds of people must be started.

This is the conclusion of church growth experts. Vergil Gerber, who studied churches around the world, said, "The ultimate evangelistic goal in the New Testament is twofold: to make (1) responsible, reproducing Christians and (2) responsible, reproducing congregations." American church analyst/consultant Lyle E. Schaller has said that starting a new church is the best way to reach new people, experience rapid growth, and realize membership increase. Church growth expert C. Peter Wagner concludes after careful research that the "planting of new churches is the most effective methodology known under heaven."

Defining the Biblical foundations. There is a good reason why the experts agree on the necessity and practicality of new-church planting: it is Biblical! God wants us to start new churches! This is seen in the progression of New Testament church growth in the Book of Acts. In 1:14, 15, the church begins with 120 disciples. In 2:41-42, 3,000 are added on the Day of Pentecost; and by 4:4, there are at least 5,000 believers in Jerusalem. In 5:14, the Scripture says that "multitudes" (KJV) were *added.*

Then, a new process begins—the process of church *multiplication.* This multiplication begins in Acts 6:1, 7. "From this point on," says Vergil Gerber, "both the Book of Acts and the New Testament Epistles underscore the *multiplication of churches* as well as church members." Then we see a geographical multiplication of churches across the Mediterranean world as the focus shifts from the mother church in Jerusalem to scores of emerging congregations in new places (Acts 9:31; 16:5; 21:20). No one can read the New Testament and escape the fact that God wants new people reached, and nothing accomplishes this goal more effectively than planting new churches in new places!

Determining a strategy. If church planting is natural and needed, and if it is expected and commanded by the Lord of the harvest, then how do we do it?

Eight Possible Options

Dr. C. Peter Wagner has identified eight possible methods of starting new churches. Four are from within the local church, and four call for *outside* help.

EIGHT CHURCH PLANTING PLANNING OPTIONS

MODALITY MODELS ("CONGREGATIONAL"): FOUR TYPES

	KEY WORDS/DESCRIPTIONS
1. Daughter Churches	
• "Hiving off"	Seperating members
• Colonization	Change of residence
• Adoption	Gathering existing churches
• Accidental Parenthood	Unplanned splits, divisions
2. Satellite Model	Connection; control
• Scattered	"away from"
• Gathered	"within the structure"
3. Multiple Campuses	One church—many locations
4. Multicongregational Church	"Together yet separate"

SODALITY MODELS ("MISSION"): FOUR TYPES

1. Mission Team	Church planting *team*
2. Catalytic Church Planter	One gathers a nucleus
3. Founding Pastor	Church Planter becomes Pastor
4. Independent Church Planter	On his own

Source: C. Peter Wagner

Inside out. From within the local church, four processes of church planting usually develop: daughter churches, satellite models, multiple campuses and the multicongregational church.

- *Daughter churches.* At least four kinds of daughter-church processes have been identified: (1) "Hiving off"— As the analogy suggests, the local church separates a number of members to start a new work (also called "tithing members"). (2) "Colonization"—This is the deliberate decision of local church members to relocate their place of residence to another city for the purpose of starting a new church. (3) "Adoption"—the gathering in of an existing congregation that wishes to join the denomination. (4) "Accidental parenthood"—the unplanned starting of a new church due to a split or division.

MODALITY MODELS ("CONGREGATIONAL STRUCTURE")
1. DAUGHTER CHURCHES: FOUR TYPES

"Hiving off"
- Separating members for a new work

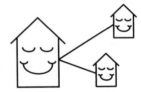

"Colonization"
- Deliberate change of residence for a new work (Paul Orjala, *Get Ready to Grow*. Beacon Hill Press, 1778).

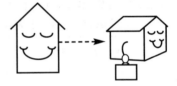

"Adoption"
- Gathering in *existing* churches (amalgamation)

"Accidental Parenthood"
- Unplanned growth due to splits or divisions

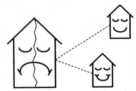

Source: C. Peter Wagner

206

• *Satellite models.* The satellite model keeps a strong mother church as the central focus. There is both the scattered satellite model, in which the newly planted congregations ("chapels," "missions," "extensions," etc.) meet away from the facilities of the mother church except for periodic visits "back home;" and there is the gathered satellite model, in which the newly formed congregation comes together regularly within the structure of the mother church. This is especially useful in understanding the growing ethnic church development across North America. If immigration or other social movements are bringing the harvest to you, your next step should be to consider ways of starting new churches among those unreached people.

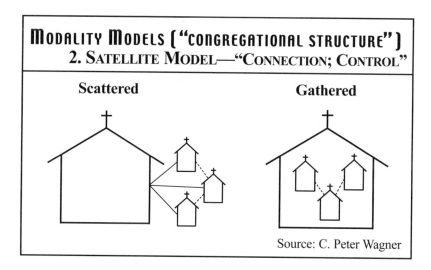

MODALITY MODELS ("CONGREGATIONAL STRUCTURE")
2. SATELLITE MODEL—"CONNECTION; CONTROL"

Scattered   **Gathered**

Source: C. Peter Wagner

• *Multiple campuses.* This model allows for one church, whose members are meeting at more than one location but which is serviced by the same pastor, staff, council, and so on.

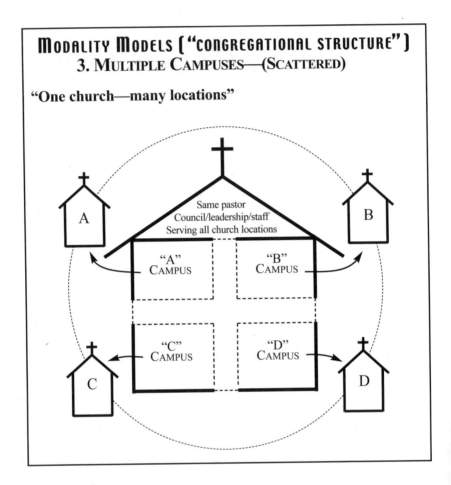

MODALITY MODELS ("CONGREGATIONAL STRUCTURE")
3. MULTIPLE CAMPUSES—(SCATTERED)

"One church—many locations"

A

B

Same pastor
Council/leadership/staff
Serving all church locations

"A" CAMPUS

"B" CAMPUS

"C" CAMPUS

"D" CAMPUS

C

D

- *Multicongregational church.* In this model there are equally independent congregations which share the same physical facilities. You may wish to offer your facilities to an unaffiliated ethnic congregation with the intention of building a relationship that will lead to their membership in your denomination or association. Creativity and stewardship demand that we make better use of our physical facilities in order to reach more people. Church facilities are not an end but a means to an end.

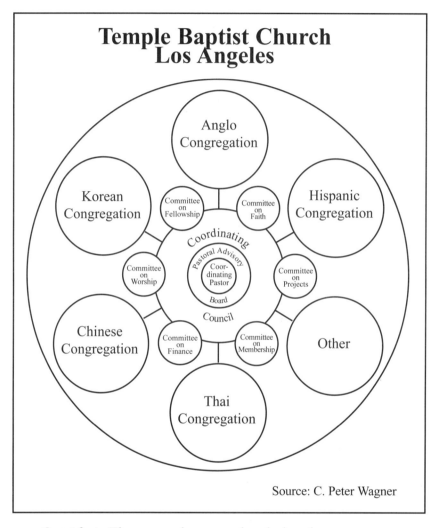

Temple Baptist Church Los Angeles

Anglo Congregation

Korean Congregation

Hispanic Congregation

Committee on Fellowship

Committee on Faith

Coordinating

Pastoral Advisory

Committee on Worship

Coor-dinating Pastor

Committee on Projects

Board

Council

Chinese Congregation

Committee on Finance

Committee on Membership

Other

Thai Congregation

Source: C. Peter Wagner

Outside in. There are also ways local churches can get outside help in starting a new church. Often it is better to begin with these methods until the vision for church planting from "inside out" (within the local congregation) is gained.

- *Mission team.* A group of church planters is brought to the area to start a new church.

- *Catalytic church planter.* Someone—usually a layperson—gathers a nucleus of people "from scratch." A church is established and a pastor is called.

- *Founding pastor.* Either full-time or "bi-vocational" (working on a secular job while preaching), a person starts a church and becomes its first pastor.

- *Independent church planter.* A person starts a church and eventually becomes its pastor. He or she is sometimes a layperson.

SODALITY MODELS ("MISSION STRUCTURE")

1. MISSION TEAM
"Church Planting *Team*"

"Ordain elders" (inside)

2. CATALYTIC CHURCH PLANTER—"ONE GATHERS A NUCLEUS"

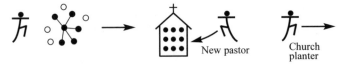

New pastor   Church planter

3. FOUNDING PASTOR—CHURCH PLANTER BECOMES PASTOR

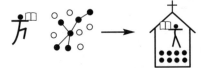

4. INDEPENDENT CHURCH PASTOR—"ON HIS OWN"

"A sodality structure is stronger for church planting"

Source: C. Peter Wagner

Three Practical Steps

How do we get started? Here are three processes that must form the outline of your approach.

Describe the people to be reached. If you try to reach everyone, you will reach no one. Know specifically your "target audience." From journalistic/broadcasting experience I have learned five questions to ask about a target audience:

1. *Who?* Who are the people you're trying to reach? What are they like? What do they do? What is their lifestyle?

2. *What?* What do they know about Christianity? What is their perception of Christ? Of the church? Of Christians? Of you? This information can be gained through neighborhood surveys, community questionnaires, informal listening, bridge-building relationships, and other methods.

3. *Where?* Where are these people (both geographically and spiritually)?

Geographically. Use demographics and research to determine a target audience and detect future trends. Here are some places to look for information: city/county planning commissions; school boards/districts; public utilities/telephone companies; local university sociology departments; lending institutions/market reports; chambers of commerce; newspaper marketing/research departments; secular media (print and broadcast); local libraries; other denominational studies. Some things to look for: population growth projections; land use projections; occupations; housing information; family statistics (married, single, divorced).

Spiritually. We know from Scripture three things about people everywhere: they are spiritual, sinful and savable. What do we know about the spiritual readiness of the specific target group? Determine the degree of their resistance or receptivity to the gospel message. They may be more receptive than we imagine if we present the gospel to them in a way that is understandable and relevant to their felt needs. The burden of communication lies upon us.

4. *When*? When were these people open to the gospel before (if ever)? Did they recently become receptive? What caused a change in their attitude toward God? Watch for key indicators of a people's readiness to change. Be perceptive and sensitive.

5. *Why*? Why do they do what they do? What motivates this people? What is their worldview? What is their philosophy of life?

The underlying principle of all these questions is "Know your audience."

Determine the people to reach them. A key question to ask at this point is, "Who do we have who can help do the job?" If it is vitally important to know the target audience you want to reach, it is equally necessary to know the people you already have who can reach them. This is commonly called the "force for evangelism." This force does not have to be large or talented. It must, however, be gifted, called and committed.

1. *It must be gifted.* Every member of the body of Christ is spiritually gifted (1 Corinthians 12:7; Ephesians 4:7; 1 Peter 4:10). Helping each member of your church discover, develop, and use his or her spiritual gift(s) is the first step in not only mobilizing your own congregation to grow but also in leading them in the planting of a new church.

2. *It must be called.* As with any ministry in the local body, the participants in church planting must be burdened and called by the Holy Spirit. Your part in that process is to help implant the vision—through sermons, teaching, workers conferences, council meetings and private conversation. Pray workers into the harvest! When a church catches the vision for church planting, God will inevitably raise up and call workers into that ministry.

3. *It must be committed.* The church-planting force for evangelism must be faithful, available and teachable. It must be committed to you, to your leadership, and to the local church's "philosophy of ministry."

Direct your attention to receptive people. A basic principle of church growth is that churches grow best among receptive people. The flow of gospel communication in the New Testament also verifies that observation. Scripture instructs us to concentrate on those who are ready to hear the message. Go where receptive people are. On a personal level, various events make a person or a family more open to the gospel: a new baby, a change in job or marital status, sickness, the death of a loved one, and so forth. In general, look for two areas in which to plant new churches: (1) where new populations of people are moving in and (2) where other churches are growing. Seek to reap the harvest when it is ripe.

Receptive Times

Moving to a new community
—new friends
—new groups
—new schedule
A new baby
Death of a loved one
A change in marital status
A change in job status
Sickness
Hospitalization
First child enters school

Summary

Church planting is a natural and normal process. Through it the local church will grow and be blessed. In leading your church toward church planting, develop a church-planting vision, define the Biblical foundations, and determine the strategy best suited for your local and regional situation.

Reflections

1. If you had to write out a sentence stating the most important thing you learned from the interview with Donald A. McGavran ("Analysis of Growth"), what would it be? Why?

2. Using the material on church planting, list three key ideas and action steps for getting yourself or your local church involved in new church planting.

*Pause now for personal or group prayer before moving to Projections/Actions.

Projections

Today's date_____

By this time next year, next month, next week, I believe God for the following ministry goals to connect to God's Work in my world (enter calendar date for accountability):

1. Next year (date_____)
2. Next month (date_____)
3. Next week (date_____)

Actions

By this time tomorrow—in the next 24 hours—I will . . .

1.

2.

CHAPTER TWELVE

YOU'VE GOT MAIL

> HE IS NO FOOL WHO GIVES WHAT HE CAN-
> NOT KEEP TO GAIN WHAT HE CANNOT LOSE.
> —JIM ELLIOT
> MISSIONARY MARTYR (ECUADOR)

You've Got Mail" is an everyday announcement in our computer-driven world. One day Bob had some "mail." Actually, it wasn't an e-mail but a telegram. It wasn't addressed to Bob but to "Robert"—a famous agnostic philosopher. You see, Robert G. Ingersoll had been at the convention of the "Freethinkers Association of America" in Chicago, saying things like, "The churches are dying out all over the earth; they are struck with death." It was 1881.

What makes the story interesting is knowing the sender of the telegram. It was Bishop C.C. McCabe, the head of new church extension for the Methodist Episcopal Church. McCabe was not an "armchair strategist." He had dodged bullets and cared for the dying on the battlefields of the U.S. Civil War. He read Ingersoll's comments in his morning newspaper he had picked up before boarding a train for the Pacific Northwest. In a matter of days, McCabe would be leading the charge for fund-raising and new church planting of Methodist churches across Washington, Oregon and Idaho. I can almost see the old warrior's blood boil and the hair rise on the back of his neck. Surely he must have thought that the heady agnostic philosopher in Chicago didn't have a clue about what was actually happening at the grassroots of frontier church life among both the Baptists and Methodists.

One hundred years prior to 1881, the Methodists and Baptists were rivals in reaching new frontier populations. In fact, Francis Asbury, the early Methodist leader, said about the Baptists, "Like ghosts they haunt us from place to place!" Now, the Methodists were starting more than one new congregation a day. Some months they averaged two new churches a day.

Old McCabe couldn't wait. He got off the train at the next stop and went straight for the telegraph office. Here is what he sent to Ingersoll, still at the convention in Chicago:

> Dear Robert:
>
> "All hail the power of Jesus' name"—we are building one Methodist church for every day in the year, and propose to make it two a day!
>
> C.C. McCabe

I love to tell this story from my friend George Hunter (*To Spread the Power: Church Growth in the Wesleyan Spirit*). In fact, George told me recently that he should start telling it more, lest people think he got it from me! But here's the rest of the story in George's own words:

Word about the telegram was leaked, and someone wrote a folk hymn that was sung throughout the Pacific Northwest in preaching missions and camp meetings, brush arbors and Sunday evening services. The song dramatized the frontier Methodist people's quiet confidence in the power of what they offered people:

> The infidels, a motley band, in counsel met, and said:
> 'The churches are dying across the land, and soon they'll all
>   be dead.'
> When suddenly, a message came and caught them with dismay:
> 'All hail the power of Jesus' name, We're building two a day!'
> We're building two a day, Dear Bob, We're building two a day!
> All hail the power of Jesus' name, We're building two a day.[1]

I don't think Bob liked his mail that day.

God has some mail for you, global believer. It reads, "Keep on praying for the nations! Keep on preaching world missions! Keep on helping people into hands-on ministry! Keep on strategizing for your global reach!"

WHAT HAPPENS WHEN WE PRAY FOR NATIONS?

Prayer is a proactive, not just a reactive, force. Prayer takes an offensive position that accomplishes things—it is not just a defensive reaction to things happening to us.

Prayer power is real. Local churches, entire denominations and interdenominational prayer movements are being called by the Holy Spirit to intercede for their own country and for the nations of the world. As a result, God is demonstrating Himself in workings of His power.

At least seven things happen when we pray for the world:

1. God is glorified as we obey His command to pray for leaders, governments and nations.

2. We follow the example of the early Christians who made this a practice in their group worship and personal devotional life.

3. An actual difference is made in the life and welfare of nations. Church history and contemporary life are filled with positive changes that happen in nations when Christians pray.

4. We are led beyond politics and geography to focus on the people in nations. We begin to pray specifically, by name, for government leaders, opinion influencers, national leaders and missionaries.

PRAYER GUIDE FOR THE MISSIONARIES

1. The missionaries personal relationship with God

2. The physical and emotional aspects of the missionary's life

3. The missionary's family

4. The ability to communicate

5. The missionary's ministry

6. The missionary's colleagues

7. The country where the missionary works

---

5. We are brought into effective spiritual warfare, reminding Satan of Christ's lordship in the world, pushing back darkness with the advance of God's kingdom, power and light.

6. Our hearts and minds are broadened. Our personal horizons expand as we are transformed from narrow to broad views of God's work in the world and our active involvement in it.

7. We are led to put "shoe leather to our prayers" in Christian activism. It's been said that every great work of God can be traced to a kneeling form. As we pray, the Holy Spirit leads us to concrete acts of witness, encouragement and service that make a difference.

Developing Global Christians in a Local Church
The Role of Prayer

Teaching people to pray:

1. Spiritually
(context of worship and praise, personal cleansing)

2. Systematically
(regular ongoing involvement as Christian discipleship)

3. Sensibly
(intelligently, knowing the facts)

4. Spontaneously
(following the creative leading of the Holy Spirit)

5. Sensitively/Specifically
(for the individual missionary and his/her family)

6. Strategically
(prayer that opens up new doors)

MULTIPLYING THE VISION: PREACHING WORLD MISSIONS

He was only 13 years old, yet he sat spellbound as the anointed preacher delivered the message in a youth revival in a little Pentecostal church in Springdale, Arkansas. The young teenager responded by going to the altar to pray. Suddenly, before his eyes, written in bold letters were the words "Go ye into all the world, and preach the gospel to every creature" (Mark 16:15, KJV).

"The impact of this vision is so imbedded in my memory, I can still see those big bold letters right now as I recall the occasion. It was something God was really driving home to me in a lasting way." So is the testimony of a man touched by the power of the preached Word. He is Loren Cunningham, who went on to preach the gospel around the world and establish a movement— Youth With A Mission (YWAM)—which eventually spread to more than 200 countries of the world.[2]

By 1985, about 20,000 people were involved in YWAM (5,000 long-term missionary workers and 15,000 annual short-term volunteers). The ministry had more than 190 locations around the world, including more than 80 missionary training schools.

It all began with a Spirit-led sermon. Indeed, the modern missionary movement began with a sermon! Some 200 years ago, young William Carey was gripped by the challenge of a larger world in need. He was artful in merging the affairs of his contemporary world with the insights of Scripture into a balanced missions appeal in his writing and preaching.

On May 30, 1792, he preached his now famous sermon from Isaiah 54:2, 3, in which he coined the familiar watchword, "Expect great things from God; attempt great things for God." The sermon had a profound effect upon his hearers. It resulted in the formation of a new missionary society that set off a chain reaction of 12 new missions organizations over the next 32 years. Since that time, Carey has become known as "The Father of Modern Missions."

The modern missionary movement and the more recent Pentecostal-Charismatic movements began with Spirit-led preaching. Spiritual preaching and the resulting missionary expansion were central elements in the Pentecostal revival that began in Los Angeles in 1906, in the Azusa Street Mission. Read accounts of the preaching and Charismatic worship in the early editions of *The Apostolic Faith* (reprinted by Fred T. Corum in *Like as of Fire*). The account shows the direct connection of preaching and the resulting evangelistic expansion.

The message you preach from your pulpit can be the spark that ignites a flame and fans the fire of intense involvement in world missions within members of your congregation. Multiplying the vision for world evangelization through the power to communicate what the Holy Spirit has given you in your pulpit should include the *motivation*, the *method* and the *material* of missions.

Motivation

Preaching is the single most important resource for multiplying ministry vision and enlisting the additional resources of the "force for evangelism" latent in congregations.

Jesus gathered His followers, proclaimed the Kingdom and multiplied His ministry through preaching. The Spirit of the Lord was upon Jesus as He preached, and He places His enduement of power upon His preachers today.

Jesus is present in our preaching and together with the Holy Spirit sends forth His people into ministry (Acts 8:29; 13:2). This same teamwork is displayed in Ephesians 4:1-13 and 1 Corinthians 12:1-11 as Jesus Christ and the Holy Spirit distribute *charismata* (gifts) for the effectual ministry of the church—both in edification and outreach. He works with you as you preach God's vision (Mark 16:20).

One of today's best-known preachers is David Yonggi Cho, pastor of Yoido Full Gospel Church in Seoul, Korea. How has this Pentecostal congregation become the world's largest church with more than 800,000 members? Certainly one of the factors has been the equipping ministry from his pulpit in anointed preaching.

Pastor Cho, "To a pastor, the message preached is life. The right interpretation of the Word of God is the most important part of the message. How to interpret the Bible determines what to preach. What to preach determines the growth of the church."[3]

Spiritual motivation that leads to a multiplication of available personnel begins with preaching.

Method

The consistent and systematic preaching of God's world mission is the best method for multiplying the church's world vision!

Preaching is here to stay. Observers have questioned its value, noting popular preference for other means of communication. Printing presses, motion pictures, or the Internet have never equaled the persuasive power of personal preaching.

This is especially true when convincing believers to become involved in missions. The preacher expresses the vision. The preacher recruits the missions candidate. The preacher raises the funds. The preacher challenges the intercessors. Some very basic decisions must be met in finding your own approach to consistent and systematic missions preaching. The world vision begins with *you*.

As you determine to preach missions, direct your attention to related Biblical passages and develop Spirit-empowered sermons. Many pastors find that a "preaching plan" helps them maintain a balanced diet. Some pastors preach on world missions once a month.

Starting points, of course, are the familiar "Great Commission" passages of the New Testament: Matthew 28:18-20; Mark 16:15; Luke 24:46-49; John 20:21; Acts 1:8 (with their surrounding contexts). A basic commentary review of such words as *nations*, *Gentiles*, *world*, and *all* yields valuable preaching materials from both the Old and New Testament.

I have followed the four guiding principles to help me in approaching, accepting and applying the Scripture: *familiarize, find, focus, formulate*.

Familiarize yourself with the text. Read the passage and reread it (not just what others say about it). Look for the general to specific context out of which the passage emerges. Ask five key questions about the Scripture reference: *Who? What? Where? When? Why?*

Find a basic pattern or structure. Look for possible natural outlines which suggest themselves out of the context of your reading. Acts 1:8, for example, forms the outline for the remainder of the book.

Focus on key words and phrases. You can use the natural construction of English grammar (verbs, nouns, prepositions, adjectives, adverbs, etc.). Look for imperatives (commands), questions (Isaiah 6:8), and for other interesting grammatical constructions (contrasts, metaphors, etc.). Compare your reading with other English translations available in such tools as *The New Testament From 26 Translations.*

I always look for nouns and verbs in a passage. They often form a natural outline for teaching or preaching. John 3:16, for example, gives us four nouns around which to build the presentation of God's world concern: *God, world, Son* and *whosoever.*

There is a powerful missions insight found in the interesting contrast in Psalm 67 between the pronoun *us* and the adjective *all* ("all nations," "all peoples").

There is a threefold exhortation describing our relationship to God, the world and the body of Christ in the "let us" commands of Hebrews 10:22-25. In fact, "let us" is a key grammatical indicator for the interpretation and outlining in Hebrews.

Formulate principles and applications. Formulate a few summary principles and applications from the passage. State one unifying principle or truth for the passage. This will tie it all together for you and for your listeners.

Material

There is much to be said about the power of illustration. Intersperse your message with biographical references or powerful anecdotes from the lives of Biblical, historical and contemporary missionaries.

A wealth of resources is available for preaching on world evangelization. We need them! No one is an island of creativity. We all rely on the thoughts, insights and ideas of others.

Entire book sources and other literature are now available to help the serious pastor develop sermon material on missions and church growth. Older classics such as Robert H. Glover's *The Bible Basis of Missions* and Alan Tippett's *Church Growth and the Word of God* have been joined by Francis M. DuBose's *God Who Sends*. Many missions and church growth titles are available at a discount (from many publishers) through the agency of Pathway Press, the Global Church Growth Book Club (P.O. Box 40129, Pasadena, CA 91104) and Church of God World Missions.

New studies are now available on the growth of Pentecostal-Charismatic missions movements, including Paul Pomerville's *The Third Force in Missions*; Gary McGee's *This Gospel Shall Be Preached*; and *Azusa Street and Beyond: Pentecostal Missions and Church Growth in the Twentieth Century*. All of these point out the growth dynamics associated with anointed preaching. Ray H. Hughes' *Pentecostal Preaching* is also helpful in this regard.

Networking is possible through a number of associations and idea sources. Contact Church of God World Missions (*www.cogwm.org*) for ideas and literature. Write the U.S. Center for World Mission, 1605 Elizabeth St., Pasadena, CA 91104 (*www.missionfrontiers.org*).

Remember that people are media, too—"network" with other pastors, seminary and Bible college personnel, missionaries and mission leaders in your area.

The modern missionary movement began with a sermon. The *motivation* for workers comes through preaching as the single most important resource for multiplying ministries. The *method* is through consistent and systematic proclamation of God's world vision. The *material* is available in a wealth of resources.

All that is needed is a man or woman sent from God to proclaim the message. "Raise your voice like a trumpet" (Isaiah 58:1); proclaim the call and heart of God for the world; multiply the vision through the power of your pulpit!

FIVE WAYS TO HELP CHILDREN HEAR GOD'S VOICE

Although a full understanding of a missions call did not come until I was a high school junior at West Coast Bible College (high school), God had prepared me earlier through childhood experiences. Without any expensive budget or elaborate materials, the following five elements can be useful to prepare children's hearts for missionary service:

1. *An atmosphere of love and concern.* I knelt as a 7-year-old to accept Christ with my dad, my pastor and a state youth leader by my side.

2. *Early opportunities for Christian service.* Whether preparing Sunday school literature and arranging chairs (my dad was the superintendent) or visiting elderly people with Mom, I knew I was doing this for Jesus.

3. *Role modeling.* Whenever teachers (such as David Bishop, Paul Lauster) at West Coast talked about missions, I watched their lives. They carried a burden. They prayed for missionaries. I tried to follow their example.

4. *Opportunities for personal contact with missionaries and other Christians.* Camp meetings, school revivals, missions conferences came alive not just because of dynamic preaching or informative lectures but because I met real people. One of those real people—James Slay—stopped in a busy camp meeting to talk to me, a 17-year-old youth. After that "divine appointment," my first application was sent to Church of God World Missions. Missionaries are often mentored into service.

5. Early cross-cultural contact. Growing up in central California, I had Hispanic, Italian, Armenian and Asian friends. Little did I know that I was being cross-culturally conditioned. Today, I watch as some of the richest experiences my family have are with ethnic friends. Having a Christian foreign student in your home is a valuable experience for your children and grandchildren.

There you have it. An ordinary kid into Little League, muddy jeans, bicycles, dogs and tree houses. No spectacular visions or Damascus road experience. But there was the context of a loving family, an involvement in the life of a living local church, and the constant example of faithful men and women. We can provide these same things and add to them the prayer of our Lord, "Pray ye therefore the Lord of the harvest, that he would send forth labourers into his harvest" (Luke 10:2, KJV).

BALANCED DISCIPLESHIP

"And Jesus *grew* . . .

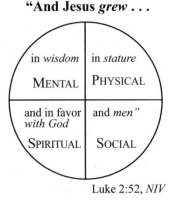

Luke 2:52, *NIV*

HELPING PEOPLE INTO POST-CAREER MINISTRY

Ray Kroc never said "quit." He knew that "it's not over 'til it's over." I guess that is why he stopped selling milkshake machines for someone else, bought a hamburger stand, and turned hard-charging business methods into an $10 billion fast-food empire with more than 25,000 outlets around the world—half of them in 120 foreign countries. Had it not been for Ray Kroc's "second start," there would never have been the American cultural phenomenon known as "McDonald's." When Ray Kroc started—again—he was 53 years old.

Sure, history always produces its *wunderkind* ("wonder child") who accomplishes much in a short time: Keats died at 26; Shelley at 30; Schubert at 31; Alexander the Great at 33; Mozart at 35. Today, in our highly technocratic society, the genius of youth is glorified as adolescent entrepreneurs spawn computer companies and design video game programs before leaving high school. Steve Jobs, the highly celebrated computer intellectual, made his mark and his millions with Apple Computer before reaching the age of 30.

Yet, history will also record significant contributions from those who did not begin, or begin again, until later in life: Grandma Moses started painting at 78; Tennyson wrote his greatest lines when he was 83; Michelangelo began building St. Peter's Cathedral at 76. Caleb the Israelite banged on Joshua's door with a proposal that would outdistance most men half his age:

> "Now then, just as the Lord promised, he has kept me alive for forty-five years since the time he said this to Moses, while Israel moved about in the desert. So here I am today, eighty-five years old! I am still as strong today as the day Moses sent me out; I'm just as vigorous to go out to battle now as I was then. Now give me this hill country that the Lord promised me that day" (Joshua 14:10-12).

There is a future for the Calebs of all ages in our congregations—whether in the pulpit or in the pew. I hope this attention on "second starters" will help us see people like the middle-aged executive whose career is on a plateau, or the retired schoolteacher who has many productive years still available, or the peaked-out professional whose career is cobwebbed and needs a change, or the ex-military man who is only halfway through life, or the empty-nest homemaker who wants to extend her service beyond the four walls of her home.

What Is Happening to the Workforce?

Change is second nature to our society. The world into which we were born is gone. The world in which our children will live is not yet evident. Transition, mobility, nomadic lifestyles and career change go with the territory of our society. An IBM executive was overheard bemoaning yet another transfer. "IBM does not mean International Business Machines," he lamented. "It means `I've Been Moved.'" Sociologists observe that the average American family moves at least six to eight times in its existence. Ministers probably surpass the national average!

Gone are the days when a person can be apprenticed for a skill, perform that job an entire lifetime and retire in one place. Changes in the labor market, technology, supply and demand, and life expectancy have made second and third careers a fact of life. Author Gail Sheehy, a researcher on adult development and change, argues for midlife career readjustment as a path toward new meaning and vitality in our work:

> Is there still any need to question, "Why a second career?" The simple fact that people are living longer in better physical condition than ever before makes commitment to a single, 40-year career almost predestinate stagnation. Added to that is the accelerated rate of technological change that makes almost any set of skills subject to obsolescence.[4]

Is God Trying to Get Our Attention?

Societal trends and secular researchers are informative, but

God may have a deeper message emerging from today's socio-economic changes. On one hand, He could be saying, "Follow Me *into* the marketplace. Do your work `as to the Lord' as an avenue of ministry" (see Colossians 3:22-25; Ephesians 6:5-8). Or, in light of international chaos and end-time conditions, He could be saying, "Follow Me *out of* the marketplace. It is time to move into a broadened ministry." He told fisherman/businessman Simon Peter, "Don't be afraid; from now on you will catch men" (Luke 5:10). Peter became a second starter.

The awesome challenge of our lost world, unparalleled response and receptivity to the gospel in many areas, and the imminent return of Jesus Christ demand a readjustment in the mobilization of our Christian workforce. Second-start Christians are desperately needed. In *Azusa Street and Beyond: Pentecostal Missions and Church Growth in the Twentieth Century*, I have noted the eschatological urgency that characterized the early Pentecostal Movement in this century. A rediscovery of that urgency is needed now.

Writers like Listen Pope have traced the phenomenal recruitment of early Pentecostal preachers from among the common workforce. Blue-collar laborers were called from the plow to the pulpits and from factories to flocks because God's Spirit was moving and they believed Jesus was coming soon. Like the prophet Amos, their second start was an unexpected and abrupt job change:

> I was neither a prophet nor a prophet's son, but I was a shepherd, and I also took care of sycamore-fig trees. But the Lord took me from tending the flock and said to me, "Go, prophesy to my people Israel" (Amos 7:14, 15).

Around us is a burgeoning lay ministry movement. We cannot keep up with the wealth of literature and programs being produced on the subject (including innovative and far-reaching ministries from the Church of God Office of Lay Affairs—*www.churchofgod.cc*).

Does all this mean that post-career lay ministers should enter the full-time pulpit preaching ministry? In most cases, probably not. In many cases, yes! In every case, Christians should be encouraged to discover, develop and use their area of giftedness and ministry in the body of Christ (1 Peter 2:5-10).

Who Are the Second Starters?

On both sides of the "clergy and laity" threshold, people are making transitions. Professional clergy retire or move into a new type of ministry. Pastors become missionaries. Missionaries return home to teach, evangelize, pastor or administrate. Members of the rank and file accept broadened responsibilities of leadership, and administrators return to the pastorate or evangelistic ministry. Military chaplains retire and continue fruitful ministries in another area of their church.

On the other hand, ministers among the laity make career changes through retirement or career readjustment. Military and government personnel finish their careers in midlife with much time left to live. Some adults are forced into early retirement through budget cutbacks, corporate restructuring or physical disability. Others must seek a new career because their work skills or jobs are obsolete.

Look at your congregation. What is happening in the work trends and career paths of your people? Where are they in their adult development? What will confront them at key transition points ten, five, or even two years down the road? If you are working with second-start Christians or upcoming post-career ministers, how can you assist them in fruitful ministry?

> ***LOOKING TO THE BEST HALF OF LIFE***
> Between the exhilaration of Beginning
> and the satisfaction of Concluding
> is the Middle Time
> of enduring, changing, trying,
> despairing, continuing, becoming.[5]
> —Lona Fowler

If I had a chance to counsel, motivate, lead or teach people in the post-career "middle time" or in the ending years, I would want to say at least six things to them.

1. *The future is now—go out to meet it.* As a project launched from their 50th birthdays (just a few months apart), authors Ray and Anne Ortlund wrote about *The Best Half of Life.* They begin with these lines:

> Friend, there's someone coming down the road toward you. Take a look. It's you, 25 years from now. Perhaps you've never before looked at your future self. Have you? If you're now anywhere from 35 to 50, this Future You walking toward you has slowed down somewhat—but it's you, all right.[6]

We can help people by motivating them to think about future transitions in life. Post-career ministry may sometimes be abrupt, but usually it is a gradual move. Second-start Christians do not go to bed one night inactive in ministry and get up the next morning with a newly found job in the Kingdom. Prepare people to think about what they will do after one phase of their growth has ended. Help them project forward to what can develop by faith. Consider with them the range of possibilities. Introduce them to their future.

2. *Move from crisis to convergence.* Studies and reports on midlife crisis abound. One of the best-known in Christian circles is Jim Conway's *Men in Mid-Life Crisis* and its sequel, *Women in Mid-Life Crisis,* by Jim and Sally Conway. There is a lot of talk about it, even in the popular media. (Last summer I saw a middle-aged man with his T-shirt message, "Don't Bother Me. I'm Having a Crisis!")

People *do* need to be bothered in their crises. They need the intervention of a pastor or friend who can help them see that they are only in the vestibule, that they are on the verge of a new, exciting phase of productivity. In fact, people in middle age enjoy special strengths and privileges unique to their phase of life. Their free time, increased financial stability, matured character and wealth of experience can now converge into a fruitful and enjoyable adventure in ministry. Help people make ministry in midlife or senior life an asset, not a liability. Help them move from crisis to convergence.

3. *Let closure be a cocoon.* Many people dread career change or retirement due to the fear of "stopping and flopping," an expression from Harvard-trained management consultant James Kelley. The concept of *closure* can move Christians beyond this fear. Closure carries with it the idea of "wrapping it up," of concluding one phase in order to begin a new one.

One must end well to begin well. Encourage second-start Christians to say good-bye and embrace a new challenge. Effective closure can be a cocoon out of which a whole new meaning in God's kingdom is discovered.

4. *Find the path through the passages.* On the way from the airport to a church-speaking appointment, a pastor in a Northern industrial city shared with me his burden for a newly retired man in his church. The man was not ready for retirement. He had been replaced by a younger foreman in his factory and he was bitter and resentful. He had not yet found the path through the passages.

"DON'T PARK HERE!" threatened a sign in a hospital parking lot to a burdened man coming to visit his ailing wife. That sign became a life sermon for that Pentecostal preacher. From it he learned through the Holy Spirit to go on, to move ahead with the Lord beyond the present difficulty. Help post-career people to see that there is more. Encourage them not to park—mentally or spiritually.

5. *Retire* to *something, not* from *something.* This is the title of one of the 11 exciting chapters in Ted Engstrom's book *The Most Important Thing a Man Needs to Know About the Rest of His Life.*[7] Engstrom discusses "the great retirement dream" and the disillusionment retirement brings because of unfulfilled expectations. He warns against "retirement me-ism," an unhealthy preoccupation with self-interests and personal ego needs.

Many local churches, denominations and Christian organizations are finding that retirees are some of the most faithful and productive personnel they can employ in God's work. Many post-career Christians are turning the condemnation of "being put out to pasture" into a commission of being "put in to pastor." Indeed, whether or not they are full-time "pastors," retirees and second-career individuals can have a significant nurturing, caring and teaching ministry.

6. *Get out of the cave and into the field.* Many midlifers and seniors retire into their own private cave of depression, cynicism and bitterness. Elijah the prophet is a case study in career transition. He is one of the few "cave dwellers" recorded in Biblical history!

Here is a nutshell version of a story with significant impact for post-career Christians. It unfolds in 1 Kings 18 and 19, where Elijah had witnessed a great victory over the prophets of Baal on Mount Carmel (18:16-40). After this, he "was afraid and ran for his life" from wicked Queen Jezebel (19:3). He hid out in the wilderness and finally came to a cave to spend the night. There God challenged him with the question, "What are you doing here, Elijah?" (v. 9). In his self-pity, he complained that he had been very zealous for the Lord and now was the only prophet left in Israel (vv. 10, 14).

But, as therapy for second starters, God said to Elijah, "Go back the way you came" (v. 15). God was not finished with His man. He had more work to do. He was to anoint Hazael king over Aram, Jehu king over Israel, and Elisha to succeed him as prophet (vv. 15, 16).

God may be telling you to "get out of the cave; get your cave dwellers out of the cave and help them reflect upon their past blessings and usefulness in the Kingdom." When cave dwellers "go back the way they came," they will see younger, inexperienced leaders coming along the same road who need the experience and encouragement of those who are older. One of the greatest gifts you can give second starters is the realization that they can move from "just making a living" to a new position of molding others to godly living. Encourage them as mentors to disciple the youth and young married couples of your church. Years ago, for example, my son and his junior high school classmates loved their Sunday school teacher, a retired minister who was "going back the way he came" to meet young, impressionable lives.

Our stewardship of God's gifts and grace calls us from being producers to reproducers. It keeps us out of the cave and places us in the field.

One Last Word

Post-career and retired lifestyles have undergone dramatic changes, and this will continue. God speaks to us through all of this. Now is the time for a change in our mind-set regarding employment and deployment in the kingdom of God. We will continue to need the idealism of youth coupled with the realism of middle age. If God has blessed us with health and longer life, increased earning power, reduction of debt loads and more leisure time, could it be that He wants our time, our ministry and ourselves in return? Look around for post-career Christians and help them get started . . . again.

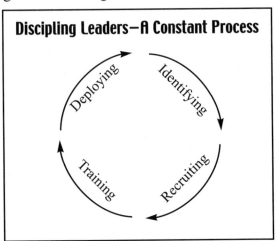

234

Reflections

1. This chapter highlighted praying, preaching, mobilizing for world Christian involvement. List three new ideas for you and your local church.

2. Two sections of this chapter dealt with children ("Five Ways to Help Children Hear God's Voice") and adults ("Helping People Into Post-Career Ministry"). Think about three concrete ways you and your church can help children and "second-start" Christians connect to God's work in their world.

*Pause now for personal or group prayer before moving to Projections/Actions.

Projections

Today's date_____

By this time next year, next month, next week, I believe God for the following ministry goals to connect to God's Work in my world (enter calendar dates for accountability):

1. Next year (date_____)
2. Next month (date_____)
3. Next week (date_____)

Actions

By this time tomorrow—in the next 24 hours—I will . . .

1.

2.

Part Three Resource Connections

1. Check with the following agencies and associations for ideas and resources:

Intent—Networking Professionals for Global Impact
5840 W. Midway Park
Chicago, IL 60644-1803
800-478-2598
Web site: *www.intent.org*
E-mail: *info@intent.org*

Tentmakers International Exchange
206-781-3151
E-mail: *tie@gati.wa.com*

International Employment Gazette
423 Townes St.
Greenville, SC 29601
800-882-9188
Web site: *www.intemployment.com*
E-mail: *intljobs@aol.com*

Nelson/Word Direct
P.O. Box 140300
Nashville, TN 37214-9831
800-933-9673, ext. 2039
Web site: *www.nelsonword.com*
Ask for: Mission Explorers Video Series (for Children)

Church Growth Institute
P.O. Box 9176
Oxnard, CA 93031
800-553-4769

Web site: *www.churchgrowth.org*
Church Growth Center
P.O. Box 145
Corunna, IN 46730
800-626-8515
Web site: *www.churchdoctor.org*

New Life Resources
101 TDK Boulevard, Suite B
Peachtree City, GA 30269-9808
800-827-2788
Web site: *www.campuscrusade.org*

MissionAmerica
The Lighthouse Movement
5666 Lincoln Drive, Suite 100
Edina, MN 55436-1673
Web site: *www.lighthousemovement.com*

2. Through your occupation, do you (or a committed Christian you know) travel or reside overseas? Check with the world missions office of your association or denomination on how to find your church overseas or how to use your occupation in missionary service.

Chairman, Personnel Committee
Church of God World Missions
P.O. Box 8016
Cleveland, TN 37320-8016
800-345-7492
Web site: *www.cogwm.org*

3. Contact your association or denominational resource offices for information on conferences, seminars, and evangelism training tools:

Evangelism and Home Missions
P.O. Box 2430
Cleveland, TN 37320-2430
423-478-7103

Office of Lay Ministries
P.O. Box 2430
Cleveland, TN 37320-2430
423-478-7286

PART FOUR

Logging On to Your Global Future

Preview
Part IV gives practical guidance in connecting to global involvement including actual steps toward developing a ministry strategy. It also provides an overall overview of the dynamics of the global Pentecostal/Charismatic Movement with forecasts of future trends.

Globalbeliever.Completion—"The Great Completion"

And this gospel of the kingdom will be preached in the whole world as a testimony to all nations, and then the end will come (Matthew 24:14).

Globalbeliever.Coming—"The Great Coming"

He who testifies to these things says, "Yes, I am coming soon." Amen. Come, Lord Jesus. The grace of the Lord Jesus be with God's people. Amen (Revelation 22:20, 21).

On any given day in Quito, Ecuador, you can hail a taxi or jump on a crowded bus to head up the winding roads to a plateau outside the city, which attracts thousands of tourists from around the world. Upon arriving at "Mitad del Mundo," you'll see the usual array of tourist shops and cafes surrounding an expansive plaza. In the center of the plaza is a museum with a tall pedestal supporting a huge model world globe. The gathering point for the whole attraction is a line drawn across the middle of the plaza. There you see tourists posing for photos while straddling the line. They are standing at "Mitad del Mundo"— the "Middle of the World." This is the imaginary line we call the equator, which girdles the center of the globe like a gigantic belt. If the painted line continued, you could follow it east to Nairobi or west to Singapore. The curiosity of putting a foot on each side of the line is to show the friends back home, "I stood at the middle of the world with one foot in the Northern Hemisphere and the other in the South." The global believer logs on to God's "missions central"—constantly keeping his or her perspective in the middle—looking back to yesterday and looking forward to tomorrow. We live in the present, remembering the past, reaching forward to our global future.

Chapter Thirteen

"Plug In" to Your Plan

> THE NOBLEST THING A MAN CAN DO IS,
> JUST HUMBLY RECEIVE, AND THEN GO
> AMONGST OTHERS AND GIVE.
> —DAVID LIVINGSTONE
> LEGENDARY MISSIONARY TO AFRICA

An overzealous vacuum cleaner salesman from the city took his sales crusade door-to-door in the country where there was no electricity. With his foot already in the door of one wide-eyed country housewife, he proclaimed as he dropped a handful of dirt on the living room rug, "I'll eat every bit of this if my machine doesn't pick up every speck of dust!"

"Start eatin'," she challenged as she returned from the kitchen with a spoon. "We ain't got no electricity, and you ain't got no place to plug it in!"

Thankfully, we're delivered from such a plight, both in terms of cleaning house and extending our church's mission! Our local churches have the machinery and the power. Many, however, are still looking for the place to plug them in! Let me offer a few guiding principles for getting and staying plugged into world missions.

To keep your congregation's interest fresh and to maintain the good works you have begun, I'm going to suggest that this happens by staying informed, interested, in touch and inquisitive.

Staying Informed

Most missionaries have communication tools to inform

245

their supporting constituencies: newsletters, magazines, video and audio reports, e-mails, annual reports, and so forth. Get on the mailing list of reputable ministries. Be willing to cut through the "hype" and generalized "verbal fog" in the generic missions reports. Look and ask for documented statistics and case histories.

Another way of staying informed is through the process of "networking," developing an interconnecting web of friendships and professional contacts who will keep you informed. We forget that people are media, too. Some of our best resources and contacts will come from other churches or leaders who can, in good conscience, recommend a ministry worthy of support.

Staying Interested

Those who look to you for support should know that your church is interested in them. You should expect reports (photos, videos, newsletters, etc.) from them regularly. You should expect them to visit your church and review the things God is doing through your support. This is the New Testament pattern exhibited in the Book of Acts. There is no substitute for face-to-face responsibility in reporting.

Staying in Touch

Likewise, you should be willing to visit the ministries you support. In fact, there is no better way of raising the interest and mission consciousness of supporters than to take them personally to the mission field when possible. This is "research through travel" and it greatly broadens the vision of supporters back home. God confirmed my missionary calling when I participated in a "missionary orientation trip" to Mexico when I was only 17. Research through traveling should never become justification for luxurious "tourist junkets" or shopping excursions in exotic places. They must be maintained as ministry trips which have evangelism encouragement and nurture at the heart of their mission.

Staying Inquisitive

Donors have the God-given responsibility to expect recipients to be upright and accountable to the Christian community. Blind giving has no Biblical precedent. As the manager of God's resources in your care, you should be willing to investigate and remain inquisitive regarding your investment in world missions.

Now is the time to get plugged into world missions by doing your homework, knowing the ministry, and determining the categories of support under the guidance of the Holy Spirit. Now is the time to stay plugged in by staying in touch and staying inquisitive. We have the machinery, the personnel and the power to evangelize the world. The church has enough financial potential to fund every major effort to disciple the nations. Let's get plugged in and get on with the job.

Seven Steps to a Strategy

What does the Lord want us to do? How are we going to do it? These are fundamental and appropriate questions in approaching the development of a plan or a strategy for world evangelization. Strategizing is more of an ongoing, developing process than a momentary idea that is ready-made and fully formed. The following "Seven Steps to a Strategy" are broader categories that may involve a number of supporting processes.

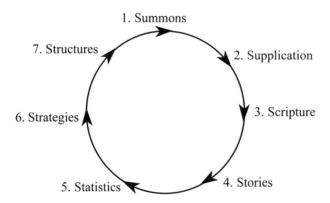

1. Summons
2. Supplication
3. Scripture
4. Stories
5. Statistics
6. Strategies
7. Structures

1. *Summons*. A *summons* is a call to attention and action. It represents an alarm that should mobilize to action. Used here in the context of strategic planning, *summons* represents the burden, calling and vision from the Lord.

As a basic starting point, fundamental questions for us should be these: What does the Lord want? Where is He leading? What is His burden and calling? This means that the initiative for strategy is divine, not human. It keeps us under the sovereign guidance of Jesus, the Lord of the harvest, and the Holy Spirit, the Supreme Strategist.

We don't begin a strategy with the mere accumulation of facts and possible methodologies but with the call of God.

2. *Supplication*. *Supplication* represents the central place of prayer in strategizing. This should not be any kind of prayer, however, but prayer that involves waiting, abiding, consecration and deep adoration. Strategies that are only "prayed over" are bound to fail. By this I mean the faulty practice of laying out a plan of our own making and then asking God to bless it with His stamp of approval.

The most productive strategies are those "prayed out"—those that emerge naturally under the careful, wise guidance of the Holy Spirit. This is best expressed in the missions maxim, "We don't pray to receive a strategy; prayer is the strategy."

Recently, researchers uncovered more than 700 strategic worldwide plans for missions propagated over the last 2,000 years of church history. No doubt every one of them has had merit and a number of good qualities. The "strategy of the Holy Spirit," however, is pungent, penetrating and lasting. It produces effective church growth—"fruit that remains" (see John 15:16) and glorifies God. "Every great move of God," said one observer of revival history, "can be traced to a kneeling form."

Supplication is essential, indispensable and integral to the strategizing process from first to last. It keeps us open to the summons of God and creates fertile ground for the Scriptural guidelines for strategic planning.

3. *Scripture.* Since God's desire and plan for world redemption is the heart of Scripture, it follows that Scripture would be central to the strategizing process. The Bible is our message book, for it has the clear revelation of the gospel. Evangelistic preaching and church planting are at the core of any successful missions strategy.

The Bible is not only a *message* book but it is also a *method* book. We look at Biblical methods and models and find where God's servants were effective. The Book of Acts, for example, has been the "operating manual" for lasting results in Pentecostal church growth around the world.

Finally, Scripture also provides the guidelines of truth that keep our *motivations* pure. A strategy is only as good as the sincere and sanctified servant who employs it. Paul had a variety of successful approaches but recognized the danger of preaching to others and losing his own spiritual experience (1 Corinthians 9:27).

4. *Stories. Story* is a key word to emphasize the importance of gathering personal experiences and testimonies, past and present. Taking time to hear the past experiences of experienced and retired cross-cultural workers will give one a depth and wealth of background. Knowing the failures and pitfalls can help avoid disappointment, lack of productivity or the waste of resources. Hearing the successes will encourage and affirm that a strategy may be on target.

From the standpoint of "tracking," it is also very important to gather current stories of what God is doing. This may indeed be a way of "hearing what the Spirit is saying to the churches" (see Revelation 2; 3). Before building a tower or going to war, Jesus said, it is important to take inventory of the current situation (Luke 14:28-32). It is instructional, for example, in building a strategy to reach Muslims, to examine other areas where Muslim evangelization is meeting with God's blessing. People are media and we learn from their stories.

5. *Statistics*. Faith and facts do not have to be incompatible. There is nothing unspiritual about getting the proper information. We do it before we buy a house or a car, entrust our children to a baby-sitter, or travel to a foreign place. The wisdom of the Old Testament says it is foolish and a shame "to decide before knowing the facts!" (Proverbs 18:13, *TLB*).

There is evidence in the New Testament that church leaders took time to do their research in advance—even if it was the informal data gathering through personal references. Paul, for example, acquired prior knowledge of situations and people before he arrived at a place. In the 27 verses of Romans 16, for example, he mentions 26 individuals by name. There is internal and external evidence in this and other epistles that Paul took the time to acquire prior knowledge of local situations before going there or sending a representative.

Before proceeding toward any plan, hear the *summons* from the Holy Spirit, continue in *supplication* with the guidelines of *Scripture*, and listen to the *stories* of what God has done and is doing. Document the need and work intelligently using *statistics*. By then, a spiritually sensitive and well-informed *strategy* will begin to emerge.

Envisioning Anticipated Outcomes
TWO BASIC QUESTIONS:

1. What is the *present* situation?
   - Accurate analysis
   - Careful consideration
   - Objective reporting
   - No "verbal fog"

2. What will the *future envisioned* situation be?
   - Faith thinking
   - Hard, bold plans
   - Concrete goal-setting
   - Definite projections

---

6. *Strategies*. A *strategy* is a working plan that moves toward predetermined goals established by faith under the guidance of

the Holy Spirit. It is a "faith projection" of what we expect to see develop under the leadership of the Holy Spirit. It is another way of expressing what the Lord is intending.

Strategic planning is a Biblical idea and model. Consider the wisdom of these Bible references:

- John 4:35—Jesus directed His disciples to "look at the fields," meaning "to examine closely, to investigate, to determine, to perceive."

- Numbers 13:2—God directed Moses to send men to do a preliminary exploration of the land of Canaan (though He could have revealed everything to them by dreams and visions).

- Jeremiah 5:1—Jeremiah was directed to look through Jerusalem to find any righteous man.

- Nehemiah 2:11-18—Nehemiah did preliminary research around Jerusalem before proceeding to rebuild.

- Luke 14:28-32—Jesus advocated preliminary research in His examples of building a tower or going to war.

Three Important Strategies

1. A GRAND STRATEGY
- Broad and Visionary
- What will we do by 2010?
- "Expect great things from God; attempt great things for God"
  —William Carey

2. A INTERMEDIATE STRATEGY
- Initial movement
- Looks for ways to implement the grand strategy

3. A SHORT-RANGE STRATEGY
- States the beginning steps

Key Question: Is this strategy appropriate?

Consider the planning wisdom from Proverbs (*TLB*):

- "A wise man thinks ahead; a fool doesn't, and even brags about it!" (13:16).

- "It is pleasant to see plans develop. That is why fools refuse to give them up even when they are wrong" (13:19).

- "The wise man looks ahead. The fool attempts to fool himself and won't face facts" (14:8).

- "Plans go wrong with too few counselors; many counselors bring success" (15:22).

- "We can make our plans, but the final outcome is in God's hands" (16:1).

- "We should make plans—counting on God to direct us" (16:9).

- "What a shame—yes, how stupid!—to decide before knowing the facts!" (18:13).

- "The intelligent man is always open to new ideas. In fact, he looks for them" (18:15).

Jesus Himself had definite goals in His ministry. He came to . . .

- *Subdue*—"The reason the Son of God appeared was to destroy the devil's work" (1 John 3:8).

- *Seek and save*—"For the Son of Man came to seek and to save what was lost" (Luke 19:10).

- *Serve*—"For even the Son of Man did not come to be served, but to serve, and to give his life as a ransom for many" (Mark 10:45).

- *Secure* (eternal life)—"The thief comes only to steal and kill and destroy; I have come that they may have life, and have it to the full" (John 10:10).

- *Sanctify and separate*—"[Christ] gave himself for us to redeem us from all wickedness and to purify for himself a people that are his very own, eager to do what is good" (Titus 2:14).

- *Send*—"As the Father has sent me, I am sending you" (John 20:21).

- *Spiritize (anoint, empower)*—"God has raised this Jesus to life, and we are all witnesses of the fact. Exalted to the right hand of God, he has received from the Father the promised Holy Spirit and has poured out what you now see and hear" (Acts 2:32, 33; see also Matthew 3:11; Mark 1:8; Luke 3:16; 24:49; John 1:33).

Paul had a plan, a strategy for growth:

- He limited himself to Rome-administered areas.

- He focused in two or three centers in each area.

- He went to centers of Jewish influence.

- In new communities, he used contacts supplied by relatives of people from established churches.

- He reached whole families.

7. *Structures*. The key word, *structure*, is meant to designate the actual methodologies, which are used to carry out a strategy. Out of the many varieties of methodologies available, here are at least three options:

- Biblical examples from Acts and other sources.

- The examples surfacing in the "stories" and "statistics" you have gathered to this point.

- Unique and creative new methods which you develop under the guidance of the Holy Spirit to meet a particular strategy opportunity.

Summary

In review, here are the "Seven Steps to a Strategy" with a definition of each of the processes:

1. *Summons*—the burden, calling, vision from the Lord

2. *Supplication*—praying, worshiping, waiting, abiding in God's presence

3. *Scripture*—finding Biblical methods and models

4. *Stories*—"tracking" what God is doing through past and current reports/testimonies

5. *Statistics*—gathering the data, knowing the people with information

6. *Strategies*—setting goals, designing a plan

7. *Structures*—developing methodologies and concrete actions

Strategizing is an ongoing Biblical process that will need constant monitoring, evaluation and readjustment. It is a stewardship of God's resources and personnel that is carried out under the lordship of Jesus Christ and the supervision of the Holy Spirit.

Reflections

1. Where are you "plugging in" to what God is doing in your world (local and international)? How can you get others to join you?

2. Think about a way to get some local church leadership together to apply the "Seven Steps to a Strategy" model to your specific ministry situation. Before you do that, take at least 30 minutes to think through the basic seven steps on your own.

*Pause now for personal or group prayer before moving to Projections/Actions.

Projections

Today's date_____

By this time next year, next month, next week, I believe God for the following ministry goals to connect to God's work in my world (enter calendar dates for accountability):
1. Next year (date_____)
2. Next month (date_____)
3. Next week (date_____)

Actions

By this time tomorrow—in the next 24 hours—I will . . .

1.

2.

THIRD MILLENNIUM— THIRD CHURCH

WE SPEAK ABOUT THE DIVINELY ORDAINED
GLOBALIZATION BECAUSE THE GOSPEL OF JESUS
CHRIST IS A UNIVERSALLY VALID, GLOBALLY
RELEVANT MESSAGE OF HOPE AND SALVATION.
—PETER KUZMIC
CROATIAN PENTECOSTAL THEOLOGIAN

North American and European Pentecostal Christians need a "wake-up call." We need to acknowledge the new *realities* in global Pentecostalism, find ways to incorporate the necessary *resources* from our worldwide family, and responsibly formulate needed *resolutions* (in word and deed) to advance our global interdependence. Neither *dependence* nor *independence* expresses the Biblical model. The key word for our time is *interdependence*, which involves the mutual and reciprocal dependence on one another as equal partners and co-laborers in the international body of Christ. Community necessitates collaboration.

New Realities: The Arrival of the Third Church

In reality there is only one universal church—"one body and one Spirit . . . one hope . . . one Lord, one faith, one baptism; one God and Father of all, who is over all and through all and in all" (Ephesians 4:4-6). The last 2,000 years of international expansion, however, have unfolded various "eras" and areas of geographical strength in the Christian movement. The vitality of Christianity (an "Eastern religion") has moved progressively from the East to the North to the West, and now to the Southern Hemisphere.

The "third church" is the language of missiologist Walbert Buhlmann. The "first church," characterized in the arch of expansion and influence from Jerusalem to Rome, was predominantly Eastern for the first millennium. Over the next 1,000 years, the "second church," the Western, prevailed from Rome northward to central Europe and then outward to European colonies in North and South America, Africa, and Southeast Asia. Now (as Jesus has tarried) we have entered the third millennium and the third church of the Southern Hemisphere.[1]

Concurrent with Buhlmann, University of Aberdeen (Scotland) Professor Andrew F. Walls was speaking in 1976 of "a complete change in the centre of gravity of Christianity, so that the heartlands of the church are no longer in Europe, decreasingly in North America, but in Latin America, in certain parts of Asia, and . . . in Africa."[2] In the years since the observation of Walls, many commentators began to speak of "the southernization of Christianity."

The "third church" is generally identified geographically with the "Third World" (my preference is to say the "Southern World"), which includes the continents of Latin America, Africa, and Asia (including Oceania)—areas Donald McGavran dubbed "Latfricasia" as compared to what he called "Eurica" (Europe and North America). It is in *this* world (actually, two-thirds of the world in population and land mass) where our Pentecostal/Charismatic family has its greatest assets ("spiritual capital" if not economic capital) with 75 percent of its adherents in those regions.

Researcher David Barrett, editor of the prestigious *World Christian Encyclopedia,* and his international research network found that the combined global Pentecostal/Charismatic family comes in an amazing variety of 38 major categories—11,000 Pentecostal denominations and 3,000 independent Charismatic denominations spread across 8,000 ethnolinguistic cultures and 7,000 languages. This overall movement is increasing by 54,000 new members per day and 19 million members per year, and are active in 80 percent of the world's 3,300 large metropolises.[3] By the end of the 20th century, the movement had increased to more than 500 million members.

Buhlmann makes a very positive projection upon this new reality:

> In the course of the third millennium—who knows?—a church historian may compare the eastern church to the morning star, silent, glittering, ever full of hope; the western church to the moon, which, after a night almost as luminous as the day, is now growing dim; and the third church to the sun, newly risen on the horizon, ruling the day.[4]

Most American Christian leaders, formed in a culture that has led the world as the ranking superpower in the 20th century (now more prominent with the demise of Soviet Marxism), would probably find the language of "growing dim" versus "ruling the day" threatening or offensive. Many American Pentecostals, for example, would not be aware that 75 percent of Church of God (Cleveland, Tennessee) membership as well as 88 percent of the Assemblies of God are living outside the United States and Canada. Most likely, this would also be surprising news for the average European Pentecostal.

This "hidden majority" are another world away for the larger part of American and European Pentecostals. In North America, for example (especially since World War II), we are now, with the exception of urban *ethnic* Pentecostalism, largely typified as rural/suburban middle class (also true of North American Charismatics). In Europe, middle-class Pentecostals and Charismatics seem to have a growing distance between themselves and the poor. As a stark contrast, Barrett's cross section of worldwide Pentecostalism reveals a composite "international Pentecostal/Charismatic" who is more urban than rural, more female than male, more Third World (66%) than Western world, more impoverished (87%) than affluent, more family-oriented than individualistic and, on the average, younger than 18.[5]

To put all of this in the historical context of the roots of American Pentecostalism, there are many similarities between our original founders and early leaders and the "international composite Pentecostal" described by Barrett. Though he writes out of a subjective "social deprivation" theory for the origins of American Pentecostalism, Robert Mapes Anderson is helpful at this point. His Ph.D. dissertation (1969) was published in 1979 as *Vision of the Disinherited: The Making of American Pentecostalism*. From their diaries, memoirs, autobiographies and informal writings, Anderson put together descriptive profiles of some 45 selected Pentecostals before 1914, most of them before 1909. As a composite, they were generally young, rural, impoverished, poorly educated. The age category is interesting:

> The Pentecostal leaders were young. More than a third of the sample joined the movement before reaching the age of 30, more than two-thirds before 40. During the movement's initial thrust in the years between 1906 and 1912, most of them ranged in age from the mid-20s to the early 40s. Aimee Semple McPherson was an 18-year-old bride when she went to China as a Pentecostal missionary, and was making national headlines while still in her 20s. Howard Goss joined in the work with Parham (who was then 29) at the age of 19, was a recognized leader of the Apostolic Faith movement in the Lower Midwest in his early 20s, and the prime mover in creating the Assemblies of God at the age of 28. . . . Goss said of the workers in those early days, "90 percent of us were so very young."[6]

What becomes disturbing with a backward look (Anderson's description) and a forward projection (based on new Southern World realities in Pentecostalism as revealed by Barrett) is that where we are presently in North American middle-class Pentecostalism (at the outset of the 21st century) is neither really at home with our past nor our future. We are in a "chronological parenthesis." With more careful analysis I suspect the same could be said for the European situation today (excluding Eastern Europe, of course).

To use the analogy of a tree to describe ourselves, many in North American and European Pentecostalism would see themselves as the full-grown trunk (stability, strength, support base) coming out of 19th-century holiness roots and would probably put the "mission colonies" we have established around the world as the fruit-bearing branches that proceed out of the "real" tree—the trunk.

Where we are frustrated, however, in moving toward true globalization and international interdependence is that we have tried to understand the *organic* church (cf. Paul's "organic" metaphors of a tree, Romans 11:13-24, and a human body, 1 Corinthians 12:12-31) in terms of an *organizational* church, using images from a technological model of modern corporate management. As the older European and North American Pentecostal bodies have grown into various regions and countries, it has not been a componental matter of opening up new regional offices, adding additional bank branches, or building new rooms onto the house. These are organizational, economic, structural models, but not wholistic organic models. In reality, it would be more realistic to see global Pentecostalism as having a common trunk and the various regional expressions (North America and Europe included) as being the branches. Jesus, the same Baptizer in the Holy Ghost for the Pentecostal reality in *all* regions, is the only Vine (trunk), and the various regional and national church movements are only the branches (John 15).

Necessary Resources: Acknowledging Global Riches

In terms of resources, most of the communication flow in the 100-year history of modern Pentecostalism has been from the Northern to the Southern Hemisphere. That day is now gone and a new reality has come. A theology (belief) and a theopraxy (action) of interdependence would lead to a more healthy engrafting of third-church resources into the older movements. Pentecostals outside Europe and North America (and their connected ethnic families in the Northern Hemisphere) have historical, theological, missiological and leadership richness to offer. They have common roots in the same tree. They are not just branches of the European/North American tree.

We need the doctrinal leadership of Southern World leaders, scholars, and pastors who not only grapple with the American and European exported doctrinal heresies (areas such as extreme faith and prosperity, Kingdom Now, New Age, etc.), but also address life-and-death issues from their own regions. An underlying truth to this whole area of acknowledging the theological contributions from all arenas of faith around the world must be stated in a maxim. I wonder if this maxim is seriously believed by North American and European Pentecostals: *We have something to learn about theology and ministry in daily life from the Southern World.*

True globalization and a theology of interdependence is a two-way street. This means the communication flow must also move from the Southern Hemisphere to the North. Two outstanding books are indispensable for those who really want to move the church in this direction: *Learning About Theology From the Third World*, by William A. Dyrness (Zondervan, 1990), and *Unexpected News: Reading the Bible With Third World Eyes*, by Robert McAfee Brown (Westminster Press, 1984).

We have something to learn about how our laity, pastors and teachers struggle with liberation theology in Latin America where socioeconomic and political issues cannot remain separate from the faith. Our South African brethren must take the lead in discerning the Biblical nature of the church and the demands of discipleship over against apartheid. Our people in Holland must help us with the integration of faith and science out of a context where euthanasia ("mercy killing") is legal. Our brethren in Eastern Europe have addressed Christian ethics under totalitarianism for years. Christians in Africa and Asia are challenged by animistic religions of power and questions of ancestor worship.

Asian Pentecostals are a minority in a sea of non-Christian religions which are increasingly intolerant and aggressively missionary. Surely we could learn something about relating to Muslim peoples from Pentecostals in Indonesia (the fourth most populated nation on earth and the largest Muslim country in the world).

Europeans must learn from Indonesians since Europe now has more than 30 million Muslim residents, and Americans must learn from them since there are now more Muslims than Presbyterians in the United States (estimates range from 8-10 million in 2000). Let's globalize the doctrinal process and ask Asian Indian Pentecostals to help us with the New Age movement (reworked Hinduism customized for a European and American audience). Let's get Asian, African and Latin American pastors and evangelists on our Bible conference and retreat programs to talk to us about spiritual warfare, signs and wonders, and "power evangelism." Let's continue to encourage faculty exchanges with the third church to learn about theology through Southern World eyes. Let's call for the aggressive missionary evangelists from the burgeoning overseas Pentecostal churches to "come over to Macedonia and help us."

Dyrness argues that the interconnectedness of the modern world ensures that issues challenging the church today—technology, medical ethics, secularism, feminism, the environment, the arms race, international indebtedness, urban deterioration, AIDS, drugs, the decline of the traditional family—are *intercultural, international* issues that cannot be properly addressed in isolation from a narrow point of view:

All of this suggests that any theology today that claims to be comprehensive must result from an interchange between theologians from many different settings and representing many different points of view. Those of us who take the authority of Scripture seriously would add that only through such interchange will the full truth of Scripture be seen.[7]

Needed Resolutions: Advancing Interdependence in Global Pentecostalism

Resolutions should not be understood to mean merely written responses that are given "rubber stamp" assent in international Pentecostal gatherings. These make for interesting reading in our denominational magazines but may not bring about change. *Resolutions* should be understood in the spirit of resolving to *do* something—a call to action. Lay leaders, pastors and church executives are in positions to enact change in our church structures—by executive appointment, by creation of new ministry possibilities, by group consensus with councils creating funding, by innovative ideas given to general boards and committees, by influencing other decision makers in church leadership. Let us move toward continued partnership and interdependence in the global Pentecostal community and demonstrate our organic unity in Christ, who has baptized us *all* into the same Body with the same Holy Spirit.

Reflections

1. There are many factors and characteristics in the global expansion of the Pentecostal/Charismatic Movement (especially in the "Southern World" of Asia, Africa and Latin America). From this chapter, list three which are the most important for you:

2. Based upon the demographic information in this chapter, the composite sketch of the global Pentecostal believer is someone who is an urban, poor, two-thirds world, family-oriented female under the age of 18. Are you and your local church out of touch, or are you in a position to identify with and minister to such a person? How could this begin globally and locally for you and your church?

*Pause now for personal or group prayer before moving to Projections/Actions.

Projections

Today's date_____

By this time next year, next month, next week, I believe God for the following ministry goals to connect to God's work in my world (enter calendar dates for accountability):

1. Next year (date_____)
2. Next month (date_____)
3. Next week (date_____)

Actions

By this time tomorrow—in the next 24 hours—I will . . .

1.

2.

CHAPTER FIFTEEN

2000–2010: TOMORROW'S FORECAST

CALLING THE WHOLE CHURCH TO TAKE THE
WHOLE GOSPEL TO THE WHOLE WORLD.
—FROM THE MANILA MANIFESTO
ON WORLD EVANGELIZATION
MANILA, PHILIPPINES

In 1977 Dr. Donald A. McGavran questioned, "What Makes Pentecostal Churches Grow?" "The question underlined above," he said, "has animated my mind since the early '60s."

McGavran's question from the early 1960s is still with us. Though there may now be more general consensus of growth factors based upon 30 plus years of research and reflection, the attempt to "understand" Pentecostal/Charismatic church growth remains a complex issue. "Forecasting" the future of these churches, like commanding the wind, is next to impossible (John 3:8)! We have already seen the extensive growth and diversity of the Pentecostal/Charismatic Movement in the statistics from David Barrett.

Commenting on the movement's diversity, Grant Wacker has observed:

> Immensity breeds confusion. Contemporary Pentecostalism is so vast and sprawling it is sometimes difficult for outsiders to know exactly what the creature is. Like the beasts in Noah's ark, Pentecostals come in a bewildering variety. Protestant, Catholic, Reformed, Wesleyan, Trinitarian, Unitarian, mainline, sectarian, white, black, Hispanic, nouveau riche, working class—the list of

adjectives that describe one subgroup or another could be extended almost indefinitely. Perhaps more than any other segment of Christendom, the boundaries of the movement seem hopelessly tangled in a maze of crisscrossing beliefs and practices.[1]

There is diversity and complexity yet also simplicity in explaining the global growth of the Holy Spirit. Note these insightful quotations:

> It is recognized by students of church growth operating within varying research paradigms that the dynamics of growth and decline are always complex. There is no one simple reason why a given church or denomination grows or declines. . . . The Holy Spirit uses sociological factors but it is not restricted by them, at least according to the theological assumptions of the Church Growth Movement. This, in itself, increases the complexity of understanding ecclesiastical growth trends (C. Peter Wagner).[2]

> The Pentecostal missionary movement is prospering for the very reason that it is Pentecostal. Some recent writers have attempted to show that the results Pentecostal churches experienced on the foreign field could be achieved by simply adopting some of the practices of Pentecostals which are most appealing to the masses without necessarily becoming "Pentecostal" in experience. It is questionable that one could find a Pentecostal who would agree with this premise (Melvin L. Hodges).[3]

> A common error on the part of the Pentecostals is to attempt to explain church growth in terms of one dimension—the Holy Spirit. But perhaps an equally deceptive error made by non-Pentecostals is the underestimation of that dimension of church growth, specifically the dynamic of the Pentecostal experience itself (Paul A. Pomerville).[4]

Often I read articles and manuscripts which quote my teaching on the subject of church growth. Sometimes I am disappointed with their perspective on what I am saying. Because I give a great many principles and techniques when I teach, some only hear the techniques and never catch the basic theology and spiritual philosophy which will make those techniques work. Church growth is more than a series of ideas and principles which will, when put into practice, automatically make your church grow numerically. (David Yonggi Cho).[5]

"Trends" and "Projections"?

After witnessing the surprises of the 1990s, I'm personally a little reluctant to predict what will become of the Pentecostal/Charismatic Movement in coming years. At the end of the 1980s, even the best of today's increasingly popular "evangelical futurists" could not have suspected the end of totalitarianism in Eastern Europe, the demise of the Soviet Union, and strident forward advances in human rights in South Africa—and all within a two-year period, from 1989 to 1991!

The Pentecostal/Charismatic branch of worldwide Christianity is far from being monolithic, homogeneous, predictable. In the science of church growth, Pentecostals and Charismatics are the laboratory animals that won't sit still under investigation. If church growth were pediatrics, the Pentecostal/Charismatic children would no doubt be among the most challenging of patients! Pentecostal/Charismatic church growth is a fire out of control (Acts 2:2, 3).

If the past and the present are any indicators, however, it seems that five processes will characterize us in the coming years: publishing, proclamation/planting, persecution, partnership, and prioritization.

Publishing. By "publishing" I mean the wider process of self-definition by insiders as well as continued research by outside observers.

269

Pentecostals have been in the missions/church growth lab for over 50 years. J. Merle Davis wrote about us in 1943 in a study commissioned by the International Missionary Council (*How the Church Grows in Brazil*). Already in 1954, Lesslie Newbigin was suggesting in *The Household of God* that Pentecostals be seen as "The Community of the Holy Spirit" (ch. 4). When McGavran (with John Huegel and Jack Taylor) wrote *Church Growth in Mexico,* he cited the church growth conclusions of Davis and also called upon Eugene Nida's earlier work on Pentecostals.[6]

A large part of Donald McGavran's genius in forming the Church Growth Movement was his ability to attract researchers of high caliber. Along the way these colleagues provided significant studies of Pentecostal church growth: William R. Read, *New Patterns of Church Growth in Brazil*; William R. Read, Victor M. Monterroso and Harmon Johnson, *Latin American Church Growth*; Jim Montgomery, *Fire in the Philippines*. By far, however, C. Peter Wagner's *Look Out! The Pentecostals Are Coming* brought the most widespread attention of the church world to the dynamics of Pentecostal church growth (the book is now revised as *Spiritual Power and Church Growth*).

Most of the publishing about Pentecostals during the first 30 years of the Church Growth Movement (1955-1985) was done primarily (not exclusively) by non-Pentecostals. The lone exception was Assemblies of God missiologist Melvin L. Hodges, who sought to articulate a Pentecostal missiology in the years following World War II (*The Indigenous Church*). His name became synonymous with indigenous church principles, even in the wider evangelical world and he became a regular dialogue partner with non-Pentecostal missiologists.[7]

This trend changed in the 1980s. The seeds of Pentecostal church growth thinking, unwittingly planted in the last century by Anglican missiologist Roland Allen and A.B. Simpson (founder of the Christian and Missionary Alliance) and nurtured by Melvin Hodges, began to sprout in a proliferation of articles and books.

These were written by *insiders* who claimed that the primary purpose and self-identity of the Pentecostal Movement centered on a
revival raised up by God for world evangelization. This was my
central point in *Azusa Street and Beyond: Pentecostal Missions
and Church Growth in the Twentieth Century.*[8]

There is a strong indication that Pentecostals and Charismatics
will continue to tell their own stories. Particularly revealing and
exciting will be the church growth interpretations from the
"Melvin Hodges" of the Pentecostal/Charismatic world in Asia,
Africa, Latin America, and from the newly visible churches of
Eastern Europe and the former Soviet Union.

As their voices are heard more and more in leading missiological journals and consultations, the whole landscape of the church
growth agenda will change. There will be more global interdependence and less North American dominance in church growth
publishing. Traditional Pentecostals and non-Pentecostals alike
may be in for a surprise!

Proclamation/Planting. From all indications, the Pentecostal/
Charismatic communities will continue to proclaim the gospel
and multiply churches (probably the understatement of the
year!). We will still hold "Great Commission" missions, personal conversion, and the growth and reproduction of churches
as our main reason for being.

Though speaking with a slightly different accent, we are learning well the "language of Lausanne." Concepts of "countdown"
and "closure" toward the completion of the Great Commission
are a part of our vocabulary. Accordingly, mainline Pentecostals
and Charismatics have set ambitious goals for this new century.

Our proclamation and planting, however, have more to do with
what we perceive as ultimate meaning than with temporary methods. Throughout our history there has been an aggressive "to the
gates of hell" mentality that has propelled the movement forward.
Anyone looking in from the outside needs to understand that
"Pentecostal/Charismatic church growth" is more than just another

style or methodology. There is an eschatological urgency about our evangelism because of firm theological convictions regarding the lostness of man, the judgment of God, the imminence of Christ's return, and the indispensability of the empowerment of the Holy Spirit to accomplish the growth of the church.

Persecution. The purpose of this observation is not to spread pessimism or gloom. But let us deal with the realities that go beyond the triumphal preaching in our superchurches and the megaplans hatched in our comfortable corporate offices.

When the grand slogans and demographic calculations that drive our enterprise forward come down to the street level in the squalor of urban barrios, favellas, and villages where the Pentecostal poor live, we will realize that there is a war in progress. U.S. Charismatics utilizing the media and marching on abortion clinics already understand this well. Inner-city Pentecostals, who go against crack houses and gang warfare, relate to the language of spiritual and physical conflict.

Consider the explosive mixture of the burgeoning worldwide growth of the Pentecostal/ Charismatic faith expression as the "second most widespread variety of Christian spiritual lifestyle" (Russell Spittler, Fuller Seminary). Add to this the wholesale membership losses of previously dominant religious move-ments, especially in the Southern Hemisphere. Consider our sometimes offensive propagational style contrasted by an equal-ly determined missionary fervor and growing intolerance from cults and non-Christian religions. These contrasts bring about one result: religious persecution. We would not wish this on any of God's people. The potential remains, however, for Barrett's estimate of 300,000 annual Christian martyrs to unfortunately multiply. The World Evangelical Fellowship, which sponsors an annual International Day of Prayer for the persecuted church, has said that more people were martyred for their Christian faith in the 20th century than in all the previous 19 centuries combined. Their Web site is *www.persecutedchurch.org*.

We believe that the most important issue we will face in the future will be how to confront the destructive supernatural evil forces that oppose the growth of the church. For this reason, look for a multiplication of "prayer and power" literature on spiritual warfare to continue. In the decade of the 1990s it became one of the most frequent topics in Pentecostal/Charismatic publications.

Partnership. Though we have been blessed by God with outstanding growth, we will have to ask ourselves if we can survive our own success. A profound sense of destiny has caused this movement to be self-assured that God is powerfully working among us. With that comes a potential for arrogance and triumphalism. University of Chicago church historian Martin Marty once observed that Pentecostals used to argue God's approval upon them because they numbered so few. But more recently, he said, the proof has shifted to the fact that they are so many. Even so, Pentecostals and Charismatics need the experience and partnership of the wider Christian community.

At the original Lausanne Congress in 1974, there were few signs of Pentecostal/Charismatic participants. Fifteen years later at Lausanne II in Manila (1989), more than half of the participants had a Pentecostal/Charismatic orientation and were highly visible as platform speakers and workshop leaders. In the closing decade of the 20th century, the Pentecostal/Charismatic churches integrated themselves into networks such as the Lausanne Movement, the "A.D. 2000 and Beyond" movement, and the "emerging missions" movement from the Southern Hemisphere. In reality, there is a symbiotic relationship between us and the Church Growth Movement. While we speak of the "Pentecostalization" of the church growth school of thought, the Pentecostal/Charismatic churches have also been helped and informed by church growth thinking. (I have discussed this at length in Part Four, "Pentecostals and the Church Growth Movement," *Azusa Street and Beyond*).

In short, most Pentecostals and Charismatics would agree with David Shibley's assessment: "World evangelization can never be accomplished by Charismatics alone. Neither can it be accomplished without us."[9]

Prioritization. Our partnership with other "Great Commission" Christians has helped us learn from them and be influenced in our church growth strategizing. Church growth strategists and missiologists are helping the Pentecostals and Charismatics focus on the "front burner" agenda items for the future: world-class cities, the poor, the Muslim world, youth and children, the unreached people groups of the 10/40 Window, and so forth.

There is a notable shift in mainline Pentecostal missions departments toward these needs. Already for years, Pentecostal/Charismatic sodalities such as Youth With A Mission, Teen Challenge, Center for Ministry to Muslims, the Sentinel Group, and others have led the way in pioneering ministries in these areas (in addition, the Charismatic influence is being felt in standard evangelical parachurch groups like Campus Crusade for Christ).

Another encouraging development is the growing missions involvement from independent Charismatic churches. Scholarly estimates indicate that some 60,000 to 100,000 such congregations grew up in the United States alone during the 1980s. Fuller researcher Edward K. Pousson charted the dramatic rise in missions involvement among these churches in his *Spreading the Flame: Charismatic Churches and Missions Today.*[10]

The "new Antiochs"—the Pentecostal/Charismatic superchurches of Asia, Africa and Latin America—will also play a key role in galvanizing the worldwide "Great Commission Community" toward discipling receptive segments of society. One of these churches, for example, is Singapore's Calvary Charismatic Center, which grew to 5,000 members in 10 years. By the mid-1980s, Calvary was sending more than 200 short-term missionaries and giving $1.2 million annually to missions.

The lessons being learned from the "new Antiochs" (also in urban "ethnic" America) may rewrite church growth theory. As Melvin Hodges and other mainline Pentecostals were suspicious of the influence of the social sciences in early church-growth thinking, there is concern today in our circles over the growing "management/marketing" paradigm, particularly on the North American church growth scene. Granted, some of the more high-profile Pentecostal/Charismatic media personalities are among the most professional marketing entrepreneurs. But the rank and file of Pentecostalism, particularly in the Two-Thirds World, would opt for a paradigm of the supernatural.

These Two-Thirds World and U.S. urban ethnic Pentecostals and Charismatics may also have some redefinitions and provide alternatives to previously held church growth assumptions regarding social sciences, social action, redemption and lift, resistance-receptivity theory, the homogeneous unit principle, and so forth.

God Is Throwing the Party

In the final analysis, the Christian church, my Pentecostal/Charismatic tradition included, will discover that the developments and initiatives of the coming years will be God's. *Charismata* (the gifts and workings of the Holy Spirit) cannot be charted or contained. The glory of the Christian mission and harvest will be God's alone (Matthew 9:38).

Let's continue to be awed by the initiative (Acts 13:1-4) and the unpredictability of God in the growth of His church (8:26ff.; 9:10ff.; 10:9ff.).

THE FUTURE OF PENTECOSTAL MISSIONS

I am excited about the future of Pentecostal missions. I am filled with optimism about what is happening. Futuristic thinking is occurring in contemporary Pentecostal missiology. These are signs of hope in our present outreach.

275

At this phase of our movement, Pentecostals now have the perspective of an extended past. The British historian E.H. Carr once observed, "You cannot look forward intelligently into the future unless you are also prepared to look back attentively into the past." Our past reminds us of our spiritual roots and helps us get "back to the future" of missions.

My observation of Pentecostal missions theology and strategy, as stated in my study of scores of Pentecostal literary sources, is that the Pentecostal missions movement is firmly set on obeying the Great Commission in this new century, should the Lord tarry.

Current Signs of Hope

Under the leadership of the Holy Spirit, the Pentecostal missions movement has moved into new areas of ministry which will set the course for coming years. Surveying the contemporary scene from my vantage point, I see at least four major reasons for hope— advancement of our worldwide mission: (1) in new places, (2) to new people, (3) for new personnel and (4) of new power.

In new places. Pentecostals believe that the Lord Jesus Christ meant it when He commanded us to "go into all the world . . . " (Mark 16:15). Pentecostal churches are not content as long as there is a nation or a people without the gospel. Pentecostals take it as a personal challenge when they learn of a country or people group that is not yet touched with the full gospel message.

At a recent international conference in Asia, a Pentecostal leader from Eastern Europe told me how the local church has sponsored missionaries into Albania, once a staunchly atheistic nation with minimal Christian presence. A Japanese Charismatic friend of mine has established a missions organization that regularly carries Bibles, literature and encouragement across Mongolia and the CIS. If there is a place without the gospel, do not tell a Pentecostal!

In addition, Pentecostal leaders have urban places upon their hearts. A review of Pentecostal ministries in urban areas indicates the burden and intention of Pentecostal missions departments and organizations to carry God's Word to the heart of the city. Pentecostal churches are experiencing dynamic growth in almost every major urban center in the world. The Spirit is in the city to stay! Pentecostal missions are advancing *in new places*.

To new people. Pentecostals are working with and opening up to the concept of "unreached peoples." The "unreached peoples" idea recognizes the fact of "peoples within a people," or "nations within a nation." It teaches that a myriad of cultural, linguistic and ethnic groups form a kaleidoscope of unevangelized people groups living within traditional geographical and political boundaries.

The Church of God, for example, is now reaching and discipling Haitians in Miami, Jamaicans in Brooklyn, Romanians in Chicago, Sikh East Indians in Vancouver, Dutch Indonesians in Rotterdam, Zairians in Brussels, ethnic Chinese Vietnamese refugees in central France, poor Miskito Indian refugees from Nicaragua in Honduras, and rich upper-middle class professionals in Hong Kong and Manila (and the list could go on and on).

For our denomination, these are only the beginnings of new kinds of people making up a growing international membership which now surpasses our original composition of "WASPS" (White Anglo-Saxon Pentecostal Southerners). Pentecostal missions are advancing *to new people*.

For new personnel. Picture in your mind a widely diverse, multiethnic, transnational force of cross-cultural witnesses coming from a variety of social classes and racial groups and from both the ranks of clergy and laity. This is the composite picture of the newly emerging breed of Pentecostal missionaries. There may be many more types, but I see at least seven kinds of new personnel for the future of Pentecostal missions:

1. *World-traveling laity.* Like Priscilla and Aquila of the early church, Pentecostal believers are scattered throughout the world in connection with civilian or military careers and occupations. They are today's "tentmakers," like the civil engineer I met in

Seoul, Korea. He had been temporarily assigned with a Korean construction outfit in Saudi Arabia and had an opportunity to spread the faith while being a "tentmaker" outside his country.

2. *Short-term professionals.* Whether it be a team of construction workers building a church in Honduras or a group of physicians on "missions of mercy" in Haiti or East Africa, our Missions Department is partnering with lay volunteer movements such as Men and Women of Action and Volunteers in Medical Missions who go at their own expense for brief, specialized ministries. This trend will grow in coming years.

3. *The newly retired.* There is a rising number of "second-start Christians" who are giving the energies of their middle and later years to ministry. Among both clergy and laity is a burgeoning force of dedicated people with vigor and experience who say with Caleb of the Old Testament, "Give me this mountain!"

4. *Pastors with a world parish.* Internationally, more pastors are traveling, observing and ministering on short-term visits to missions work. They are returning to their pulpits with a new message of God's heart and vision for the world.

Domestically, a growing number of pastors are envisioning ways to reach the ethnic mosaic of North America—a mission field at their doorstep. My files are filled with feasibility studies from Pentecostal pastors seeking ways to plant new ethnic churches or expand their local church into a multicongregational or international assembly of believers. Church growth pastors are the missions motivators of the future.

5. *Career missionaries from North America.* This reserve force continues to grow, although today's career missionary is finding new servant roles of leadership in cooperation with mature national church administrations.

6. *Overseas missionaries from overseas churches.* This rapidly expanding cadre of leadership is being called by various names: Third World missionaries, non-Western missionaries, emerging missionaries. Whatever you call them, do not forget to count

them. By the year 2000 there were more than 150,000 non-North American, non-European evangelical missionaries originating from overseas churches!

Keep your eyes on this dynamic trend. The "mission field" is becoming a "missions force." The understatement of the year would be, "God is doing something in the non-Western World."

7. *A newly emerging world Christian student movement.* We are witnessing what may be unprecedented in the history of the Pentecostal Movement. There is a dramatic upswing in the number of students (internationally) who are not only interested in world missions, but are actually being called to and preparing for cross-cultural witness. The network of Pentecostal Bible schools and seminaries around the world are becoming "new Antiochs"— inspiring, training, and deploying another generation of missionary recruits for the 21st century. With a variety of gifts and callings, Pentecostal missions are advancing with a place *for new personnel.*

Of new power. Actually, this is that same power spoken of by the prophet Joel and experienced by our Pentecostal mothers and fathers. But God's same power is being experienced in new ways and among new kinds of people through Pentecostal missions efforts. It is incumbent on us as century-old Pentecostals to ensure that we are totally saturated with, baptized in, dependent upon and led by the Holy Spirit of God!

It is important for Pentecostals not to depend on the heritage and experiences of another generation, but to missionize in the power of the Holy Spirit today and tomorrow. Pentecostal missions are advancing with a strategy *of new power.*

I am optimistic about the future of Pentecostal missions because of these four major signs of hope that will continue to unfold into future multifaceted international ministries. We are advancing a mission *in new places, to new people, for new personnel*, and *of new power.* We are "global believers," connecting to God's work in our world!

Reflections

1. The following words were used in this chapter to forecast future global trends: publishing, proclamation/planting, persecution, partnership and prioritization. How do you see yourself and your church connecting with and being involved in these trends?

2. In discussing optimism about the future of Pentecostal missions, four expressions were used: in new places; to new people; for new personnel; and of new power. How do you see yourself and your church connecting with and being involved in these four expressions for the future?

*Pause now for personal or group prayer before moving to Projections/Actions.

 Projections

Today's date_____

By this time next year, next month, next week, I believe God for the following ministry goals to connect to God's work in my world (enter calendar dates for accountability):

1. Next year (date_____)
2. Next month (date_____)
3. Next week (date_____)

Actions

By this time tomorrow—in the next 24 hours—I will . . .

1.
2.

Part Four Resource Connections

1. Check with Pentecostal/Charismatic research agencies, seminaries and colleges for resources on Pentecostal/Charismatic missions ministries. Ask for catalogs, newsletters, lists of publications, seminars, courses, and so forth.

Pentecostal Resource Center
260 11th St., N.E.
Cleveland, TN 37311
423-614-8576
Web site: *www.leeuniversity.edu*

Church of God Theological Seminary
P.O. Box 3330
Cleveland, TN 37320-3330
423-478-1131
Web site: *www.cogts.edu*

Lee University
1120 N. Ocoee St.
Cleveland, TN 37311
423-614-8000
Web site: *www.leeuniversity.edu*

Patten College
2433 Coolidge Ave.
Oakland, CA 94601
510-533-8300
Web site: *www.patten.edu*

2. Check at your local bookstore or library for resources on Pentecostal/Charismatic missions and church growth.

FINAL WORD—GOD'S WORD

> HE WHO TESTIFIES TO THESE THINGS SAYS, "YES, I AM COMING SOON." AMEN. COME, LORD JESUS. THE GRACE OF THE LORD JESUS BE WITH GOD'S PEOPLE. AMEN.
> —REVELATION 22:20, 21

"Tomorrow" was on the minds of the Hickory Huskers as they filed anxiously into the Butler Field House in South Bend, Indiana. It was 1952. The true story of the Huskers (who in rags-to-riches style won the state basketball championship) is told in *Hoosiers*, one of my favorite family films. The Huskers were from a small country high school of 64 students in the rural heartland of Indiana. The film records victory after successive Husker victory in the crowded, hot, cracker-box gymnasiums of small-town high schools. The scene etched in my memory is when they step off of their rattletrap school bus on practice day before the tournament and walk for the first time into Butler Field House, a massive arena with row upon intimidating row of thousands of seats.

"Tomorrow," in this new and imposing environment they would face off with the Mighty Bears of South Bend Central High School, a modern urban high school which had 2,800 students. One by one, the camera captures the expressions of these farm boys—wide-eyed with mouths open—who have never seen a place like this before (1952 . . . before the urban omnipresence of television). In their faces you can see fear, anxiety, intimidation. Their coach (played by Gene Hackman) was ready for this moment. Pulling a tape measure from his overcoat, he said, "Charlie, come over here." Handing Charlie one end of the line and holding the other under the basket, he told his player to walk to the foul line. He deliberately measured and called out the distance. Then, he called his shortest player to be hoisted up with the tape measure to the rim of the basket. They carefully measured from the rim to the floor. "Ten feet, Coach," came the surprised response from his player.

To their relief and reassurance, the coach gathered his team around him, looked them in the eyes and said, "I think you'll find it's the exact same court as ours back in Hickory." He was saying to them that regardless of the overwhelming size of the arena and the massive, sometimes hostile crowd, the dimensions of the court were exactly the same as the one at home. The court belonged to them.

Accessing your global future and connecting to God's work in your world may seem to be an insecure risky pursuit. The future may appear intimidating . . . but for the "global believer," online with the global, universal God, it will be exhilarating! The enemies of Christ's mission advance may be hostile and threatening, but the size of the court is, and will always be, the same. The dimension and the despair of the human heart have never changed, and "Jesus Christ is the same yesterday and today and forever" (Hebrews 13:8).

ENDNOTES

CHAPTER 1

[1] John Piper, *Let the Nations Be Glad! The Supremacy of God in Missions* (Grand Rapids: Baker, 1993) 11.

[2] J. Herbert Kane, *Christian Missions in Biblical Perspective* (Grand Rapids: Baker, 1976) 26.

CHAPTER 2

[1] Robert Hall Glover, *The Bible Basis of Mission* (Los Angeles: Bible House, 1946) 13.

[2] J. Herbert Kane, *Understanding Christian Missions*, revised ed. (Grand Rapids: Baker, 1974).

[3] Ferdinand Hahn, *Mission in the New Testament*, transl. by Frank Clarke from the German (Naperville, IL: Alec R. Allenson, 1965).

[4] George Peters, *A Biblical Theology of Missions* (Chicago: Moody, 1972) 116.

[5] Walter C. Kaiser Jr., "Israel's Missionary Call," *Perspectives on the World Christian Movement: A Reader*, 3rd ed., ed. Ralph D. Winter and Steven C. Hawthorne (Pasadena, CA: William Carey Library, 1999) 15.

[6] Glover, 20.

[7] Kane, *Christian Missions in Biblical Perspective* (Grand Rapids: Baker, 1976) 26-29.

[8] Kane, *Christian Missions in Biblical Perspective*, 31-33.

Chapter 3

[1] "Call Upon Me . . . How God Answered a Father's Desperate Prayer," *InSpirit: Church of God European News Journal*, Spring 1999.

[2] William Owen Carver, *Missions in the Plan of the Ages* (1909; New York: Revell; Nashville: Broadman, 1951) 254.

[3] George F. MacLeod, *Only One Way Left* (Glasgow, Scotland: Iona Community, n.d.) 38.

Chapter 5

[1] "The Two Structures of God's Redemptive Mission," *Perspectives on the World Christian Movement: A Reader,* 3rd ed., ed. Ralph D. Winter and Steven C. Hawthorne (Pasadena, CA: William Carey Library, 1999), 220-230.

[2] Helen Barrett Montgomery, *Western Women in Eastern Lands* (New York: Macmillan, 1910) 243-244.

[3] Gary McGee, "Missions, Overseas (North American)," *Dictionary of Pentecostal and Charismatic Movements* (Grand Rapids: Zondervan, 1988) 613.

[4] David J. duPlessis, in *Azusa Street and Beyond: Pentecostal Missions and Church Growth in the Twentieth Century*, ed. L. Grant McClung Jr. (South Plainfield, NJ: Bridge, 1986) 77.

Chapter 6

[1] Donald A. McGavran, *The Bridges of God* (New York: Friendship, 1955).

[2] Edward Dayton and David Fraser, *Planning Strategies for World Evangelization* (Grand Rapids: Eerdmans, 1990) 28. See also John D. Robb, *Focus! The Power of People Group Thinking* (Monrovia, CA: MARC/World Vision, 1994).

CHAPTER 7

[1] James A. Cross, ed., *A Treasury of Pentecostal Classics: Writings From the First Century of the Church of God* (Cleveland, TN: Pathway, 1985).

[2] *World Pulse* report from the Evangelical Missions Information Service early in 1992. In Stan Guthrie's article, "Conversions Among Turks Suggest Gospel Lift Off Near," Guthrie interviewed Steve Hagerman, director of "Friends of Turkey" in Grand Junction, Colorado.

[3] Reported by *World Christian News*, Youth With A Mission, Nov. 1989.

CHAPTER 8

[1] Robert Linthicum, "Towards a Biblical Urban Theology," *Together*, April-June 1988: 4.

[2] George MacDonald, *Urban Mission*, Jan. 1986.

[3] Ralph Earle, *Word Meanings in the New Testament*, vol. 3 (Kansas City, MO: Beacon Hill, 1974) 29.

[4] John W. Sanday, *A Critical and Exegetical Commentary of the Epistle to the Romans* (Edinburgh, Scotland: T & T Clark, 1895) 229.

Chapter 9

[1] *World Vision* magazine article by an African church leader, Gottfried Osai-Mensah of Kenya.

[2] L. Grant McClung Jr., ed., *Azusa Street and Beyond: Pentecostal Missions and Church Growth in the Twentieth Century* (South Plainfield, NJ: Bridge, 1986) 77.

[3] John Wimber, *Power Evangelism* (New York: Harper, 1986) 35.

Chapter 10

[1] C. Peter Wagner, *Your Church Can Grow* (Ventura, CA: Regal, 1984) 14.

[2] Wagner, ed., with Win Arn and Elmer Towns, *Church Growth: State of the Art* (Wheaton: Tyndale, 1988) 284.

[3] Donald A. McGavran, *Effective Evangelism: A Theological Mandate* (Phillipsburg, NJ: Presbyterian and Reformed, 1988).

[4] McGavran, *The Bridges of God* (New York: Friendship, 1955).

[5] McGavran and George G. Hunter III, *Church Growth: Strategies That Work* (Nashville: Abingdon, 1980).

[6] McGavran, *Understanding Church Growth*, 3rd ed. (Grand Rapids: Eerdmans, 1990) 21-23.

[7] McGavran, *Effective Evangelism: A Theological Mandate*.

[8] L. Grant McClung Jr., ed., *Azusa Street and Beyond:*

Pentecostal Missions and Church Growth in the Twentieth Century (South Plainfield, NJ: Bridge, 1986) 109-136.

[9] McGavran, "What Makes Pentecostal Churches Grow?," *Church Growth Bulletin*, Jan. 1977.

[10] Wagner, "The Characteristics of Pentecostal Church Growth," *The Pentecostal Minister*, Summer 1982: 4-9.

[11] Wagner, *Spiritual Power and Church Growth* (Altamonte Springs, FL: Strang Communications, 1986).

[12] William R. Read, Victor M. Monterosso, and Herman A. Johnson, *Latin American Church Growth* (Grand Rapids: Eerdmans, 1969).

CHAPTER 11
[1] Donald A. McGavran, *Understanding Church Growth* (Grand Rapids: Eerdmans, 1980).

CHAPTER 12
[1] George Hunter, *To Spread the Power: Church Growth in the Wesleyan Spirit* (Nashville: Abingdon, 1987) 19.

[2] Loren Cunningham, *Ministries*, Summer 1986.

[3] David (Paul) Yonggi Cho, *Global Church Growth Bulletin*, March-April 1984.

[4] Gail Sheehy, *Pathfinders* (New York: Bantam, 1981).

[5] Ray and Ann Ortlund, *The Best Half of Life* (Ventura, CA: Regal, 1976) 90.

[6] Ortlund, 7.

[7] Ted Engstrom, *The Most Important Thing a Man Needs to Know About the Rest of His Life*.

Chapter 14
[1] Walbert Buhlmann, *The Coming of the Third Church: An Analysis of the Present and Future of the Church* (Maryknoll, NY: Orbis, 1977).

[2] Andrew F. Walls, "Towards an Understanding of Africa's Place in Christian History," *Religion in a Pluralistic Society,* ed. J.S. Pobee (Leiden, Holland: Brill, 1976) 180.

[3] David B. Barrett, "Statistics, Global," *Dictionary of Pentecostal and Charismatic Movements*, ed. Stanley M. Burgess and Gary B. McGee (Grand Rapids: Zondervan, 1988) 811.

[4] Buhlmann, 24.

[5] Barrett, 811.

[6] Robert Mapes Anderson, *Vision of the Disinherited: The Making of American Pentecostalism* (New York: Oxford UP, 1969) 98-113.

[7] William A. Dyrness, *Learning About Theology From the Third World* (Grand Rapids: Zondervan, 1990) 20.

Chapter 15
[1] Grant Wacker, "Wild Theories and Mad Excitement," *Pentecostals From the Inside Out*, ed. Harold B. Smith (Wheaton, IL: Scripture Press/Christianity Today, 1990) 20-21.

[2] C. Peter Wagner, *Understanding Church Growth and Decline: 1950-1978*, ed. Dean R. Hoge and David A. Roozen (Pilgrim, 1979).

[3] Melvin L. Hodges, *A Theology of the Church and Its Mission: A Pentecostal Perspective* (Gospel Publishing, 1977).

[4] Paul A. Pomerville, *The Third Force in Mission* (Hendrickson, 1985).

[5] David (Paul) Yonggi Cho and R. Whitney Manzano, *More Than Numbers* (Waco, TX: Word, 1984).

[6] Donald A. McGavran, with John Huegel and Jack Taylor, *Church Growth in Mexico* (Grand Rapids: Eerdmans, 1963).

[7] Hodges, *The Indigenous Church* (Springfield, MO: Gospel Publishing, 1953).

[8] L. Grant McClung Jr., ed., *Azusa Street and Beyond: Pentecostal Missions and Church Growth in the Twentieth Century* (South Plainfield, NJ: Bridge, 1986). One of the book's special features is an "Annotated Bibliography of Pentecostal Missions," which has more than 300 listings of references—books, articles and research papers—on the global growth dynamics of Pentecostal missions. In addition to the books already mentioned in this chapter, listed at the end of this section are several other examples of Pentecostal/Charismatic thinking on missions and church growth since 1986.

[9] David Shibley, *A Force in the Earth: The Move of the Holy Spirit in World Evangelization* (Orlando, FL: Creation, 1997).

[10] Edward K. Pousson, *Spreading the Flame: Charismatic*

Churches and Missions Today (Grand Rapids: Zondervan, 1992).

Additional Resource Material:

Burgess, Stanley M., and Gary B. McGee, eds. *Dictionary of Pentecostal and Charismatic Movements.* Grand Rapids: Zondervan, 1988.

Dawson, John. *Taking Our Cities for God.* Altamonte Springs, FL: Creation, 1989.

Klaus, Byron D., Murray W. Dempster, and Douglas Peterson. *Called and Empowered: Pentecostal Perspectives on Global Mission.* Peabody, MA: Hendrickson, 1991.

May, F.J. *The Book of Acts and Church Growth.* Cleveland, TN: Pathway, 1990.

McClung, L. Grant Jr. "The Pentecostal/Charismatic Contribution to World Evangelization." *Mission in the 1990s.* Ed. Gerald H. Anderson, James M. Phillips, Robert T. Coote. Grand Rapids: Eerdmans, 1991.

Pennoyer, F. Douglas, and C. Peter Wagner, eds. *Wrestling With Dark Angels.* Ventura, CA: Regal, 1990.

Reddin, Opal L., ed. *Power Encounter: A Pentecostal Perspective.* Springfield, MO: Central Bible College Press, 1989.

Smith, Harold, ed. *Pentecostals From the Inside Out.* Carol Stream, IL: Christianity Today Institute, 1990.

Stockwell, Eugene L., ed. *International Review of Mission*

(vol. LXXV, nos. 297, 298, Jan. and April 1986—special editions on Pentecostals and Charismatics in the world today).

Synan, Vinson. *The Twentieth-Century Pentecostal Explosion.* Altamonte Springs, FL: Creation, 1987.

Underwood, B.E. *Sixteen New Testament Principles for World Evangelization.* Franklin Springs, GA: Advocate, 1988.